BY BRENÉ BROWN

Dare to Lead

Braving the Wilderness

Rising Strong

Daring Greatly

The Gifts of Imperfection

I Thought It Was Just Me

dare to lead

dare to lead

BRAVE WORK.
TOUGH CONVERSATIONS.
WHOLE HEARTS.

Brené Brown

RANDOM HOUSE | NEW YORK

This is a work of nonfiction. Nonetheless, some of the names and personal characteristics of the individuals involved have been changed in order to disguise their identities. Any resulting resemblance to persons living or dead is entirely coincidental and unintentional.

Published in the United States by Random House, an imprint and division of Penguin Random House LLC, New York.

Random House and the House colophon are registered trademarks of Penguin Random House LLC.

Library of Congress Cataloging-in-Publication Data
Names: Brown, Brené, author.
Title: Dare to lead: brave work, tough conversations, whole hearts / Brené Brown.
Description: New York: Random House, [2018] | Includes index.
Identifiers: LCCN 2018038094 | ISBN 9780399592522 (hardback) | ISBN 9780399592546 (ebook) | ISBN 9781984854032 (international edition)
Subjects: LCSH: Leadership.
Classification: LCC HD57.7 .B764 2018 | DDC 658.4/092—dc23
LC record available at https://lccn.loc.gov/2018038094

Printed in the United States of America on acid-free paper

randomhousebooks.com

16 17 18 19 20

To my friend Charles Kiley. Who would have thought we'd go from waiting tables, to selling copies of my first, self-published book out of the extra room in your house, to working and leading together today? I couldn't have done it without you. #outrageous #pingpong #playsomecheap

CONTENTS

a note from Brené

People often ask me if I still get nervous when I speak in public. The answer is yes. I'm always nervous. Experience keeps me from being scared, but I'm still nervous. First, people are offering me their most precious gift—their time. Time is, hands down, our most coveted, most unrenewable resource. If being on the receiving end of one of life's most valuable gifts fails to leave you with a lump in your throat or butterflies in your stomach, then you're not paying attention.

Second, speaking is vulnerable. I don't memorize my lines or have a set shtick that I do verbatim. Effective speaking is about the unpredictable and uncontrollable art of connection. Even though it's just me onstage and possibly ten thousand people sitting in folding chairs in a convention center, I try to look into as many pairs of eyes as I can. So, yes. I'm always nervous.

I have a couple of tricks that I've developed over the past several years that help me stay centered. Even though it makes event production teams crazy, I always ask for the stage lights to be at 50 percent. When they're at 100 percent, you can't see the audience at all, and I don't like talking into the void. I need to see enough faces to know if we're in sync. *Are the words and images pulling us together or pushing us apart? Are they recognizing their experiences in my stories?* People make very specific faces when they're hearing something that rings true for them. They nod and smile and sometimes cover their faces with their hands. When it's not landing, I get the side tilt. And less laughter.

I have another trick I use when anxious event organizers try encouraging me to up my game by describing the status of the audience members. An organizer might say, "Hey, Brené, just so you know, the audience tonight includes top military brass." They'll mention the high-level corporate leaders, elite members of this or that super special group, the top glass-ceiling breakers in the world, or, my favorite, "These actually are rocket scientists who will probably hate what you're saying, so stick to the data." This strategy is often employed when the audience seems somewhat resistant because they don't know why I'm there, or, worst-case scenario, they don't know why they've been forced to be there with me.

In these cases, my strategy is a take on the classic "picture the audience naked" trick. Rather than picturing naked people sitting in auditorium chairs, which just doesn't work for me, I picture people without the armor of their titles, positions, power, or influence. When I spot the woman in the audience who has her lips pursed and her arms tightly folded across her chest, I picture what she looked like in third grade. If I'm hooked by the guy who keeps shaking his head and making comments like "Winners aren't weak at work," I try to picture him holding a child or sitting with his therapist. *Or, honestly, sitting with the therapist I think he should see.*

Before I go onstage, I whisper the word *people,* three or four times to myself. "People. People, people, people." This strategy was born out of desperation a decade ago, back in 2008, when I gave what I consider my first talk to a corporate leadership audience. I had lectured at grand rounds in hospitals and done many behavioral health talks, but the difference between those experiences and even just standing in that green room was palpable.

I was trying to find a place to set up camp in a room with twenty other speakers, each of us waiting to be called to do our TED-style twenty-minute talk at this day-long event, when that lonely feeling of not belonging and being out of place started washing over me. I first checked if it was a gender thing, because, to date, I'm often still the only female speaker backstage. That wasn't it. It wasn't homesickness, because I was thirty minutes from my house in Houston.

When I heard the event organizers talking to the audience, I pulled back a small section of the heavy velvet curtains that separated the green room from the auditorium and peeked out. It was like a Brooks Brothers convention—rows of mostly men in white shirts and very dark suits.

I shut the curtain and started to panic. The guy standing closest to me was a young, super energetic speaker who, you could tell, had never met a stranger. I'm not even sure what he was saying to me when I cut him off in midsentence: "Oh, my God. These are all businesspeople—executives. Or FBI agents."

He chuckled. "Yeah, mate. It's a conference for C-levels. Didn't they tell you that?"

The blood drained out of my face as I slowly sat down on the empty chair next to me.

He explained, "You know, CEOs, COOs, CFOs, CMOs, CHROs . . ."

All I could think was, *There is no way I'm going to tell this guy the truth.*

He knelt next to me and put his arm on my shoulder. "You okay, mate?"

Maybe it was the Australian accent, or the big smile, or the name Pete that made this guy instantly trustworthy, but I turned to him and said, "They did tell me it was a C-level audience. But I thought that meant down-to-earth. Like these are real sea-level people. Salt of the earth. S-E-A-level."

Through a huge, booming laugh he said, "That's brilliant! You should use that!"

I looked him in the eye and said, "It's not funny. I'm talking about shame and the danger of not believing we're enough."

There was a long pause before I added, "Ironically."

By that time a woman from Washington, D.C., who was doing her twenty-minute talk on the oil trade, was standing beside us. She looked at me and said, "Shame—as in the emotion? Like I'm *ashamed*?"

Before I could even admit that was true, she said, "Interesting. Better you than me," and walked off.

I'll never forget Pete's response. "Look out into that audience again. These are people. Just people. And no one talks to them about shame, and every single one of them is in it up to their eyeballs. Just like the rest of us. Look at them. They are people."

I think either the truth of his advice or the thought of my topic got to him, because he stood up, squeezed my shoulder, and walked away. I quickly pulled out my laptop and searched "popular MBA and business terms." *Maybe I can put some hard corners on my topic by weaving in a little business lingo.*

Damn. It was like reading *Old Hat, New Hat,* the Berenstain Bears book that my kids loved when they were little. It's the story of Papa Bear going to the hat store and trying on fifty different hats to replace his old, ragged hat. But of course all of the new hats have issues: "Too loose. Too tight. Too heavy. Too light." It goes on for pages until it reaches the logical conclusion of keeping the old, ugly hat that fits perfectly.

I started whispering some of the terms to myself to see if I could pull it off.

Long pole item? Too tall.

Critical pathway? Too trafficky.

Skip-level? Too hopscotchy.

Incentive? Maybe?

Incentivize? Wait. What? I call bullshit. You can't just add "ize" to stuff.

Mercifully, my husband, Steve, called and interrupted my Berenstain Bears business search.

"How are you? Are you ready?" he asked.

"*No!* It's a total cluster," I said. After I explained the situation, he was very quiet.

Using his serious voice—the one reserved for panicked parents calling for medical advice (he's a pediatrician), or for me when I'm losing my mind—he said, "Brené, promise me that you will not use any of those dumb-ass words. I mean it."

I was near tears at this point. I whispered, "I promise. But you should see these people. It's like a funeral. And not a funeral in my family, not a fancy-Wranglers-and-an-appropriately-somber-cowboy-hat funeral. It's like a British funeral. Or a graveside service on *The Sopranos*."

He said, "Take that guy's advice and look out at the audience again. They're really just people. Like you and me. Like our friends. There are people there you know, right? These are real people with real lives and real problems. Do *your* thing."

He told me he loved me, and we hung up. I stood up and pulled the curtain back one more time. The room was darker, and a speaker was talking from the stage. I wanted to see the audience members' faces but my side view made it tough. Then, like a slow motion scene from a movie, a large bald guy turned to whisper something to the guy sitting next to him, and I saw his face.

I gasped and pulled the curtains closed. *I know that guy*. We got sober around the same time, and we used to go to the same AA meetings in the mid-'90s. I couldn't believe it. As I sat there wondering if I was in the middle of a miracle, my new friend Pete walked up.

"You doing okay?" he asked.

I smiled. "Yeah. I think so. Just people, right?"

He patted me on the shoulder and told me that a woman was standing outside the green room door asking to talk to me. I thanked him again and went to check on my visitor. It was my neighbor! At the time she was a managing partner at a law firm, and she was attending the event with several other partners and a few clients. She told me that she just wanted to say hello and wish me luck. I gave her a quick hug, and she went back toward the auditorium doors. I walked across the lobby and stepped outside for some fresh air.

She may never know what it meant for me to see her that day. I appreciated the kindness and connection, but it was the simple act of seeing her that made all the difference for me. Yes, she's a partner in a prestigious law firm, but she's also a daughter who I know recently moved her mother from assisted living to hospice. She's also a mother and a wife going through a difficult divorce.

People. People. People.

The experience that day was electric. The audience and I were totally in sync and deeply connected. We belly-laughed. We cried. The audience leaned in so hard to what I was sharing about shame, unattainable expectations, and perfectionism that I thought they would fall out of their seats. We experienced the surge.

Before I went back to school to study social work in the early '90s, I was climbing the corporate ladder at a Fortune 10 company. I left that job to study social work, and I didn't think then that I would return to that world, which, in my mind, was the opposite of what I cared about—courage, connection, and meaning.

For the first several years of my doctoral work, I focused on systems change management and organizational environmental scanning. I eventually shifted direction and wrote my dissertation on connection and vulnerability. I never thought I'd return to the field of organizational development, because I didn't really love it at that time.

The talk I gave that day marked a significant turning point in my career. The heartfelt experience I had with that audience made me question whether I had made a mistake by framing two of my interests as mutually exclusive. *What would it look like to combine courage, connection, and meaning with the world of work?*

The other weird thing that happened that day resulted in a major shift in my speaking career. There were several speaking agents at the event, and after the audience evaluations were shared with the speakers and their agents, I got calls from all of them asking about my career goals. After a couple of months of soul searching, I decided to find my way back to the world of leadership and organizational development. But this time, with a new focus: people, people, people.

It's Not the Critic Who Counts

In 2010, two years after that event, I wrote *The Gifts of Imperfection,* a book that introduced my research on the ten guideposts for wholeheartedness. It had a very wide audience including corporate, community, faith, and nonprofit leaders.

Two years after that, in 2012, I sharpened my focus on vulnerability and courage and wrote *Daring Greatly.* This was my first book that included findings on what I was learning about leadership and what I was observing in my work with organizations.

The epigraph of *Daring Greatly* is this quote from Theodore Roosevelt:

> It is not the critic who counts; not the man who points out how the strong man stumbles, or where the doer of deeds could have done them better. The credit belongs to the man who is actually in the arena, whose face is marred by dust and sweat and blood; who strives valiantly; who errs, who comes short again and again . . . who at the best knows in the end the triumph of high achievement, and who at the worst, if he fails, at least fails while daring greatly.

I found this quote during a particularly challenging time in my career. My TEDxHouston talk on vulnerability was going viral, and while there was a groundswell of support for the talk, many of the criticisms were cruel and personal, confirming my biggest fears about putting myself out there. This was the perfect quote to capture how I felt and my growing resolve to go full-on Tom Petty and not back down.

The courage to be vulnerable is not about winning or losing, it's about the courage to show up when you can't predict or control the outcome. Just as the quote resonated so deeply with my desire to live a brave life despite the growing cynicism and fearmongering in the world, it resonated with leaders everywhere. For many, *Daring Greatly* was their introduction to the quote, while others had it hanging in their offices or homes for years and felt a kindred connection. I recently saw a picture of LeBron James's game shoes, and "Man in the Arena" was written on the side.

I followed up *Daring Greatly* very quickly with *Rising Strong*—a book that explores the process that the most resilient of my research participants use to get up after a fall. It felt like a mandate to write it, because the only thing I know for sure after all of this research is that if you're going to dare greatly, you're going to get your ass kicked at some point. If you choose courage, you will absolutely know failure, disappointment, setback, even heartbreak. That's why we call it courage. That's why it's so rare.

In 2016, I combined the research from *Daring Greatly* and *Rising Strong* to develop a courage-building program, and we launched Brave Leaders Inc. to offer online learning and in-person facilitation of the work. Within one year, we were working with fifty companies and close to ten thousand leaders. The next year brought *Braving the Wilderness,* a book about the courage to belong to ourselves as a prerequisite for true belonging, and the dangers of spending our lives trying to fit in and hustle for acceptance. It was a topic I felt called to research and write in the midst of increased polarization, rampant dehumanization of people who are different from us, and our growing inability to ditch the echo chambers for real critical thinking.

Over the past two years, our team has researched, evaluated, failed, iterated, listened, observed, watched, grown, and learned more than we could ever have imagined. And if that wasn't enough, I've had the opportunity to sit with and learn from some of the greatest leaders in the world. I can't wait to share what I've learned, how it can completely change how we show up with each other, why it works, why it's really hard in places, and where I keep screwing up (*just to keep it real*).

dare to lead

You can't get to courage without rumbling with vulnerability.

EMBRACE THE SUCK.

introduction

BRAVE LEADERS AND COURAGE CULTURES

I have one deceptively simple and somewhat selfish goal for this book: I desperately want to share everything I've learned with you. I want to take my two decades of research and my experiences inside hundreds of organizations to give you a practical, *no-BS,* actionable book about what it takes to be a daring leader.

I say "deceptively simple" because the data informing what's presented in this book are the culmination of:

- Interview data collected over the past twenty years
- New research including interviews with 150 global C-level (and sea-level) leaders on the future of leadership
- Program evaluation research from our Brave Leaders Inc. courage-building work
- Data collected during a three-year instrument development study on daring leadership

Coding and making sense of 400,000 pieces of data is already complex, and the more committed I am to translating the data into actionable, research-based practices, the more painstakingly precise I need to be with the data and the more testing I need to do.

The selfish part of my goal stems from wanting to be a better leader myself. Over the past five years, I've transitioned from research professor to research professor *and* founder and CEO. The first hard and humbling lesson? Regardless of the complexity of the concepts, studying leadership is way easier than leading.

When I think about my personal experiences with leading over the past few years, the only endeavors that have required the same level of self-awareness and equally high-level "comms plans" are being married for twenty-four years and parenting. And that's saying something. I completely underestimated the pull on my emotional bandwidth, the sheer determination it takes to stay calm under pressure, and the weight of continuous problem solving and decision making. Oh, yeah—and the sleepless nights.

My other quasi-selfish goal is this: I want to live in a world with braver, bolder leaders, and I want to be able to pass that kind of world on to my children. **I define a leader as anyone who takes responsibility for finding the potential in people and processes, and who has the courage to develop that potential.** From corporations, nonprofits, and public sector organizations to governments, activist groups, schools, and faith communities, we desperately need more leaders who are committed to courageous, wholehearted leadership and who are self-aware enough to lead from their hearts, rather than unevolved leaders who lead from hurt and fear.

We've got a lot of ground to cover, and I told Steve that I wanted to write a book that would change how the reader thinks about leading, would result in at least one meaningful behavior change, and could be read cover to cover on one flight. He laughed and asked, "Houston to Singapore?"

He knows that's the longest flight I've ever endured (Moscow was just halfway). I smiled and said, "No. New York to L.A. With a short delay."

Brave Leaders and Courage Cultures

I've always been told, "Write what you need to read." What I need as a leader, and what every leader I've worked with over the past several years has asked for, is a practical playbook for putting the lessons from *Daring Greatly* and *Rising Strong* into action. There are even a few learnings from *Braving the Wilderness* that can help us create a culture of belonging at work. If you've read these books, expect some familiar lessons with new context, stories, tools, and examples related to our work lives. If you haven't read these books—no problem. I'll cover everything you need to know.

The language, tools, and skills described in these chapters require courage and serious practice. Yet they are straightforward and, I believe, accessible and actionable to everyone holding this book. The barriers and obstacles to daring leadership are real and sometimes fierce. But what I've learned from both the research and my own life is that as long as we name them, stay curious, and keep showing up, they don't have the power to stop us from being brave.

We've built a *Dare to Lead* hub on brenebrown.com where you can find resources including a free downloadable workbook for anyone who wants to put this book further into action as you read. I highly recommend it. As we learned from the research we did for *Rising Strong*: **We know that the way to**

move information from your head to your heart is through your hands.

There are also leadership book recommendations and role-play videos that you can watch as part of building your own courage skills. The videos won't take the place of putting this work into practice, but they will give you some idea of what it can look like, of where it gets hard, and of how to circle back when you inevitably make a mistake.

Additionally, you'll find a downloadable glossary of the language, tools, and skills that I'm discussing in the book. (Terms included in the glossary are bolded throughout the book.)

WHAT STANDS IN THE WAY BECOMES THE WAY

We started our interviews with senior leaders with one question: *What, if anything, about the way people are leading today needs to change in order for leaders to be successful in a complex, rapidly changing environment where we're faced with seemingly intractable challenges and an insatiable demand for innovation?*

There was one answer across the interviews: **We need braver leaders and more courageous cultures.**

When we followed up to understand the specific "why" behind the call for braver leadership, the research took a critical turn. There wasn't just one answer. There were close to fifty answers, and many of them weren't intuitively connected to courage. Leaders talked about everything from critical thinking and the ability to synthesize and analyze information to building trust, rethinking educational systems, inspiring innovation, finding common political ground amid growing polarization, making tough decisions, and the importance of empathy and relationship-building in the context of machine learning and artificial intelligence.

We kept peeling the metaphorical onion by asking: *Can you break down the specific skills that you believe underpin brave leadership?*

I was surprised by how much the research participants struggled to answer this question. Just under half of the leaders we interviewed initially talked about courage as a personality trait, not a skill. They typically approached the question about specific skills with a "Well, you either have it or you don't" answer. We stayed curious and kept pushing for observable behaviors: *What does it look like if you have it?*

Just over 80 percent of the leaders, including those who believed that courage is behavioral, couldn't identify the specific skills; however, they could immediately and passionately talk about problematic behaviors and cultural norms that corrode trust and courage. Luckily, the idea of "starting where people are" is a tenet of both grounded theory research and social work, and it's exactly what I do. As much time as I spend trying to understand *the way,* I spend ten times as much researching *what gets in the way.*

For example, I didn't set out to study shame; I wanted to understand connection and empathy. But if you don't understand how shame can unravel connection in a split second, you don't really get connection. I didn't set out to study vulnerability; it just happens to be the big barrier to almost everything we want from our lives, especially courage. As Marcus Aurelius taught us, "What stands in the way becomes the way."

Here are the ten behaviors and cultural issues that leaders identified as getting in our way in organizations across the world:

1. We avoid tough conversations, including giving honest, productive feedback. Some leaders attributed this to a

lack of courage, others to a lack of skills, and, shockingly, more than half talked about a cultural norm of "nice and polite" that's leveraged as an excuse to avoid tough conversations. Whatever the reason, there was saturation across the data that the consequence is a lack of clarity, diminishing trust and engagement, and an increase in problematic behavior, including passive-aggressive behavior, talking behind people's backs, pervasive back-channel communication (or "the meeting after the meeting"), gossip, and the "dirty yes" (when I say yes to your face and then no behind your back).

2. Rather than spending a reasonable amount of time proactively acknowledging and addressing the fears and feelings that show up during change and upheaval, we spend an unreasonable amount of time managing problematic behaviors.
3. Diminishing trust caused by a lack of connection and empathy.
4. Not enough people are taking smart risks or creating and sharing bold ideas to meet changing demands and the insatiable need for innovation. When people are afraid of being put down or ridiculed for trying something and failing, or even for putting forward a radical new idea, the best you can expect is status quo and groupthink.
5. We get stuck and defined by setbacks, disappointments, and failures, so instead of spending resources on cleanup to ensure that consumers, stakeholders, or internal processes are made whole, we are spending too much time and energy reassuring team members who are questioning their contribution and value.

6. Too much shame and blame, not enough accountability and learning.
7. People are opting out of vital conversations about diversity and inclusivity because they fear looking wrong, saying something wrong, or being wrong. Choosing our own comfort over hard conversations is the epitome of privilege, and it corrodes trust and moves us away from meaningful and lasting change.
8. When something goes wrong, individuals and teams are rushing into ineffective or unsustainable solutions rather than staying with problem identification and solving. When we fix the wrong thing for the wrong reason, the same problems continue to surface. It's costly and demoralizing.
9. Organizational values are gauzy and assessed in terms of aspirations rather than actual behaviors that can be taught, measured, and evaluated.
10. Perfectionism and fear are keeping people from learning and growing.

I think most of us can look at this list and quickly recognize not only the challenges in our organizations, but our own internal struggles to show up and lead through discomfort. These may be work behaviors and organizational culture concerns, but what underlies all of them are deeply human issues.

After finding the roadblocks, our job was to identify the specific courage-building skill sets that people need to address these problems. We conducted more interviews, developed instruments, and tested them with MBA and EMBA students enrolled at the Jones Graduate School of Business at Rice University, the Kellogg School of Management at Northwestern University, and the Wharton

School at the University of Pennsylvania. We worked until we found the answers. Then we tested it, improved it, and tested it again. Let's unpack what we learned.

The Heart of Daring Leadership

1. You can't get to courage without rumbling with vulnerability. Embrace the suck.

At the heart of daring leadership is a deeply human truth that is rarely acknowledged, especially at work: Courage and fear are not mutually exclusive. Most of us feel brave and afraid at the exact same time. We feel vulnerable. Sometimes all day long. During those "in the arena" moments that Roosevelt described, when we're pulled between our fear and our call to courage, we need shared language, skills, tools, and daily practices that can support us through the rumble.

The word **rumble** has become more than just a weird *West Side Story* way to say, "Let's have a real conversation, even if it's tough." It's become a serious intention and a behavioral cue or reminder.

A rumble is a discussion, conversation, or meeting defined by a commitment to lean into vulnerability, to stay curious and generous, to stick with the messy middle of problem identification and solving, to take a break and circle back when necessary, to be fearless in owning our parts, and, as psychologist Harriet Lerner teaches, to listen with the same passion with which we want to be heard. More than anything else, when someone says, "Let's rumble," it cues me to show up with an open heart and mind so we can serve the work and each other, not our egos.

Our research led to a very clear, very hopeful finding: Courage is a collection of four skill sets that can be taught, observed, and measured. The four skill sets are:

Rumbling with Vulnerability
Living into Our Values
Braving Trust
Learning to Rise

The foundational skill of courage-building is the willingness and ability to rumble with vulnerability. Without this core skill, the other three skill sets are impossible to put into practice. Consider this carefully: Our ability to be daring leaders will never be greater than our capacity for vulnerability. Once we start to build vulnerability skills, we can start to develop the other skill sets. The goal of this book is to give you language and specifics on the tools, practices, and behaviors that are critical for building the muscle memory for living these concepts.

We've now tested this approach in more than fifty organizations and with approximately ten thousand individuals who are learning these skills on their own or in teams. From the Gates Foundation to Shell, from small family-owned businesses to Fortune 50 companies, to multiple branches of the U.S. military, we have found this process to have significant positive impact, not just on the way leaders show up with their teams, but also on how their teams perform.

2. Self-awareness and self-love matter. Who we are is how we lead.

So often we think of courage as an inherent trait; however, it is less about *who* people are, and more about *how* they behave and show up in difficult situations. Fear is the emotion at the center of that list of problematic behaviors and culture issues—it's precisely what you'd expect to find as the underlying barrier to courage. However, all of the daring leaders we interviewed talked about experiencing many types of fear on a regular basis, which means that *feeling fear* is not the barrier.

The true underlying obstacle to brave leadership is *how we respond* to our fear. The real barrier to daring leadership is our armor—the thoughts, emotions, and behaviors that we use to protect ourselves when we aren't willing and able to rumble with vulnerability. While we'll learn tools and build skills in the following chapters, we'll also assess what gets in the way of building courage, especially because we can expect our armor to show up and pose resistance to new ways of doing things and new ways of being. Practicing self-compassion and having patience with ourselves are essential in this process.

3. Courage is contagious. To scale daring leadership and build courage in teams and organizations, we have to cultivate a culture in which brave work, tough conversations, and whole hearts are the expectation, and armor is not necessary or rewarded.

If we want people to fully show up, to bring their whole selves including their unarmored, whole hearts—so that we can innovate, solve problems, and serve people—we have to be vigilant about creating a culture in which people feel safe, seen, heard, and respected.

Daring leaders must care for and be connected to the people they lead.

The data made clear that care and connection are irreducible requirements for wholehearted, productive relationships between leaders and team members. This means that if we do not have a sense of caring toward someone we lead and/or we don't feel connected to that person, we have two options: Develop the caring and connection or find a leader who's a better fit. There's no shame in this—we've all experienced the kind of disconnection that doesn't get better despite our strongest efforts. Understanding that commitment to care and connection is the minimum threshold, we need real courage to recognize when we can't fully serve the people we lead.

Given the reality of the world we live in today, that means leaders—you and I—must create and hold spaces that rise to a higher standard of behavior than what we experience in the news, on TV, and in the streets. And for many, the culture at work may even need to be better than what they experience in their own home. Sometimes leadership strategies make us better partners and parents.

As I often tell teachers—some of our most important leaders—we can't always ask our students to take off the armor at home, or even on their way to school, because their emotional and physical safety may require self-protection. But what we can do, and what we are ethically called to do, is create a space in our schools and classrooms where all students can walk in and, for that day or hour, take off the crushing weight of their armor, hang it on a rack, and open their heart to truly being seen.

We must be guardians of a space that allows students to breathe and be curious and explore the world and be who they are without suffocation. They deserve one place where they can rumble with vulnerability and their hearts can exhale. And what I know from the research is that we should never underestimate the benefit to a child of having a place to belong—even one—where they can take off their armor. It can and often does change the trajectory of their life.

If the culture in our school, organization, place of worship, or even family requires armor because of issues like racism, classism, sexism, or any manifestation of fear-based leadership, we can't expect wholehearted engagement. Likewise, when our organization rewards armoring behaviors like blaming, shaming, cynicism, perfectionism, and emotional stoicism, we can't expect innovative work. You can't fully grow and contribute behind armor. It takes a massive amount of energy just to carry it around—sometimes it takes *all* of our energy.

The most powerful part of this process for us was seeing a list of behaviors emerge that are not "hardwired." Everything above is teachable, observable, and measurable, whether you're fourteen or forty. For the research participants who were initially convinced that courage is determined by genetic destiny, the interview process alone proved to be a catalyst for change.

One leader told me, "I'm in my late fifties and it wasn't until today that I realized I was taught every single one of these behaviors growing up—by either my parents or my coaches. When I get down to the nitty-gritty, I can almost remember each lesson—how and when I learned it. We could and should be teaching this to everyone." This conversation was an important reminder to me that time can wear down our memories of tough lessons until what was once a difficult learning fades into "This is just who I am as a person."

The skill sets that make up courage are not new; they've been aspirational leadership skills for as long as there have been leaders. Yet we haven't made great progress in developing these skills in leaders, because we don't dig into the humanity of this work—it's too messy. It's much easier to talk about what we want and need than it is to talk about the fears, feelings, and **scarcity** (the belief that there's not enough) that get in the way of achieving all of it. Basically, and perhaps ironically, we don't have the courage for real talk about courage. But it's time. And if you want to call these "soft skills" after you've tried putting them into practice—go for it. *I dare you.* Until then, find a home for your armor, and I'll see you in the arena.

part one RUMBLING WITH VULNERABILITY

Courage is contagious.

section one THE MOMENT AND THE MYTHS

The moment the universe put the Roosevelt quote in front of me, three lessons came into sharp focus. The first one is what I call "the physics of vulnerability." It's pretty simple: If we are brave enough often enough, we will fall. Daring is not saying "I'm willing to risk failure." Daring is saying "I know I will eventually fail, and I'm still *all in*." I've never met a brave person who hasn't known disappointment, failure, even heartbreak.

Second, the Roosevelt quote captures everything I've learned about vulnerability. **The definition of vulnerability as the emotion that we experience during times of uncertainty, risk, and emotional exposure** first emerged in my work two decades ago, and has been validated by every study I've done since, including this research on leadership. Vulnerability is not winning or losing. It's having the courage to show up when you can't control the outcome.

We've asked thousands of people to describe vulnerability to us over the years, and these are a few of the answers that directly pierce the emotion: the first date after my divorce, talking about race with my team, trying to get pregnant after my second miscarriage, starting my own business, watching my child leave for college, apologizing to a colleague about how I spoke to him in a meeting, sending my son to orchestra practice knowing how badly he wants to make first chair and knowing there's a really good chance he will not make the orchestra at all, waiting for the doctor to call back, giving feedback, getting feedback, getting fired, firing someone.

Across all of our data there's not a shred of empirical evidence that vulnerability is weakness.

Are vulnerable experiences easy? No.

Can they make us feel anxious and uncertain? Yes.

Do they make us want to self-protect? Always.

Does showing up for these experiences with a whole heart and no armor require courage? Absolutely.

The third thing I learned has turned into a mandate by which I live: If you are not in the arena getting your ass kicked on occasion, I'm not interested in or open to your feedback. There are a million cheap seats in the world today filled with people who will never be brave with their lives but who will spend every ounce of energy they have hurling advice and judgment at those who dare greatly. Their only contributions are criticism, cynicism, and fearmongering. If you're criticizing from a place where you're not also putting yourself on the line, I'm not interested in what you have to say.

We have to avoid the cheap-seats feedback *and* stay armor-free. The research participants who do both of those well have one hack in common: Get clear on whose opinions of you matter.

We need to seek feedback from *those* people. And even if it's really hard to hear, we must bring it in and hold it until we learn from it. This is what the research taught me:

> Don't grab hurtful comments and pull them close to you by rereading them and ruminating on them. Don't play with them by rehearsing your badass comeback. And whatever you do, don't pull hatefulness close to your heart.
>
> Let what's unproductive and hurtful drop at the feet of your unarmored self. And no matter how much your self-doubt wants to scoop up the criticism and snuggle with the negativity so it can confirm its worst fears, or how eager the shame gremlins are to use the hurt to fortify your armor, take a deep breath and find the strength to leave what's mean-spirited on the ground. You don't even need to stomp it or kick it away. Cruelty is cheap, easy, and chickenshit. It doesn't deserve your energy or engagement. Just step over the comments and keep daring, always remembering that armor is too heavy a price to pay to engage with cheap-seat feedback.

Again, if we shield ourselves from all feedback, we stop growing. If we engage with all feedback, regardless of the quality and intention, it hurts too much, and we will ultimately armor up by pretending it doesn't hurt, or, worse yet, we'll disconnect from vulnerability and emotion so fully that we stop feeling hurt. When we get to the place that the armor is so thick that we no longer feel anything, we experience a real death. We've paid for self-protection by sealing off our heart from everyone, and from everything—not just hurt, but love.

No one captures the consequences of choosing that level of self-protection over love better than C. S. Lewis:

> To love at all is to be vulnerable. Love anything, and your heart will certainly be wrung and possibly be broken. If you want to make sure of keeping it intact, you must give your heart to no one, not even to an animal. Wrap it carefully round with hobbies and little luxuries; avoid all entanglements; lock it up safe in the casket or coffin of your selfishness. But in that casket—safe, dark, motionless, airless—it will change. It will not be broken; it will become unbreakable, impenetrable, irredeemable.

To love is to be vulnerable.

Rumble Tool: The Square Squad

When we define ourselves by what everyone thinks, it's hard to be brave. When we stop caring about what anyone thinks, we're too armored for authentic connection. So how do we get clear on whose opinions of us matter?

Here's the solution we shared in *Daring Greatly:* Get a one-inch by one-inch piece of paper and write down the names of the people whose opinions of you matter. It needs to be small because it forces you to edit. Fold it and put it in your wallet. Then take ten minutes to reach out to those people—your **square squad**—and share a little gratitude. You can keep it simple: *I'm getting clear on whose opinions matter to me. Thank you for being one of those people. I'm grateful that you care enough to be honest and real with me.*

If you need a rubric for choosing the people, here's the best I have: The people on your list should be the people who love you not *despite* your vulnerability and imperfections, but *because* of them.

The people on your list should *not* be "yes" people. This is not the suck-up squad. They should be people who respect you enough to rumble with the vulnerability of saying "I think you were out of your integrity in that situation, and you need to clean it up and apologize. I'll be here to support you through that." Or "Yes, that was a huge setback, but you were brave and I'll dust you off and cheer you on when you go back into the arena."

The ~~Four~~ Six Myths of Vulnerability

In *Daring Greatly,* I wrote about four myths surrounding vulnerability, but since I've brought the courage-building work into organizations and have been doing it with leaders, the data have spoken, and there are clearly *six* misguided myths that persist across wide variables including gender, age, race, country, ability, and culture.

Myth #1: Vulnerability is weakness.
It used to take me a long time to dispel the myths that surround vulnerability, especially the myth that vulnerability is weakness. But in 2014, standing across from several hundred military special forces soldiers on a base in the Midwest, I decided to stop evangelizing, and I nailed my argument with a single question.

I looked at these brave soldiers and said, "Vulnerability is the emotion that we experience during times of uncertainty, risk, and emotional exposure. Can you give me a single example of courage that you've witnessed in another soldier or experienced in your own life that did not require experiencing vulnerability?"

Complete silence. Crickets.

Finally, a young man spoke up. He said, "No, ma'am. Three tours. I can't think of a single act of courage that doesn't require managing massive vulnerability."

I've asked that question now a couple of hundred times in meeting rooms across the globe. I've asked fighter pilots and software engineers, teachers and accountants, CIA agents and CEOs, clergy and professional athletes, artists and activists, and not one person has been able to give me an example of courage without vulnerability. The weakness myth simply crumbles under the weight of the data and people's lived experiences of courage.

Myth #2: I don't do vulnerability.

Our daily lives are defined by experiences of uncertainty, risk, and emotional exposure. There is no opting out, but there are two options: You can do vulnerability, or it can do you. Choosing to own our vulnerability and *do it* consciously means learning how to rumble with this emotion and understand how it drives our thinking and behavior so we can stay aligned with our values and live in our integrity. Pretending that we *don't do vulnerability* means letting fear drive our thinking and behavior without our input or even awareness, which almost always leads to acting out or shutting down.

If you don't believe the data, ask someone from your square squad this question: *How do I act when I'm feeling vulnerable?* If you're rumbling with vulnerability from a place of awareness, you won't hear anything you don't know and that you aren't actively addressing. If you subscribe to the idea of terminal uniqueness (everyone in the world *but you*), you will probably be on the receiving end of some tough feedback.

And as much as we'd like to believe that wisdom and experience can replace the need to "do" vulnerability, they don't. If anything, wisdom and experience validate the importance of rumbling with vulnerability. I love this quote by Madeleine L'Engle: "When we were children, we used to think that when we were grown-up we would no longer be vulnerable. But to grow up is to accept vulnerability."

Myth #3: I can go it alone.

The third myth surrounding vulnerability is "I can go it alone." One line of defense that I encounter is "I don't need to be vulnerable because I don't need anyone." I'm with you. Some days I wish it were true. The problem, however, is that *needing no one* pushes against everything we know about human neurobiology. We are hardwired for connection. From our mirror neurons to language, we are a social species. In the absence of authentic connection, we suffer. And by *authentic* I mean the kind of connection that doesn't require hustling for acceptance and changing who we are to fit in.

I dug deep into the work of the neuroscience researcher John Cacioppo when I was writing *Braving the Wilderness*. He dedicated his career to understanding loneliness, belonging, and connection, and he makes the argument that we don't derive strength from our rugged individualism, but rather from our collective ability to plan, communicate, and work together. Our neural, hormonal, and genetic makeup support interdependence over independence. He explained, "To grow to adulthood as a social species, including humans, is not to become autonomous and solitary, it's to become the one on whom others can depend. Whether we know it or not, our brain and biology have been shaped to favor this outcome." No matter how much we love Whitesnake—and, as many of you know, I do—we really weren't born to walk alone.

Myth #4: You can engineer the uncertainty and discomfort out of vulnerability.

I love working with tech companies and engineers. There is almost always a moment when someone suggests that we should make vulnerability easier by engineering the uncertainty and emotion right out of it. I've had people recommend everything from a texting app for hard conversations to an algorithm to predict when it's safe to be vulnerable with someone.

As I mentioned in the introduction, what sometimes underpins this urge is how we think about vulnerability and the way we use the word. Many people walk into work every day with one clear task: Engineer the vulnerability and uncertainty out of systems and/or mitigate risk. This is true of everyone from lawyers, who often equate vulnerability with loopholes and liabilities, to engineers and other people who work in operations, security, and technology, who think of vulnerabilities as potential systems failures, to combat soldiers and surgeons, who may literally equate vulnerabilities with death.

When I start talking about engaging with vulnerability and even embracing it, there can be real resistance until I clarify that I'm talking about relational vulnerability, not systemic vulnerability. Several years ago, I was working with a group of rocket scientists (actual ones). During a break an engineer walked up to me and said, "I don't do vulnerability. I can't. And that's a good thing. If I get all vulnerable, shit might fall from the sky. Literally."

I smiled and said, "Tell me about the toughest part of your job. Is it keeping shit from falling from the sky?"

He said, "No. We've created sophisticated systems that control for human error. It's hard work, but not the part I hate the most."

Wait for it.

He thought for a minute and said, "It's leading the team and all the people stuff. I've got a guy who is just not a good fit. His deliverables have been off for a year. I've tried everything. I got really tough this last time, but he almost started crying, so I wrapped up the meeting. It just didn't feel right. But now it's like I'm going to get in trouble because I'm not even turning in his performance sheets."

I said, "Yeah. That sounds hard. How does it feel?"

His response: "Got it. I'll sit down now."

Those fields in which systemic vulnerability is equated with failure (or worse) are often the ones in which I see people struggling the most for daring leadership skills and, interestingly, the ones in which people, once they understand, are willing to really dig deep and rumble hard. Can you imagine how hard it can be to wrap your brain around the critical role vulnerability plays in leadership when you're rewarded for eliminating vulnerability every day?

Another example of this comes from Canary Wharf—London's financial district—where I spent an afternoon with some very proper bankers who wondered what I was doing there and weren't afraid to ask me directly. They explained that banking is completely compliance driven and there's no place for vulnerability. Neither the frustrated bankers nor the wonderful and forward-thinking learning and development team who invited me expected my answer.

I was honest: "Tomorrow is my last day in London, and I really want to visit James Smith & Sons"—the famous umbrella shop that's been around since the early 1800s—"so let's try to figure out why I'm here, and if we can't, I'm out."

They seemed a little miffed but interested in the deal. So I asked one question: "What's the biggest issue you're facing here and in your industry?"

There was a pause filled with some back-and-forth between people before the self-elected spokesperson shouted out "Ethical decision making."

Bloody hell. I'm not going anywhere.

I took a deep breath and asked, "Has anyone here ever stood up to a team or group of people and said, 'This is outside our values' or 'This is not in line with our ethics'?"

Most people in the room raised a hand.

"And how does that feel?"

The room got quiet. I answered for them. "There's probably not a single act at work that requires more vulnerability than holding people responsible for ethics and values, especially when you're alone in it or there's a lot of money, power, or influence at stake. People will put you down, question your intentions, hate you, and sometimes try to discredit you in the process of protecting themselves. So if you don't 'do' vulnerability, and/or you have a culture that thinks vulnerability is weakness, then it's no wonder that ethical decision making is a problem."

There was nothing but the sound of people getting out pens and journals to take notes and settling into their seats until a woman in the front said, "Sorry about the umbrella shop. You'll have to come back. London is lovely in the spring."

Regardless of how we approach systemic vulnerability, once we try to strip uncertainty, risk, and emotional exposure from the relational experience, we bankrupt courage by definition. Again, we know that courage is four skill sets with vulnerability at the center. So the bad news is that there's no app for it, and regardless of what you do and where you work, you're called to be brave in vulnerability even if your job is engineering the vulnerability out of systems.

The good news is that if we can successfully develop the four courage-building skills, starting with how to rumble with vulnerability, we will have the capacity for something deeply human, invaluable to leadership, and unattainable by machines.

Myth #5: Trust comes before vulnerability.

We sometimes do an exercise with groups where we give people sentence stems and they fill out the answers on a Post-it note. An example:

> I grew up believing that vulnerability is:
> ______________________.

If the group is big enough to ensure that comments will be anonymous, we stick them up for everyone to read. It's incredibly powerful because, without fail, people are stunned by how similar the answers are. We too often believe that we're the only ones wrestling with some of these issues.

I'll never forget a sticky note that someone shared a couple of years ago. It said, "I grew up believing that vulnerability is: *The first step to betrayal.*"

I was with a group of community leaders and activists, and we spent an hour talking about how so many of us were taught that vulnerability is for suckers. While some of us were raised hearing that explicit message loud and clear, and others learned it through quiet observation, the message was the same: If you're stupid enough to let someone know where you're tender or what you care about the most, it's just a matter of time before someone uses that to hurt you.

These conversations always bring up the chicken-egg debate about trust and vulnerability.

> **How do I know if I can trust someone enough to be vulnerable?**
> **Can I build trust without ever risking vulnerability?**

The research is clear, but not a huge relief for those of us who would prefer a scoring system or failproof trust test. Or that app we just talked about.

We need to trust to be vulnerable, and we need to be vulnerable in order to build trust.

The research participants described trust as a slow-building, iterative, and layered process that happens over time. Both trust-building and rumbling with vulnerability involve risk. That's what makes courage hard and rare. In our work we use the metaphor of **the marble jar**. I first wrote about this in *Daring Greatly,* but I'll tell the story again here.

When my daughter, Ellen, was in third grade, she came home from school one day, closed the door behind her, looked at me, and then literally slid down the front door, buried her face in her hands, and started sobbing.

My response, of course, was, "Oh, my God, Ellen, are you okay? What happened?"

"Something really embarrassing happened at school today, and I shared it with my friends and they promised not to tell anyone, but by the time we got back to class, everyone in my whole class knew."

I could feel the slow rising of my internal Mama Bear. Ellen told me that it had been so bad that Ms. Baucum, her third-grade teacher, took half of the marbles out of the marble jar. In her classroom, there is a big jar for marbles—when the class collectively makes good decisions, they get to put marbles into the jar; when the class collectively makes bad decisions, marbles come out. Ms. Baucum took marbles out because everyone was laughing, apparently at Ellen. I told my daughter how sorry I was, and then she looked at me and said: "I will never trust anyone again in my life."

My heart was breaking with hers. My first thought was, *Damn straight—you trust your mama and that's it. And when you go to college I'm going to get a little apartment right next to the dorm and you can come and talk to me*. An appealing idea at the time. But instead, I put my fears and anger aside and started trying to figure out how to talk to her about trust and connection. As I was searching for the right way to translate my own experiences of trust, and what I was learning about trust from the research, I thought, *Ah, the marble jar. Perfect.*

I told Ellen, "We trust the people who have earned marbles over time in our life. Whenever someone supports you, or is kind to you, or sticks up for you, or honors what you share with them as private, you put marbles in the jar. When people are mean, or disrespectful, or share your secrets, marbles come out. We look for the people who, over time, put marbles in, and in, and in, until you look up one day and they're holding a full jar. Those are the folks you can tell your secrets to. Those are the folks you trust with information that's important to you."

And then I asked her if she had a friend with a full marble jar. "Yes, I've got marble jar friends. Hanna and Lorna are my marble jar friends." And I asked her to tell me how they earn marbles. I was really curious, and I expected her to recount dramatic stories of the girls doing heroic things for her. Instead, she said something that shocked me even more. "Well, I was at the soccer game last weekend, and Hanna looked up and told me that she saw Oma and Opa." Oma and Opa are my mom and stepdad.

I pushed Ellen for more details. "Then what?"

"No, that's it. I gave her a marble."

"Why?"

"Well, not everyone has eight grandparents." My parents are divorced and remarried, and Steve's parents are divorced and remarried. "I think it's really cool that Hanna remembers all of their names."

She continued, "Well, Lorna is also my marble jar friend because she will do the half-butt sit with me."

My very understandable response: "Lord have mercy, what is that?"

"If I come in too late to the cafeteria and all the tables are full, she'll scoot over and just take half the seat and give me the other half of the seat so I can sit at the friend table." I had to agree with her that a half-butt sit was really great, and certainly deserving of a marble. Perking up, she asked me if I have marble jar friends and how they earn their marbles.

"Well, I think it might be different for grown-ups." But then I thought back to the soccer game that Ellen was referring to. When my parents arrived, my friend Eileen had walked up and said, "Hey, David and Deanne, it's great to see you." And I remember feeling how much it meant to me that Eileen had remembered their names.

I tell you this story because I had always assumed that trust is earned in big moments and through really grand gestures, not the more simple things like a friend remembering small details in your life. Later that night, I called the doctoral students on my team, and we spent five days going through all the research around trust. We started looking into trust-earning behaviors, which enforced what Ellen had taught me after school that day. It turns out that trust is in fact earned in the smallest of moments. It is earned not through heroic deeds, or even highly visible actions, but through paying attention, listening, and gestures of genuine care and connection.

My job as a grounded theory researcher is to figure out what the data say and then jump into the literature to see how my findings fit or don't fit with what other researchers are reporting. Either way, the theory that emerges doesn't change, but if there's a conflict—which happens often—the researcher has to acknowledge it. Most quantitative researchers go the other way, looking first at what existing research says and then trying to confirm whether it is true. In my approach, I develop theories based on lived experiences, not existing theories. Only after I capture the participants' experiences do I try to place my theories in the existing research. Grounded theory researchers do it in that order so that our conclusions about the data aren't skewed by existing theories that may or may not reflect real experiences by diverse populations.

The first place I turned to see what was in the existing literature was John Gottman's research, which is based on forty years of studying intimate relationships. For those who are unfamiliar with Gottman's work on marriages, he was able to predict an outcome of divorce with 90 percent accuracy based on responses to a series of questions. His team screened for what he called the Four Horsemen of the Apocalypse—criticism, defensiveness, stonewalling, and contempt, with contempt being the most damning in a romantic partnership.

In an article on one of my go-to websites, the University of California, Berkeley's "Greater Good" (greatergood.berkeley.edu), Gottman describes trust-building with our partners in a manner totally consistent with what I found in my research. Gottman writes,

> What I've found through research is that trust is built in very small moments, which I call "sliding door" moments, after the movie *Sliding Doors*. In any interaction, there is a possibility of connecting with your partner or turning away from your partner.
>
> Let me give you an example of that from my own relationship. One night, I really wanted to finish a mystery

novel. I thought I knew who the killer was, but I was anxious to find out. At one point in the night, I put the novel on my bedside and walked into the bathroom.

As I passed the mirror, I saw my wife's face in the reflection, and she looked sad, brushing her hair. There was a sliding door moment.

I had a choice. I could sneak out of the bathroom and think, I don't want to deal with her sadness tonight; I want to read my novel. But instead, because I'm a sensitive researcher of relationships, I decided to go into the bathroom. I took the brush from her hand and asked, "What's the matter, baby?" And she told me why she was sad.

Now, at that moment, I was building trust; I was there for her. I was connecting with her rather than choosing to think only about what I wanted. These are the moments, we've discovered, that build trust.

One such moment is not that important, but if you're always choosing to turn away, then trust erodes in a relationship—very gradually, very slowly.

Trust is the stacking and layering of small moments and reciprocal vulnerability over time. Trust and vulnerability grow together, and to betray one is to destroy both.

Myth #6: Vulnerability is disclosure.

Apparently there is a misconception in some circles that I am a proponent of leaders disclosing personal experiences and openly sharing emotions in all cases. I think that notion stems from people having only a peripheral understanding of the key themes of my TEDxHouston talk on vulnerability and the book *Daring Greatly,* combined with the fact that 80 percent of the work I do today is about vulnerability and leadership. It's a bad case of the

2+2=57 craziness that we see in the world today. We all know people (and we've all been the people) who add up a couple of things that we *think* we understand and come to a clear, somewhat interesting, and totally false conclusion. Let's dispel that myth right off the bat with two seemingly conflicting statements:

1. I am not a proponent of oversharing, indiscriminate disclosure as a leadership tool, or vulnerability for vulnerability's sake.
2. There is no daring leadership without vulnerability.

Both of these are true statements.

I know there's a problem when people ask me, "How much should leaders share with their colleagues or employees?" Some of the most daring leaders I know have incredible vulnerability rumbling skills and yet disclose very little. I've also worked with leaders who share way more than they should and demonstrate little to no rumbling skills.

During a time of difficult change and uncertainty, daring leaders might sit with their teams and say,

> These changes are coming in hard and fast, and I know there's a lot of anxiety—I'm feeling it too, and it's hard to work through. It's hard not to take it home, it's hard not to worry, and it's easy to want to look for someone to blame. I will share everything I can about the changes with you, as soon as I can.
>
> I want to spend the next forty-five minutes rumbling on how we're all managing the changes. Specifically, *What does support from me look like? What questions can I try to answer? Are there any stories you want to check out with me? And any other questions you have?*

> I'm asking everyone to stay connected and lean into each other during this churn so we can really rumble with what's going on. In the midst of all of this we still need to produce work that makes us proud. Let's each write down one thing we need from this group in order to feel okay sharing and asking questions, and one thing that will get in the way.

This is a great example of rumbling with vulnerability. The leader is naming some of the unsaid emotions and creating what we call a **safe container** by asking the team what they need to feel open and safe in the conversation. This is one of the easiest practices to implement, and the return on the time investment is huge in terms of trust-building and improving the quality of feedback and conversation; yet I rarely see team, project, or group leaders take that time.

Google's five-year study on highly productive teams, Project Aristotle, found that psychological safety—team members feeling safe to take risks and be vulnerable in front of each other—was "far and away the most important of the five dynamics that set successful teams apart." Harvard Business School professor Amy Edmondson coined the phrase *psychological safety*. In her book *Teaming,* she writes,

> Simply put, psychological safety makes it possible to give tough feedback and have difficult conversations without the need to tiptoe around the truth. In psychologically safe environments, people believe that if they make a mistake others will not penalize or think less of them for it. They also believe that others will not resent or humiliate them when they ask for help or information. This belief comes about when people both trust and respect each other, and

> it produces a sense of confidence that the group won't embarrass, reject, or punish someone for speaking up. Thus psychological safety is a taken-for-granted belief about how others will respond when you ask a question, seek feedback, admit a mistake, or propose a possibly wacky idea. Most people feel a need to "manage" interpersonal risk to retain a good image, especially at work, and especially in the presence of those who formally evaluate them. This need is both instrumental (promotions and rewards may depend on impressions held by bosses and others) and socio-emotional (we simply prefer approval over disapproval).
>
> Psychological safety does not imply a cozy situation in which people are necessarily close friends. Nor does it suggest an absence of pressure or problems.

In our container-building work, the team would review all of the items that they wrote down, then work together to consolidate and match items to come up with some ground rules.

Items that frequently show up as things that get in the way of psychological safety in teams and groups include judgment, unsolicited advice giving, interrupting, and sharing outside the team meeting. The behaviors that people need from their team or group almost always include listening, staying curious, being honest, and keeping confidence. Dare to lead by investing twenty minutes in creating psychological safety when you need to rumble. Make your intention of creating safety explicit and get your team's help on how to do it effectively.

What I also love about this example is how the leader is being honest about the struggle, staying calm while naming the anxiety and how it might be showing up, and giving people the opportunity to ask questions and reality-check the rumor mill. What I really appreciate about this approach is one of my favorite rumble tools: **"What does support from me look like?"** Not only does it offer the opportunity for clarity and set up the team for success, asking people for specific examples of what supportive behaviors look like—and what they do *not* look like—it also holds them accountable for asking for what they need.

When you put this question into practice, expect to see people struggling to come up with examples of supportive behaviors. We're much more accustomed to not asking for exactly what we need and then being resentful or disappointed that we didn't get it. Also, most of us can tell you what support does *not* look like more easily than we can come up with what it does look like. Over time, this practice is a huge grounded-confidence builder (we'll talk about that concept later).

In this rumble example, the leader is not oversharing or disclosing inappropriately as a mechanism for hotwiring connection or trust with other people. There's also no fake vulnerability. Fake vulnerability can look like a leader telling us that we can ask questions but not taking the time to create the psychological safety to do it, or not offering a pause in the conversation for anyone else to speak at all.

This leader is also not shirking the responsibility of attending to the team's fears and feelings by oversharing and sympathy seeking with statements like "I'm really falling apart too. I don't know what to do either. I'm not the enemy here." Basically, *Feel sorry for me and don't hold me accountable for leading through this hard time because I'm scared too.* Blech.

Not only is fake vulnerability ineffective—but it breeds distrust. There's no faster way to piss off people than to try to manipulate them with vulnerability. Vulnerability is not a personal marketing tool. It's not an oversharing strategy. Rumbling with vulnerability is about leaning into rather than walking away from the situations that make us feel uncertain, at risk, or emotionally exposed.

We should always be clear about our intention, understand the limits of vulnerability in the context of roles and relationships, and set boundaries. **Boundaries** is a slippery word, but I love how my friend Kelly Rae Roberts makes it simple and powerful. She's an artist, and several years ago she wrote a blog post about how people can and can't use her copyrighted work. The post had two lists: what's okay and what's not okay. It was crystal clear and completely captured what had emerged from the data we collected on effective boundary setting. Today, we teach that **setting boundaries is making clear what's okay and what's not okay, and why.**

Vulnerability minus boundaries is not vulnerability. It's confession, manipulation, desperation, or shock and awe, but it's not vulnerability.

As an example of what vulnerability is not, I sometimes tell the story of a young CEO who was six months into his first round of investment funding. He came up to me after a talk and said, "I get it! I'm in. I'm drinking the Kool-Aid! *I'm gonna get really vulnerable with my people.*"

My first thought was *Oh, man. Here we go.* First, when people talk about "drinking the Kool-Aid," I get skeptical. It's a pretty terrible reference, and if you have to turn off your critical thinking and chug the groupthink juice to be down with an idea or get on board with a plan, I'm already concerned. Second, if you run up to me excited about becoming more vulnerable, you must not really understand the concept. If, on the other hand, you come up to me and say, "Okay. I think I get it and I'm going to try to embrace the suck of vulnerability," I'm pretty sure you understand what's involved.

The conversation started with multiple flags. Not enough for a parade, but close.

I gave him a nervous smile and said **"Say more."** *Another favorite rumble tool.* Asking someone to "say more" often leads to profoundly deeper and more productive rumbling. Context and details matter. Peel the onion. Stephen Covey's sage advice still stands: "Seek first to understand, then to be understood."

The excited CEO explained, "I'm just going to tell the investors and my team the truth: I'm completely in over my head, we're bleeding money, and I have no idea what I'm doing."

He paused and looked at me. "What do you think?"

I took his hand and led him to the side of the room, and we sat down. I looked at him and repeated what I had said in the talk, but what he apparently missed: "What do I think? I think you won't secure any more funding and you're going to scare the shit out of some people. Vulnerability without boundaries is not vulnerability. It might be fear or anxiety. We have to think about why we're sharing and, equally important, with whom. *What are their roles? What is our role? Is this sharing productive and appropriate?*"

Before I go any further when I'm telling the story to a group, I always ask the audience this question: *We probably all agree that standing in front of your employees and investors with this confession is not smart. But here's a question for you: If everyone here had a full year's salary invested in this guy's company, how many of you would be hoping he was sitting down across from* someone *saying, "I'm completely in over my head, we're bleeding money, and I have no idea what I'm doing?"*

If there are a thousand people in the room, two or three might nervously raise their hand as they become increasingly aware of being in a tiny minority. The only exception was a room of fifty venture capitalists. They all raised their hand.

I break the tension by raising my hand and explaining my

thinking: "If I've got money invested in his company, I pray that he's sitting down with a mentor or an advisor or a board member and being really honest about what's happening. Why? Because we all know the alternative. He keeps pretending and hustling and grinding on the same ineffective changes until everything is gone."

Now, if I were the guy, I wouldn't stand up in front of all of my investors or my team of friends and colleagues who left great jobs to come work with me to turn my vision into a reality and spill my guts like that—that's not good judgment. When I asked him why he'd share that with them rather than an advisor or mentor who might be able to help without becoming personally panicked, he revealed what I call the **stealth intention** and the **stealth expectation.**

The stealth intention is a self-protection need that lurks beneath the surface and often drives behavior outside our values. Closely related is the stealth expectation—a desire or expectation that exists outside our awareness and typically includes a dangerous combination of fear and magical thinking. Stealth expectations almost always lead to disappointment, resentment, and more fear.

He said, "I'm not sure. I guess I want them to know I'm trying. I want them to know that I'm doing the best I can and I'm a good guy, but I'm failing. If I tell them the truth and get really vulnerable, they won't blame me or hate me. They'll understand."

Stealth intention: I can protect myself from rejection, shame, judgment, and people turning away from me and thinking I'm a bad person.

Stealth expectation: They won't turn away from me and think I'm a bad person.

Trust me when I tell you that stealth intentions and expectations are things I have to wrestle with often in myself, sometimes on a daily basis. I've wanted to shout the same type of thing to my team for the same reasons, but I've had enough practice to know that vulnerability is not a sympathy-seeking tool. As a leader, he needs to stay honest with his team and investors, *and* this vulnerable conversation needs to happen with someone who can help him lead through it. Sharing just to share without understanding your role, recognizing your professional boundaries, and getting clear on your intentions and expectations (especially those flying under the radar) is just purging or venting or gossip or a million other things that are often propelled by hidden needs.

More than occasionally, I find that the people who misrepresent my work on vulnerability and conflate it with disclosure or emotional purging either don't understand it, or they have so much personal resistance to the notion of being vulnerable that they stretch the concept until it appears ridiculous and easy to discount. In either case, if you come across an explanation of vulnerability that doesn't include setting boundaries or being clear on intentions, proceed with caution. Vulnerability for vulnerability's sake is not effective, useful, or smart.

TO FEEL IS TO BE VULNERABLE

For those of us who were raised with a healthy (or unhealthy) dose of "suck it up and get 'er done," rumbling with vulnerability is a challenge. The myths I outlined above work together to lead us to believe that vulnerability is the gooey center of the hard emotions that we work full time to avoid feeling, much less discussing (even when our avoidance causes us and the people around us pain)—emotions like fear, shame, grief, disappointment, and sadness. But vulnerability isn't just the center of hard emotions, it's the core of all emotions. **To feel is to be vulnerable. Believing that vulnerability is weakness is believing that feeling is weakness.** And, like it or not, we are emotional beings.

What most of us fail to understand, and what took me a decade of research to learn, is that vulnerability is the cradle of the emotions and experiences that we crave. Vulnerability is the birthplace of love, belonging, and joy.

We know that vulnerability is the cornerstone of courage-building, but we often fail to realize that without vulnerability there is no creativity or innovation. Why? Because there is nothing more uncertain than the creative process, and there is absolutely no innovation without failure. Show me a culture in which vulnerability is framed as weakness and I'll show you a culture struggling to come up with fresh ideas and new perspectives. I love what Amy Poehler had to say in her web series *Smart Girls: Ask Amy*:

> It's very hard to have ideas. It's very hard to put yourself out there, it's very hard to be vulnerable, but those people who do that are the dreamers, the thinkers, and the creators. They are the magic people of the world.

Adaptability to change, hard conversations, feedback, problem solving, ethical decision making, recognition, resilience, and all of the other skills that underpin daring leadership are born of vulnerability. To foreclose on vulnerability and our emotional life out of fear that the costs will be too high is to walk away from the very thing that gives purpose and meaning to living. As the neuroscientist Antonio Damasio reminds us, "We are not necessarily thinking machines. We are feeling machines that think."

In the next section we'll break down one of my own leadership stories to better understand how fear and feelings left unattended can cause major problems, and we'll explore more rumbling language, skills, tools, and practices.

Clear is kind.

UNCLEAR
IS UNKIND.

section two THE CALL TO COURAGE

In the earliest days of building our company, I found myself sitting at a table with my team after they asked if we could meet for an hour. When I realized there was no agenda, I got that sinking *What now?* feeling. Charles, our CFO, looked at me and said, "We need to rumble with you on a growing concern about how we're working together."

For years, my first thought in a situation like this would have been *Oh, God. It's an intervention. And I'm the intervenee.* But I trust my team, and I trust the rumble process.

Chaz, as I've called him for twenty-five years, cut right to the chase. "We keep setting unrealistic timelines, working frantically to meet them, failing, setting new timelines, and still not meeting them. It's keeping us in constant chaos and people are burning out. When you set a timeline and we push back because we know it's unattainable, you get so insistent that we stop pushing. It's not working. You have a lot of strengths, but you're not good at estimating time, and we need to find a new process that works for all of us."

As my team sat there looking anxious for me to respond and relieved that the issue was on the table regardless of my response, I thought about the first time I heard someone say "You're not good at estimating time," and I drifted off to the memory of an almost-fight I had with Steve a decade before this meeting.

Steve and I, along with our next-door neighbors, signed up to host a progressive dinner party to raise money for our daughter's PTO. Steve and I were in charge of appetizers and salad at our house, then the guests would walk next door for dinner, then back to our house for dessert and coffee. Very retro and very fun.

Everything sounds easy when it's months away.

I remember exactly where I was standing when I looked at Steve and said, "This is going to be great. I'm excited about the new recipes. All we need to do is get the house ready. I can do a little paint touch-up in the dining room, and I need you to add some pops of color in the front yard. I need the yard to say, *Welcome! We're glad you're here! These flowers are evidence that we're awesome neighbors who have our shit together!*"

Steve just stared at me.

I glared back at him. "What? Why are you looking at me like that?"

Steve said, "The dinner party starts in two hours."

"I know," I said. "I've thought about it. It'll take you fifteen minutes to get to Home Depot, thirty minutes to pick out the right combination of flowers, fifteen minutes to get home, forty-five minutes to plant them, and then fifteen minutes to take a shower."

Steve couldn't speak. He just stood there shaking his head until I said, "What? What's wrong?"

Steve said, "You're not good at estimating time, Brené."

I quipped back without thinking, "Maybe I'm just faster than most people."

I drew a deep breath, immediately regretting being a smart-ass when I needed him to hightail it to Home Depot. I responded to my own comment before he could. "Really? Why do you think that I'm bad at estimating time?"

"Well, for starters," he said, "you didn't factor in the hour we're going to need for the fight that's going to break out when I say 'Hell, no, I'm not going to landscape the front yard two hours before company comes' and you respond by accusing me of never caring about the details or worrying about the little things. You'll say my lack of attention to detail is why you're so stressed out all the time. Then you'll say something like 'It must be nice not to have to worry about the little things that make a big difference.' "

I just stood there.

The fact that he was saying all of this in a kind way and not being crappy made it worse.

He continued, "Your 'must be nice' comment is going to feel like blame and criticism, and it's going to piss me off. All of the stress of hosting this party is going to escalate things. You'll try not to cry because you don't want puffy eyes, but we'll both end up in tears. We'll spend the rest of the night just wanting it to be over. So we're not going to get flowers, and I think we should skip the fight, given our tight timeline."

His prophecy forced me into a weepy laugh. "Okay. That was painful. And funny."

Steve said, "The best thing you can do right now is go for a short run and take a shower. What people see is what they get."

As I pulled myself back from this memory and into my seat at the table with my team, I found myself deeply grateful for Chaz's clarity. Over our years of researching and working together, we've learned something about clarity that has changed everything from the way we talk to each other to the way we negotiate with external partners. It's simple but transformative: **Clear is kind. Unclear is unkind.** I first heard this saying two decades ago in a 12-step meeting, but I was on slogan overload at the time and didn't even think about it again until I saw the data about how most of us avoid clarity because we tell ourselves that we're being kind, when what we're actually doing is being unkind and unfair.

Feeding people half-truths or bullshit to make them feel better (which is almost always about making ourselves feel more comfortable) is unkind. Not getting clear with a colleague about your expectations because it feels too hard, yet holding them accountable or blaming them for not delivering is unkind. Talking *about* people rather than *to* them is unkind. This lesson has so wildly transformed my life that we live by it at home. If Ellen is trying to figure out how to handle a college roommate issue or Charlie needs to talk to a friend about something . . . clear is kind. Unclear is unkind.

I looked at my team and said, "Thank you for trusting me enough to tell me this. It's not the first or even hundredth time I've heard this feedback about my sucky time estimation skills. I'm going to work on it. I'm going to get better."

I could tell they were a little disappointed in my response. The "Okay, I get it and I'll work on it" is a common shut-down technique. I took a deep breath and leaned into the mother of all rumble tools—curiosity. "Tell me more about how this plays out for y'all. I want to understand."

I'm glad I asked. I needed to hear what they had to say, and they needed me to hear how frustrating, demoralizing, and unproductive it was for me to continue pitching ideas and timelines that were completely unrealistic and then looking at them like they were crushing my dream when they did their jobs by being honest and saying, "That will take at least twelve months, not two months, and it will require a significant cash investment."

It was painful and uncomfortable. Which is exactly why we try to wrap things up quickly and get the hell out of conversations like this. It's so much easier to say "Got it, on it," and run.

After listening, I thanked them for their courage and honesty and promised again that I would think about it. I asked if we could **circle back** the next day. In my research and in my life, I've found absolutely no benefit to pushing through a hard conversation unless there's an urgent, time-sensitive issue at hand. I've never regretted taking a short break or circling back after a few hours of thinking time. I have, however, regretted many instances where I pushed through to get it over and done with. Those self-serving instincts end up costing way more time than a short break.

When I got home that evening, I downloaded a couple of books on project management, and for some reason, maybe something I read on LinkedIn, I convinced myself that I needed a "Six Sigma black belt." I had no idea what that even meant, but I googled it, and after I read for a few minutes, the thought of it made me want to knock myself unconscious with my laptop.

It didn't take long before I realized that my plan wasn't going to work. I'm not good at time or things with hard edges, like Tetris or Blokus. I don't think that way or see the world that way. I see projects in constellations, not lines. I see plans the way I see data—relationally and with rounded corners and a million connection ports. As much as I read and tried, it felt like a strange and terrible spreadsheet world to me.

Interested in an example of how I think? *Brace yourself.*

When I realized that I couldn't return to my team and impress them with my shiny new black belt and laserlike time estimations, it made me think immediately of Luke Skywalker struggling to become a Jedi warrior in *The Empire Strikes Back*.

I share my love for this story in *Rising Strong,* but I'll share it again here because there's no such thing as too much *Star Wars.*

Yoda is trying to teach Luke how to use the Force and how the dark side of the Force—anger, fear, and aggression—is holding him back. Luke and Yoda are in the swamp where they've been training when Luke points toward a dark cave at the base of a giant tree and, looking at Yoda, says, "There's something not right here . . . I feel cold. Death."

Yoda explains to Luke that the cave is dangerous and strong with the dark side of the Force. Luke looks confused and afraid, but Yoda's response is simply, "In you must go."

When Luke asks what's in the cave, Yoda explains, "Only what you take with you."

As Luke straps on his weapons, Yoda hauntingly advises, "Your weapons, you will not need them." Luke grabs his light saber anyway.

The cave is dark and scary. As Luke slowly makes his way through it, he is confronted by his enemy, Darth Vader. They both draw their light sabers, and Luke quickly cuts off Vader's helmeted head. The head rolls to the ground and the face guard blows off the helmet. Only it isn't Darth Vader's face that's revealed; it's Luke's. Luke is staring at his own head on the ground.

This parable got me thinking about the possibility that maybe the problem was less about my time estimation and project management skills and more about my fears. So I wrote down a couple of very specific examples of timelines that I forced on my reluctant team, and sure enough, the biggest enemy was not a lack of estimation skills but a lack of personal awareness. Was I cutting off my own head with a light saber?

I discovered that my unreasonable timelines were seldom driven by excitement or ambition. I drive these unattainable timelines for two reasons: (1) I'm feeling fear, scarcity, and anxiety (e.g., *We're not doing enough, someone else is going to think of this idea before we get it done, look what everyone else is doing*), or (2) In addition to the daily work we do together, I'm often holding visions of longer-term university commitments, publishing contracts, and a dozen potential collaboration conversations in my head. Sometimes I'm pushing timelines because I'm trying to sync up the timing on projects and deadlines that my team doesn't even know about because I've failed to share.

It was powerful to figure out the source of the issue, but that didn't translate to my wanting to circle back with my team about these **key learnings**. I didn't want to say "I'm actually not good at the time estimation piece, and the more I understand that skill set, the less confident I am that I will actually get much better."

I didn't want to share the truth about my fear. *What if the scarcity and anxiety are happening because I have no business being a leader?* Even being honest about my failure to communicate larger strategy was daunting. *What if my communication fails are just symptomatic of my being in over my head trying to run businesses?* The most critical thing that the shame gremlins kept whispering was *You don't belong in this job. You study leadership, but you can't lead. You're a joke!*

When we're in fear, or an emotion is driving self-protection, there's a fairly predictable pattern of how we assemble our armor, piece by piece:

1. I'm not enough.
2. If I'm honest with them about what's happening, they'll think less of me or maybe even use it against me.
3. No way am I going to be honest about this. No one else does it. Why do I have to put myself out there?

4. Yeah. Screw them. I don't see them being honest about what scares them. And they've got plenty of issues.
5. It's actually their issues and shortcomings that make me act this way. This is their fault, and they're trying to blame me.
6. In fact, now that I think about it, I'm actually better than them.

People think it's a long walk from "I'm not enough" to "I'm better than them," but it's actually just standing still. In the exact same place. In fear. Assembling the armor.

I don't want to live in fear or lead from fear, and I'm sick to death of the armor. Courage and faith are my core values, and when I'm in fear I show up in ways that leave me feeling out of alignment with these values and outside my integrity. This is when I remember Joseph Campbell's quote, which I believe is one of the purest calls to courage for leaders: **"The cave you fear to enter holds the treasure you seek."**

Campbell consulted with George Lucas on *Star Wars,* and there's no question in my mind that my favorite scene is Lucas bringing this wisdom to life.

This is how I think. No black belt, but I have to believe that the Force is with me.

Treasure Hunting

What is the treasure I seek? Less fear, scarcity, and anxiety. Less feeling alone. More working together toward goals that excite all of us.

What is the cave I fear to enter? I'm afraid to admit that I don't know how to do some of the things that I think all "real leaders" know how to do. I don't want to share that when I'm scared I make bad decisions, and I've felt stuck and scared, tired and lonely, a lot lately.

When I sat down with my team for our circle back, we started the meeting with one of our rituals: **permission slips**. We each wrote down one thing that we gave ourselves permission to do or feel for this meeting. Sometimes we do it on Post-it notes, but I prefer to write in my journal so that, in addition to my meeting notes, I have a reminder of what I was feeling that day.

That afternoon I gave myself permission to be honest with my team about my experiences and the stories I make up about sharing my feelings. Two of the other permissions I remember my team sharing that day were "Listen with passion" and "Ask for breaks if we need them."

Permission slips are powerful. I've seen people, after coming into meetings hell-bent on getting approval for their idea or plan, instead give themselves permission to stay open-minded or to listen more than they talk. I've also heard "I give myself permission to ask for more time to think about something before I share my point of view" or "I give myself permission to be present here even though I'm getting pulled in another direction today."

We love permission slips. Because, just like when I used to sign a permission slip to allow Ellen or Charlie to go to the zoo with their class, they still had to get it to the teacher and get on the bus. Just because you write down "Permission to speak up even though I'm the only person here who isn't a content expert" doesn't mean that you're going to do it. Permission slips aren't promissory notes, they are for stating and writing down intentions only, so there are no repercussions if you fail to deliver; however, they are useful for increasing accountability and the potential for support, and also for understanding where everyone in the room is coming from.

After we shared permission slips, I told them about my unsuccessful experience reading the business books. I explained how I had discovered that fear, anxiety, and scarcity were driving my unrealistic timelines, and how I got even more fearful when they responded with the realities of "contingencies and critical paths."

I walked them through what it felt like for me when they pushed back about timelines that I'd calculated based on a million moving pieces, some of which were completely off their radar. Because we're a close group and they work their asses off, it was hard to tell them that I can feel completely alone in trying to keep and coordinate all of the balls in the air. Basically, I owned that all my timeline pushing stemmed from fear, and that rather than being honest about those feelings and owning them, I would **offload the emotions** on them with anger and the really shitty behavior of looking at them like they were dream crushers.

I told them about trying to read the books on project management and estimation skills, and believing that the time estimation part of my brain might be missing. They didn't respond with "No, it's not missing!" Instead, they actually agreed. Murdoch, my manager, kindly said, "Yes, it could be missing. But the good news is that it makes more room in your brain for all that creativity." And we all laughed hard about the black belt.

We identified four **key learnings** during our rumble. First, as a leadership team, we need a shared understanding of all the moving pieces so no single person is the connective tissue. We've fixed this with new communication processes that include the team continuing to meet—across all areas of the businesses—when I'm locked away writing, researching, or on the road. We also have a new **meeting minutes** process. Everyone takes their own notes, but one person in the meeting volunteers to capture minutes.

These are narrowed down to:

Date:
Meeting intention:
Attendees:
Key decisions:
Tasks and ownership:

The great thing about this new practice is that everyone in the meeting is responsible for stopping to say "Let's capture this in the minutes"—not just the minute taker. And we now stop meetings five minutes early to review and agree on the minutes before we leave. Before we walk out of the meeting, the minute taker Slacks them to all of us and puts them in any other relevant channel so there isn't any clean-up or synthesizing guesswork after we've dispersed.

The minutes process also solved several other ongoing problems, including subjective minutes (as a result of one person writing them up from memory hours after the meeting) and keeping our dispersed teams up to speed on the frequent pivots that define a start-up environment. This new meeting documentation process, combined with my commitment to copy my team on planning emails with potential collaborators and my publisher, means that everyone has much more access to what's going on across the different areas of our work.

We also agreed that we'd work together on estimating timelines and due dates, rumbling on them until we all owned them as a team. Today we've started using a time estimation and project priority practice that seems simple but is effective and wildly telling. We call it the **Turn & Learn**. We all get Post-it notes and write down how long we think a project is going to take, and if we're looking at several projects that we need to prioritize, we'll write the projects in priority order. Once everyone has written down an estimate or priority ranking in private, we count to three and show our answers.

This practice controls for the **"halo effect"** created when everyone sees what the person with the most influence in the room wants and follows suit. It also controls for the **"bandwagon effect"**—that very human instinct to follow suit even when you disagree. It's tough to be the last to share when everyone is on board and getting increasingly excited about an idea.

We call it Turn & Learn because it's not about being right or wrong, it's about creating space to understand different perspectives, learning from everyone around the table, and identifying areas where we need to get clear on expectations. Most often, we learn that we're all working off different data and assumptions, or that we don't fully understand the lift, or we don't get the load certain people are already carrying. It's a huge connection tool.

It was clear that I had some serious personal work to do, and we also unearthed a dangerous pattern that we needed to name and deconstruct—a pattern that I observe in organizations all the time but was in my blind spot. It's operations versus marketing. Finance versus creative. The spenders versus the savers. The hearts versus the analytics. The dreamers versus the sticks-in-the-mud. This type of binary thinking is very dangerous because we're not leveraging the fullness of people. The roles become caricatures and stereotypes: *Juan is such an optimist with his sales projections, but it's all right because Kari will come in hard with worst-case-scenario numbers and kill those fantasies.* We should all be held accountable for being both optimistic *and* realistic. If you gain a reputation for being an idealist, you lose credibility and trust. If you're forced to be the reality-checker, you never get the opportunity to take chances and risk.

This insight took us straight to the pages of Jim Collins's classic book *Good to Great*. We had done a companywide read of the book, and even at the time, the Stockdale Paradox was something that stuck with us. As Collins explained, the Stockdale Paradox was named after Admiral Jim Stockdale, who spent eight years as a prisoner of war in Vietnam. He was tortured more than twenty times during his imprisonment from 1965 to 1973. In addition to fighting to stay alive, he worked every day to help the other prisoners survive the physical and emotional torment.

When he interviewed Stockdale, Collins asked him, "Who didn't make it out?"

Stockdale replied, "Oh, that's easy. The optimists."

Stockdale explained that the optimists would believe they'd be out by Christmas, and Christmas would come and go. Then they would believe they'd be out by Easter, and that date would come and go. And the years would tick by like that. He explained to Collins, "They died of a broken heart."

Stockdale told Collins, "This is a very important lesson. You must never confuse faith that you will prevail in the end—which you can never afford to lose—with the discipline to confront the most brutal facts of your current reality, whatever they might be." We named this third key learning **gritty faith and gritty facts,** and today we all work to take responsibility for both dreaming and reality-checking those dreams with facts.

When stress is high, we can still find ourselves slipping into some of these patterns, especially failing to communicate all of these pieces and to maintain connective tissue. What's powerful about doing this work is that we now recognize it very quickly and we can name it. Once that happens, we know what rumble needs to happen and why.

At the end of the meeting, I apologized for offloading my emotions on them. And, of equal importance, I made a commitment to make good on that apology by talking about my fears when they creep up and staying aware of the behaviors that fear drives in me. I also checked with my team to make sure we agreed that if I was successful changing those behaviors, it would address the key learnings that we discussed. Apologizing and backing that up with behavior change is normalized in our organization from onboarding. While some leaders consider apologizing to be a sign of weakness, we teach it as a skill and frame the willingness to apologize and make amends as brave leadership.

Reflecting on the key learnings, all of us owned our parts and talked about how we would incorporate those learnings going forward. Examining "our part" is also critical to our rumble process. I've yet to be in a rumble, or any tough conversation—even one where I'm 99 percent sure I'm totally in the clear—in which, after digging in, I didn't have a part. Even if my part was not speaking up or staying curious. We're big believers in **"What's my part?"**

The Power and Wisdom to Serve Others

Joseph Campbell's lesson was that when you find the courage to enter that cave, you're never going in to secure your own treasure or your own wealth; you face your fears to find the power and wisdom to serve others.

In that spirit, I want to introduce you to Colonel DeDe Halfhill. She is currently the director of innovation, analysis, and leadership development for Air Force Global Strike Command, which comprises 33,000 officers and enlisted and civilian airmen. Prior to her current position she commanded the 2nd Mission Support Group at Barksdale Air Force Base, Louisiana, and was responsible for 1,800 airmen and the day-to-day sustainment operations of Barksdale Air Force Base. It was during her tenure as the commander of that organization that the following incident took place. DeDe Halfhill is one of my leadership heroes and a total badass. I often think about this story when I need inspiration to choose courage over comfort so I can serve others.

DeDe writes:

> I think one of the most helpful things I've learned from Brené's work is the importance of using the right language to talk about hard things and tackle tough subjects. Conceptually, as leaders, I think we understand vulnerability, and are even personally willing to be vulnerable, but we don't always have the right language or practice in applying such concepts. It doesn't really work to say: "I'm going to be vulnerable here with you right now."
>
> During the first year of my command, I was presenting an award to an airman at a squadron event. At the end of the presentation, I asked if anyone had any questions. A young airman raised his hand and asked, "Ma'am, when is the ops tempo [the pace of current operations] going to slow down, because we are really tired?"
>
> "Yeah," I said. "It has been very busy, and we ask a lot of you." I explained, "It's not just here at Barksdale, though. I just came from a different command, where I heard the same thing. Across our Air Force, leaders know we're asking a lot of you, and they know you're tired."
>
> "Yes, ma'am, we're tired."
>
> While the squadron itself is larger, there were probably about forty airmen at the event that day. I asked everyone who was tired to raise their hands, and pretty much every hand went up.
>
> I thought about Brené's work, and the power it has given me to talk about things that are uncomfortable.
>
> I went on: "I want to share something with all of you

that I read recently that has really made me stop and think. Three days ago, I was reading an article in the *Harvard Business Review,* and it was talking about an organization that was researching companies that were reporting high levels of exhaustion. This team went into these companies to see what was driving such high levels of exhaustion. What they found was that while these employees were in fact exhausted, it wasn't just because of the ops tempo. They were actually exhausted because people were lonely. Their workforces were lonely, and that loneliness was manifesting itself in a feeling of exhaustion."

I stopped for a second and looked out at the group, then continued, "Because that's what happens, right?

"When we're lonely, we just feel lethargic. We don't really want to do anything; we think we're tired, and we just want to sleep." I paused: "So, if I were to ask you, instead of who's tired, who's lonely? How many of you would raise your hand?"

At least fifteen people raised their hand.

Loneliness is such a hard thing for many of us to admit. I thought maybe one person would raise a hand. But when fifteen people raised their hands, I was shocked. For lack of better language, I had an "Oh shit" moment. I really didn't know what to do.

I stood there, stunned, in front of everyone, thinking: I'm not a therapist. I'm not equipped for this. I certainly wasn't prepared for nearly a quarter of the group to admit such a raw emotion to me. And truthfully, I'm trying to get through some of the same emotions myself. It was uncomfortable, and the discomfort was making me want to move on to a different topic. But that's where Brené's work has given me courage. Five years ago, before hearing her work,

I would never have had the courage to ask that question, and I certainly wouldn't have been prepared to hold space for the answers.

Our Air Force, our military in general, is facing challenges with suicide, with people feeling isolated and hopeless. As leaders we are trying everything we can to reach our airmen and ensure they know that suicide is not the answer. We spend so much time talking with them about available resources, but I'm not sure enough of us are talking about the fact that in the end, a lot of people are just lonely. They're not connecting, and they're not reaching out.

Before I even asked the question, I knew it was going to be very uncomfortable, but I also knew it was an important question to ask. So, I decided to call on courage and vulnerability and stay in the moment.

I decided to be honest with them.

"This breaks my heart. Loneliness isn't something I've talked about with you before. But seeing so many of you raise your hands today scares me a little because I'm not entirely sure what to do with this information. As a leader, if you tell me you're tired, I'm going to send you home, tell you to take some leave, to take some time away and get some rest. But if what's really going on is you're lonely, then sending you off to be by yourself, yet again, means that I could possibly exacerbate the very problem we are so desperately trying to combat in our Air Force, which is that some people are so out of hope, feeling so isolated, that they are doing something irreversible."

My willingness to ask an uncomfortable question opened the door to a great conversation. We ended the afternoon event having had a very candid discussion about how we build relationships in the unit, how we reach out to others when we're feeling alone, and how we create a community of inclusion. It also provided invaluable insight for the squadron commander and set him on a path to address the right issue: connection and inclusion versus busyness and exhaustion.

It was also a pivotal moment in my own leadership growth. I realized that day that as a leader, if I am comfortable enough to use the right language and say "Are you lonely?" I may be able to create a connection that gives someone hope. It's possible that by using the right language I'll create a connection where maybe, just maybe, they will come and talk to me. And then we can do something about it. Most of the time, if I'm not comfortable with the discomfort that can come from such a moment, and I encounter someone who is having trouble, I send them—and rightly so—to helping professionals, to trained therapists.

Sometimes I fear, though, that in doing so, I am sending the message "I don't know how to deal with this" or "I don't have the space to handle the heaviness of this" or "I have so many other demands that I just can't deal with it." As leaders I certainly believe we all want to do the right thing, but we don't always have the bandwidth or experience to take care of someone the way they need to be taken care of. Sending them to helping professionals is absolutely the right thing to do, but I also think it can add to the feeling of isolation. In some sense, it may feel as if I'm pushing that airman away, and I'm telling them to let the professionals "deal with it." The subconscious message that I could be sending is: You are not with me, and I am not with you.

That day, when I saw all those hands go up, it affected me so much that I tell the story every chance I get. I want leaders, I want fellow airmen, to hear and feel for themselves how it feels when we use words like *lonely* versus *exhausted*. I've now told the story at least thirty to forty times to different groups, to people of different ranks and professions in the Air Force. I know I've hit a nerve because every time I tell the story, as I look out at the crowd, I see people nodding in agreement. They're connected. You can see it. You can feel it. They are relating to what it feels like to be in the military, to be away from home, and how hard it is to build community with every new assignment. They're enthralled in what I'm saying in that moment, because they too have had their own moments of loneliness. I tear up every time I tell the story because I know it's resonating with them, and I'm sad that we don't talk openly about it more often. In some cases, our lives depend on it.

Now, after almost every presentation, someone will come up to me and ask: "What do I do when I'm lonely?"

I am certainly not an expert on this topic, which in itself is intimidating. I've opened the door to a conversation I don't always feel equipped to address. But that is why Brené's work is so important. We have to have the hard conversations even when we're not ready. I always use Brené's words and tell the asker, "I am a traveler, not a mapmaker. I am going down this path same as and with you." I tell everyone who shares this moment with me that I try to be very deliberate in scheduling plans, that I am very deliberate in building relationships so that when that feeling of loneliness strikes, I have someone I can reach out to. More than anything, I tell them I'm honest about the way I'm feeling and when I'm struggling. Never once, before this event, did an airman of mine come up to me and tell me they were lonely. By starting the conversation, I believe I've given them permission; I've conveyed that it's a safe topic to discuss. Now when they come to me, and they themselves are vulnerable, I have an opportunity to address it before their loneliness gets to a level of overwhelm and they see no other way out.

Once when I was telling the story, another commander came up to me and said, "I talk to my folks all the time about being disconnected." I looked at her and said, "Why do you use the word *disconnected*? It's such a sterile word. Why not just use the word *lonely*?" I can't say for certain but she appeared uncomfortable with that. I went on, "If I ask an airman 'Are you feeling disconnected?' I don't feel like that airman knows that I truly see them, that I understand what it is they're going through. Because again, *disconnected* is a sterile word. It's a safe word. It's not a word that conveys the true depth of shared human experience like loneliness. Whereas if I ask an airman 'Are you lonely?' I feel as if I am reaching them at a deeper level. I am letting them know in that moment, I am comfortable addressing the messy parts of life and I won't shy away from their loneliness. In a sense I'm telling them: Let's go there together. I am strong enough to hold this for the both of us."

The words we use really matter. But words like *loneliness, empathy, compassion,* are not words often discussed in our leadership training, nor are they included in our leadership literature.

The Air Force's most current manual on leadership, Air Force Doctrine Document 1–1: Leadership and Force Development, was written in 2011. In the document it explains that our Air Force's current core values are an evolution of seven leadership traits identified in the Air Force's very first manual on leadership, Air Force Manual 35–15, which was written in 1948. One of the seven traits was humanness.

My first reaction was "Huh? What is humanness?" Intrigued and curious, I set out to find the 1948 document. Interestingly, it took me a few hours to find the 1948 manual because it was not located in any of the leadership files. It was actually buried in the historical documents of the Air Force Chaplain Corps. As I was reading the document, I was struck by how much emotion I was feeling from the words on the page. So I started to pay more attention. The pages were full of words and phrases like: *to belong, a sense of belonging, feeling, fear, compassion, confidence, kindness, friendliness,* and *mercy*. I was amazed.

Here's this military document that's talking about leadership with mercy, and kindness, and belonging, and love. Yes, the word *love* was in this military leadership manual. I decided to do a word search for these words and phrases to see how often they were used. A discussion of feeling—how men would feel—was referred to 147 times. The importance of creating a sense of belonging was mentioned 21 times. The fear of combat, the fear of exclusion, the fear a life in the profession of arms will bring was mentioned 35 times. Love—what it means as a leader to love your men—was brought up 13 times. I won't go through the entire document, but suffice it to say this document used a language that speaks to the human experience when it was instructing leaders on how to lead people.

I went back to our current manual on leadership and searched for the same words. Unfortunately, such words weren't used. Over and over again each search turned up zero. These words that address the real emotions of people have been completely removed from our language on leadership.

Our most current manual on leadership uses phrases like *tactical leadership, operational leadership, strategic leadership.* Important concepts, no doubt, but the concepts provide little guidance to our young leaders on how to deal with the many complexities of how people, of how our airmen, process the experience of being in the military during a time of war. In sanitizing our language, I think we've decreased our comfort with expressing those feelings and holding that same space for others.

I'm comfortable using a word like *lonely*—a sometimes awkward and uncomfortable feeling and word for us to talk about—because I am willing to sit in that discomfort and give them permission to be in it with me.

When I first started learning from Brené's work and talking about it, specifically the power of vulnerability in leadership, people would look at me like I was crazy. I realized then I wasn't going to be able to talk about it on a large scale, so I decided I would start small, and I would use her work with just my six squadron commanders. I felt that if I did nothing more than help these six people become leaders with different tools to navigate the challenges of leadership, then I would have done enough.

With these six leaders, we have dug in—and because of that, there have been a million moments where Brené's work has changed the way we are leading people.

If you read either DeDe's story or the story about how my team and I worked through our rumble and think *This is way too kumbaya,* ask yourself if you're underestimating the courage these types of conversations take, or maybe diminishing the effort so you don't have to give it a shot.

If you read these stories and think *I'm not sure I could ever do this work with my team,* I have a suggestion. Make copies of this section, ask your team to read it, then bring them together for forty-five minutes. Ask a few questions: What did you think? Would putting any of this language or these tools into practice be helpful for us? If so, what would we need to do it? This is a great opportunity for **container-building.** If the team thinks there's nothing helpful here, ask why not. This is a daring opportunity to surface fears, feelings, and stealth expectations and intentions, or just to hear better ideas.

If you read these stories and think *Who has the time?* I'd ask you to calculate the cost of distrust and disconnection in terms of productivity, performance, and engagement. Here's what I know to be true from my experience and what I consider to be one of the most important learnings from this research: **Leaders must either invest a reasonable amount of time attending to fears and feelings, or squander an unreasonable amount of time trying to manage ineffective and unproductive behavior.**

What this means is that we must find the courage to get curious and possibly surface emotions and emotional experiences that people can't articulate or that might be happening outside their awareness. If we find ourselves addressing the same problematic behaviors over and over, we may need to dig deeper to the thinking and feeling driving those behaviors.

After the third one-on-one addressing the same issue, it's easy to make up the story that this person is just being difficult or even testing us. But what I've found in my own experience is that we haven't gone deep enough. We haven't peeled away enough layers of the onion. And once we start peeling, we have to leave long pauses and empty space. I know the conversation is hard enough, but people need white space. Stop talking. Even if it's awkward—which it will be the first fifteen times.

And when they start talking (which they normally will), listen. Really listen. Don't formulate your response while they're talking. If you have a great insight—hold it. Don't do that thing where the listener starts nodding faster and faster, not because they're actively listening but because they're trying to unconsciously signal the talker to wrap up so they can talk. Keep a lot of space in the conversation.

Another thing: When we're in tough rumbles with people, we can't take responsibility for their emotions. They're allowed to be pissed or sad or surprised or elated. But if their *behaviors* are not okay, we set the boundaries:

- I know this is a tough conversation. Being angry is okay. Yelling is not okay.
- I know we're tired and stressed. This has been a long meeting. Being frustrated is okay. Interrupting people and rolling your eyes is not okay.
- I appreciate the passion around these different opinions and ideas. The emotion is okay. Passive-aggressive comments and put-downs are not okay.

Also, don't forget one of our favorite rumble tools: the **time-out.** When rumbles become unproductive, call a time-out. Give everyone ten minutes to walk around outside or catch their breath. In our organization, everyone is empowered to call a time-out. And we all do it when we need it.

Sometimes a team member will say, "I need time to think about what I'm hearing. Can we take an hour and circle back after lunch?" I really appreciate that because it leads to better decision making. And giving people a reasonable amount of thinking time cuts down on the meeting-after-the-meeting and back-channeling behaviors, which are both outside what's okay in our culture.

Just remember, we can't do our jobs when we own other people's emotions or take responsibility for them as a way to control the related behaviors, for one simple reason: Other people's emotions are not our jobs. We can't both serve people and try to control their feelings.

Daring leadership is ultimately about serving other people, not ourselves. That's why we choose courage.

Leaders must either invest a reasonable amount of time attending to fears and feelings,

OR SQUANDER AN UNREASONABLE AMOUNT OF TIME TRYING TO MANAGE INEFFECTIVE AND UNPRODUCTIVE BEHAVIOR.

section three THE ARMORY

In the past, jobs were about muscles, now they're about brains, but in the future they'll be about the heart.

—MINOUCHE SHAFIK, director, London School of Economics

I have a thirteen-year-old son, which means I've seen every spy thriller and Marvel movie ever made (*Black Panther* and *Guardians of the Galaxy* at least three times). When I think about how and why we self-protect against vulnerability, I picture those movie scenes where, even after penetrating the heavily fortified perimeter, you find there are ten more obstacles to navigate to get to the treasure. You've got the infrared security beams, floors that drop out beneath you, hidden traps, and of course you have the fake contact lens to get past the retina scan. Once

you shimmy, leap, and fight your way past those impossible hurdles, the holy grail is within reach. After all of these Herculean power moves, the camera zooms in to show the small, unassuming stone that holds within it all the power in the world, or the magical elixir that grants its owner immortality.

At the center of all our elaborate personal security measures and protection schemes lies the most precious treasure of the human experience: the heart. In addition to serving as the life-giving muscle that keeps blood pumping through our body, it's the universal metaphor for our capacity to love and be loved, and it's the symbolic gateway to our emotional lives.

I've always talked about living with an unarmored heart as **wholeheartedness.** In *The Gifts of Imperfection,* I define wholeheartedness as "engaging in our lives from a place of worthiness. It means cultivating the courage, compassion, and connection to wake up in the morning and think, *No matter what gets done and how much is left undone, I am enough.* It's going to bed at night thinking, *Yes, I am imperfect and vulnerable and sometimes afraid, but that doesn't change the truth that I am brave, and worthy of love and belonging.*"

Wholeheartedness captures the essence of a fully examined emotional life and a liberated heart, one that is free and vulnerable enough to love and be loved. And a heart that is equally free and vulnerable to be broken and hurt.

Rather than protecting and hiding our heart behind bulletproof glass, wholeheartedness is about **integration.** It's integrating our thinking, feeling, and behavior. It's putting down the armor and bringing forth all of the scraggly, misshapen pieces of our history and folding in all of the different roles that, when falsely separated, keep us feeling exhausted and torn, to make a complex, messy, awesome, whole person. I love that the Latin root of the word *integrate* is *integrare,* "to make whole."

Today we pay a lot of lip service to the idea of "bringing your whole self to work"—yet the organizations that actually allow employees to do that are few and far between. I don't see a tremendous amount of meaningful, actionable support for integration and wholeheartedness in most companies. The slogan is easy. The behaviors to support the slogan are not.

There are definitely some companies that embrace wholeheartedness, but what I often observe is that many organizational cultures and leaders still subscribe to the myth that if we sever the heart (vulnerability and other emotions) from our work, we'll be more productive, efficient, and (don't forget) easier to manage. Or, at the very least, we'll be less messy and less . . . well, human. These beliefs lead us to consciously or unconsciously build cultures that require and reward armor.

In teams and organizations where heart and emotion, especially vulnerability, are seen as liabilities, the culture or in some cases individual leaders strike a bargain with our grifter egos to lock up the heart and seal off feelings. They reward armor like perfectionism, emotional stoicism, the false compartmentalizing of our lives and our work, keeping things easy and comfortable instead of embracing the necessary tough and awkward conversations, and they value all-knowing over always learning and staying curious.

The problem is that when we imprison the heart, we kill courage. In the same way that we depend on our physical heart to pump life-giving blood to every part of our body, we depend on our emotional heart to keep vulnerability coursing through the veins of courage and to engage all of the behaviors we talked about in the prior section, including trust, innovation, creativity, and accountability.

And when we become disembodied from our emotions to the point that we literally don't recognize which physical feelings are connected to which emotional feelings, we don't gain control, we lose it. Without our understanding or consent, emotions start driving our decision making and behavior while thinking is tied up in the trunk. On the other hand, when the heart is open and free and we're connected to our emotions and understand what they're telling us, new worlds open up for us, including better decision making and critical thinking, and the powerful experiences of empathy, self-compassion, and resilience.

Ego is an eager and willing conspirator when it comes to locking away the heart. I think of my ego as my inner hustler. It's that voice in my head that drives pretending, performing, pleasing, and perfecting. The ego loves gold stars and craves acceptance and approval. It has no interest in wholeheartedness, just self-protection and admiration.

Our ego will do almost anything to avoid or minimize the discomfort associated with feeling vulnerable or even being curious, because it's too risky. *What will people think? What if I learn something unpleasant or uncomfortable about myself?*

While the ego is powerful and demanding, it's just a tiny part of who we are. The heart is giant by comparison, and its free, wholehearted wisdom can drown out the smallness of needing to be liked. I love how the Jungian analyst Jim Hollis describes the ego as "that thin wafer of consciousness floating on an iridescent ocean called the soul."

He writes, "We are not here to fit in, be well balanced, or provide exempla for others. We are here to be eccentric, different, perhaps strange, perhaps merely to add our small piece, our little clunky, chunky selves, to the great mosaic of being. As the gods intended, we are here to become more and more ourselves."

Protecting our ego and fitting in is why we reach for armor in situations where we think being liked or respected is at risk because we may be wrong, or not have all of the answers, or might get in over our heads and not look smart enough. We also go on lockdown when our emotions may be perceived by others in a way that we can't manage or control. *If I'm honest about how I'm feeling, will I be misunderstood, judged, seen as weak? Will my vulnerability change the way you think of me or my ability?*

All of these situations lead to the biggest threat to our ego and our sense of self-worth: shame. **Shame** is the feeling that washes over us and makes us feel so flawed that we question whether we're worthy of love, belonging, and connection. It's such a powerful experience and so potentially debilitating that I will spend the next section walking us through shame and its antidote, empathy.

But back to the armory: The irony across all self-protection is that at the same time as we're worrying about machine learning and artificial intelligence taking jobs and dehumanizing work, we're intentionally or unintentionally creating cultures that, instead of leveraging the unique gifts of the human heart like vulnerability, empathy, and emotional literacy, are trying to lock those gifts away. There are some things that machines and algorithms do better than us for the simple reasons of computing power, quicker elimination of variables that humans either don't see or won't readily dismiss, and the fact that machines have no ego. They don't need to be right to protect their self-worth, so they don't defend or rationalize, they simply recalculate and recalibrate in an instant.

The hopeful news is that there are some tasks that humans will always be able to do better than machines *if* we are willing to take off our armor and leverage our greatest and most unique asset—the human heart. Those of us who are willing to rumble with vulnerability, live into our values, build trust, and learn to reset will not be threatened by the rise of the machines, because we will be part of the rise of daring leaders.

Armored Leadership

01. DRIVING PERFECTIONISM AND FOSTERING FEAR OF FAILURE
02. WORKING FROM SCARCITY AND SQUANDERING OPPORTUNITIES FOR JOY AND RECOGNITION
03. NUMBING
04. PROPAGATING THE FALSE DICHOTOMY OF VICTIM OR VIKING, CRUSH OR BE CRUSHED
05. BEING A KNOWER AND BEING RIGHT
06. HIDING BEHIND CYNICISM
07. USING CRITICISM AS SELF-PROTECTION
08. USING POWER OVER
09. HUSTLING FOR OUR WORTH
10. LEADING FOR COMPLIANCE AND CONTROL
11. WEAPONIZING FEAR AND UNCERTAINTY
12. REWARDING EXHAUSTION AS A STATUS SYMBOL AND ATTACHING PRODUCTIVITY TO SELF-WORTH
13. TOLERATING DISCRIMINATION, ECHO CHAMBERS, AND A “FITTING IN” CULTURE
14. COLLECTING GOLD STARS
15. ZIGZAGGING AND AVOIDING
16. LEADING FROM HURT

Daring Leadership

MODELING AND ENCOURAGING HEALTHY STRIVING, EMPATHY, AND SELF-COMPASSION	*01.*
PRACTICING GRATITUDE AND CELEBRATING MILESTONES AND VICTORIES	*02.*
SETTING BOUNDARIES AND FINDING REAL COMFORT	*03.*
PRACTICING INTEGRATION—STRONG BACK, SOFT FRONT, WILD HEART	*04.*
BEING A LEARNER AND GETTING IT RIGHT	*05.*
MODELING CLARITY, KINDNESS, AND HOPE	*06.*
MAKING CONTRIBUTIONS AND TAKING RISKS	*07.*
USING POWER WITH, POWER TO, AND POWER WITHIN	*08.*
KNOWING OUR VALUE	*09.*
CULTIVATING COMMITMENT AND SHARED PURPOSE	*10.*
ACKNOWLEDGING, NAMING, AND NORMALIZING COLLECTIVE FEAR AND UNCERTAINTY	*11.*
MODELING AND SUPPORTING REST, PLAY, AND RECOVERY	*12.*
CULTIVATING A CULTURE OF BELONGING, INCLUSIVITY, AND DIVERSE PERSPECTIVES	*13.*
GIVING GOLD STARS	*14.*
STRAIGHT TALKING AND TAKING ACTION	*15.*
LEADING FROM HEART	*16.*

Brené Brown

The Vulnerability Armory

> As children we found ways to protect ourselves from vulnerability, from being hurt, diminished, and disappointed. We put on armor; we used our thoughts, emotions, and behaviors as weapons; and we learned how to make ourselves scarce, even to disappear. Now as adults we realize that to live with courage, purpose, and connection—to be the person who we long to be—we must again be vulnerable. We must take off the armor, put down the weapons, show up, and let ourselves be seen.
>
> —*Daring Greatly*

Below are sixteen specific examples of armored leadership that emerged from our current research, along with the daring leadership response to each. The remainder of this section defines each type of armor and then digs into what it means to dare to lead. *How do we put down the armor, and how do we inspire our teams to do the same?*

The first three—perfectionism, foreboding joy, and numbing—were the top forms of armor in the original research we did on vulnerability (published in *Daring Greatly*), and they made it onto this list as well. The remaining thirteen emerged as the most common forms of self-protection we see in organizations; however, I find that they have major application across my life and probably will in yours.

1. Armored Leadership

Driving Perfectionism and Fostering Fear of Failure

For obvious reasons, I've been writing about perfectionism for as long as I've been writing: *Researcher, heal thyself.* There are also some not so obvious reasons: As a shame researcher, I've learned that wherever perfectionism is driving us, shame is riding shotgun.

Like vulnerability, perfectionism is surrounded by mythology. Below is what I've learned over the years and shared in some of my other work. Let's start with what perfectionism is *not:*

- Perfectionism is not the same thing as striving for excellence. Perfectionism is not about healthy achievement and growth. Perfectionism is a defensive move.
- Perfectionism is not the self-protection we think it is. It is a twenty-ton shield that we lug around, thinking it will protect us, when in fact it's the thing that's really preventing us from being seen.
- Perfectionism is not self-improvement. Perfectionism is, at its core, about trying to earn approval. Most perfectionists grew up being praised for achievement and performance (grades, manners, rule following, people pleasing, appearance, sports). Somewhere along the way, they adopted this dangerous and debilitating belief system: *I am what I accomplish and how well I accomplish it. Please. Perform. Perfect. Prove.* **Healthy striving** is self-focused: *How can I improve?* Perfectionism is other-focused: *What will people think?* Perfectionism is a hustle.
- Perfectionism is not the key to success. In fact, research shows that perfectionism hampers achievement. Perfectionism is correlated with depression, anxiety, addiction, and life paralysis, or missed opportunities. The fear of failing, making mistakes, not meeting people's expectations, and being criticized keeps us outside the arena where healthy competition and striving unfolds.
- Last, perfectionism is not a way to avoid shame. Perfectionism is a function of shame.

Here's how I define perfectionism:

- Perfectionism is a self-destructive and addictive belief system that fuels this primary thought: *If I look perfect and do everything perfectly, I can avoid or minimize the painful feelings of blame, judgment, and shame.*
- Perfectionism is self-destructive simply because perfection doesn't exist. It's an unattainable goal. Perfectionism is more about perception than internal motivation, and there is no way to control perception, no matter how much time and energy we spend trying.
- Perfectionism is addictive, because when we invariably do experience shame, judgment, and blame, we often believe it's because we weren't perfect enough. Rather than questioning the faulty logic of perfectionism, we become even more entrenched in our quest to look and do everything just right.
- Perfectionism actually sets us up to feel shame, judgment, and blame, which then leads to even more shame and self-blame: *It's my fault. I'm feeling this way because I'm not good enough.*

Daring Leadership

Modeling and Encouraging Healthy Striving, Empathy, and Self-Compassion

Conversations about perfectionism within trusting and brave teams can be healing and powerful. The goal is to get very clear about where, as a team, we're the most likely to get swallowed by perfectionism, how it shows up, and how we distinguish perfectionism from healthy striving for excellence. Are there ways that we can check in with one another that work for everyone? Are there flags, warning signs, or indicator lights that we can all take responsibility for spotting? I've seen teams that are willing to have these conversations make profound changes, grow closer, increase their performance, and build trust in the process.

2. Armored Leadership

Working from Scarcity and Squandering Opportunities for Joy and Recognition

When I'm speaking to big groups, I always ask: When something great happens in your life, how many of you start to celebrate only to find yourself thinking, *Don't get too happy, that's just inviting disaster*? Arms fly up. You got promoted, you're really excited. You got engaged. You found out you're pregnant. You found out you're going to be a grandparent. Something wonderful happens, and for a brief second you let the joy wash over you—and then five seconds later, the excitement is gone and you're panicked about a bad thing that's going to happen to counter the positive. *When's the other shoe going to drop?*

For the parents reading this: How many of you have stood over your child while they were sleeping and thought, *Oh, God, I love this kid more than I knew was possible,* and in that same second felt fear wash over you and pictured something horrible happening to your child? Statistically, it's about 90 percent of us.

Why do we insist on dress-rehearsing tragedy in moments of deep joy?

Because joy is the most vulnerable emotion we feel. And that's saying something, given that I study fear and shame.

When we feel joy, it is a place of incredible vulnerability—it's beauty and fragility and deep gratitude and impermanence all wrapped up in one experience. When we can't tolerate that level of vulnerability, joy actually becomes foreboding, and we immediately move to self-protection. It's as if we grab vulnerability by the shoulders and say, "You will not catch me off guard. You will not sucker-punch me with pain. I will be prepared and ready for you."

So when something joyful happens, we start planning on being hurt. We start planning to deal with the fear of disappointment. Is this helpful? Of course not.

We cannot plan for painful moments—we know this for a fact, because people who have been forced to live through those moments tell us that there is no amount of catastrophizing or planning for disaster that prepares you for them. The collateral damage of this instinct is that we squander the joy we need to build up an emotional reserve, the joy that allows us to build up resilience for when tragic things do happen.

At work, foreboding joy often shows up in more subtle and pernicious ways. It shows up by making us hesitant to celebrate victories, for two primary reasons. The first is that we're afraid if we celebrate with our team, or have a moment where we just breathe, we're inviting disaster and something will go wrong. You can likely identify with that feeling of getting a project up and out the door and then refusing to celebrate it with high-fives because you think, *We can't celebrate right now because we don't know if it's going to be perfect, we don't know if it's going to work, we don't know if the site will stay up . . .*

The second way foreboding joy shows up at work is withholding recognition. We don't want our employees to get too excited because there's still so much work to be done. We don't want them to take their foot off the gas, to get complacent. So we don't celebrate achievements. We think we'll do it someday, but these same factors persist in the wake of joy. This is how foreboding joy shows up at the office, and it is a costly mistake.

Daring Leadership

Practicing Gratitude and Celebrating Milestones and Victories

What is the one thing that people who can fully lean into joy have in common?

Gratitude. They practice gratitude. It's not an "attitude of gratitude"—it's an actual practice. They keep a journal, or make a note of what they're grateful for on their phones, or share it with family members.

From the day the finding about gratitude emerged from the data, our family put it into practice at the dinner table. Now, after we sing grace (summer camp style), we each share one specific instance of gratitude with the table. It's changed us. And it's given us an invaluable window into our kids' lives and hearts.

Embodying and practicing gratitude changes everything. It is not a personal construct, it's a human construct—a unifying part of our existence—and it's the antidote to foreboding joy, plain and simple. It's allowing yourself the pleasure of accomplishment, or love, or joy—of really feeling it, of basking in it—by conjuring up gratitude for the moment and for the opportunity.

It's allowing yourself to recognize the shiver of vulnerability—that "Oh, shit, I have something worth losing now" feeling—and to just sit with it, and be grateful that you have something you want, in your hand, that it feels good to hold and recognize. Something as simple as starting or ending meetings with a gratitude check, when everyone shares one thing they're grateful for, can build trust and connection, serve as container-building, and give your group permission to lean into joy.

Earlier this year I gave the opening keynote address at Work-Human, an HR conference put on by Globoforce, a provider of recognition programs and solutions. I said yes to the invitation to speak because recognition has emerged from our daring leadership data as essential to developing brave leaders and courage cultures. I had read several articles that show recognition is a factor in increasing employee engagement, satisfaction, and retention in an increasingly competitive global talent market. But I hadn't read any case studies, so I jumped into some of the leader and peer recognition work that Globoforce has been doing.

Globoforce worked with Cisco to use recognition to boost employee engagement by 5 percent, and with Intuit to achieve and sustain a double-digit increase in employee engagement over a large employee base that spans six countries. Hershey's recognition approach helped increase employee satisfaction by 11 percent. And for LinkedIn, retention rates are nearly 10 percentage points higher for new hires who are recognized four or more times.

Whether we're leading a group or a member of the team, whether we're working in a formal or informal recognition program, it is our responsibility to say to the people who work alongside us: "We've got to stop and celebrate one another and our victories, no matter how small. Yes, there's more work to be done, and things could go sideways in an hour, but that will never take away from the fact that we need to celebrate an accomplishment right now."

3. Armored Leadership

Numbing

We all numb. We all have different numbing agents of choice—food, work, social media, shopping, television, video games, porn, booze (from beer in a brown paper bag to the socially acceptable but equally dangerous "fine wine" hobby)—but we all do it. And when we chronically and compulsively turn to these numbing agents, it's addiction, not just taking the edge off.

Statistically, every person holding this book is affected by addiction. If it's not you, then it could be a friend, colleague, or family member. No matter who or how, if you're paying attention, you've had a front row seat to the pain, the suffering, and the costs. According to the National Council on Alcoholism and Drug Dependence, Inc., 70 percent of the estimated 14.8 million Americans who use illegal drugs are employed, and drug abuse costs employers $81 billion annually. There is no us and them when it comes to numbing—we all do it. The question is to what degree. And, when we're talking about the pain surrounding addiction, it's never a self-contained storm, it's a tornado.

Numbing or taking the edge off doesn't have the same consequences as addiction, but they are nonetheless severe and life-altering for one reason: We *cannot* selectively numb emotion. If we numb the dark, we numb the light. If we take the edge off pain and discomfort, we are, by default, taking the edge off joy, love, belonging, and the other emotions that give meaning to our lives.

Think of hard emotions as thorns with very sharp points. When they prick us, they cause discomfort, even pain. Just the anticipation or fear of these feelings can trigger intolerable levels of vulnerability in us. We know it's coming.

For many of us, the first response to the vulnerability and discomfort of these sharp points is not to lean into the discomfort and feel our way through, but to make it go away. We do that by numbing and taking the edge off the pain with whatever provides the quickest relief. Again, we can anesthetize with a whole bunch of stuff including alcohol, drugs, food, sex, relationships, money, work, caretaking, gambling, staying busy, affairs, chaos, shopping, planning, perfectionism, constant change, and the Internet.

I've been sober for over twenty years, and I've always struggled to figure out where I fit into the recovery system. We're almost back to the Berenstain Bears—nothing fit quite right. I wasn't quite drunk enough for the old-timers at AA; the OA people sent me to a meeting on codependency; and there they said I needed to start with AA. I wanted to take the frustrating process as a sign that I was just fine and celebrate with a few beers, but I knew better. My life was out of control, and a family history exercise during my final month of grad school was an unexpected addiction shitshow, so I asked a friend to take me to a meeting.

Two meetings in, my first sponsor said, "You have the pupu platter of addictions—a little bit of everything. Just to be safe, it would be best if you just quit drinking, smoking, comfort eating, and getting in your family's business."

Awesome. I'll definitely have some free time for meetings.

I never found "my" meeting, but I did quit drinking and smoking the day after I finished my master's degree on May 12, 1996, and I haven't touched alcohol or tobacco since. Confession: I still fantasize about smoking when I'm driving and Bob Seger or the Rolling Stones come on. If you see me holding a pen like a cigarette driving down the road, know that there's something great on the radio.

I ultimately worked the AA program for a year, and let me just tell you, all the slogans are true. It does look like a *Saturday Night Live* skit where there are ten posters hanging in a row on a wood-paneled wall in a church basement, but they are the damn truth, and if you live by them, they will rock your world. A friend of mine, who is also in recovery, said, "Leave it to a bunch of drunks in recovery to unlock the secrets of life." Among them:

Wherever you go, there you are.
You're only as sick as your secrets.
Easy does it.
One day at a time.
Live and let live.

To thine own self be true.
HALT: Don't get too hungry, angry, lonely, or tired.
Let go and let God. (I knew I was in trouble when my therapist reminded me that this is the saying—not "Let go and let Brené." *Ouch.*)

Daring Leadership

Setting Boundaries and Finding Real Comfort

Our research shows that participants named vulnerability, resentment, and anxiety as the biggest drivers of numbing, and resentment is almost always related to a lack of boundaries. We're knee-high in vulnerability now, and we'll dig into anxiety in a later section, and then the relationship between resentment and boundaries in the part on trust-building. For now, stay on the lookout for resentment in your life when you're into hour three on Facebook, when you are about to finish off the entire pint of Ben & Jerry's, or when you have just spent most of your paycheck online shopping.

The bottom line? Like most of you, I wasn't raised with the skills and emotional practice needed to rumble with vulnerability. So I resorted to numbing—over time I basically became an anything-to-take-the-edge-off-aholic. But there are no specific programs for that, so I cobbled together a plan of meetings, a great therapist, and new spiritual practices that work for me.

In the end, the cure for numbing is developing tools and practices that allow you to lean into discomfort and renew your spirit.

First, when we're feeling that edge, instead of asking ourselves "What's the quickest way to make these feelings go away?," ask, "What are these feelings and where did they come from?"

Second, figure out what brings you real comfort and renewal, not just numbing. We deserve real comfort. The author Jennifer Louden calls our numbing devices "shadow comforts." When we're anxious, disconnected, vulnerable, alone, and feeling helpless, booze and food and work and binge-watching endless hours of TV feel like comfort, but in reality they're only casting their long shadows over our lives.

Louden writes, "Shadow comforts can take any form. . . . It's not what you do; it's why you do it that makes the difference. You can eat a piece of chocolate as a holy wafer of sweetness—a real comfort—or you can cram an entire chocolate bar into your mouth without even tasting it in a frantic attempt to soothe yourself—a shadow comfort. You can chat on message boards for half an hour and be energized by community and ready to go back to work, or you can chat on message boards because you're avoiding talking to your partner about how angry he or she made you last night."

What emerged from the data on numbing was exactly what Louden speaks to: "It's not what you do; it's why you do it that makes the difference." The invitation is to think about the intention behind our numbing choices and, if helpful, to discuss these issues with family, close friends, or a helping professional.

Curbing comfort eating is a lifelong project for me, but I still work the steps and keep the posters hanging in the church basement of my mind. One of my most important self-care behaviors is my daily walking routine. So one tangible thing I do to avoid numbing with food is keep a Polaroid picture of my walking shoes in the pantry. *Am I actually hungry, or would a walk bring me more real comfort?*

I've also spent over a decade working on setting and maintaining appropriate boundaries, especially with regard to my overachiever role as family caretaker. I may never get my Six Sigma project management certification, but I've earned a black belt in boundaries. Funny story: Apparently my secret nickname with one of our external partners was BB—not for my name, but for "Boundaries Brown." When they learned that the secret was out and I knew about the nickname, they were embarrassed and apologetic. My reply: "No apologies necessary. Best compliment of my life."

At work, we need to support healthy rumbles with vulnerability, to respect boundaries, and to practice calm in the sea of anxiety. And when it comes to addiction, employers with successful employee assistance programs report improvements in morale and productivity and decreases in absenteeism, accidents, downtime, turnover, and theft. Employers with long-standing programs also report better health status among employees and family members.

4. Armored Leadership

Propagating the False Dichotomy of Victim or Viking, Crush or Be Crushed

Winner or loser, survive or die, kill or be killed, strong or weak, leaders or followers, success or failure, crush or be crushed. Sound familiar? This is the philosophy of people who subscribe to the paradigm of Victim or Viking. In this binary world of paired opposites, you're either a sucker/loser who always gets the short end of the stick, or you're a Viking who refuses to be victimized. You'll do whatever is required—control, dominate, exert power, shut down emotion—to ensure that you're never vulnerable.

This win-lose zero-sum power dynamic is pervasive in some professions, but it's also attributable to how people were raised. If it was your primary model growing up, you are liable to believe in a false and extreme dichotomy: that if you don't do the crushing, you won't survive.

When I interview people who operate from a Victim or Viking perspective, I often ask them to define success. While survival or winning may mean success in some contexts, when you strip away real threat, survival is not living. We all need to belong, and we all need love, and neither is possible without vulnerability and integration.

Daring Leadership

Practicing Integration—Strong Back, Soft Front, Wild Heart

The opposite of living in a world of false binaries is practicing integration—the act of bringing together all the parts of ourselves, as we talked about earlier. We are all tough and tender, scared and brave, grace and grit. The most powerful example of integration—a practice that I wrote about in *Braving the Wilderness* and that I try to live by—is strong back, soft front, wild heart. Here's what my teacher Roshi Joan Halifax says about the integration of strong back and soft front:

> All too often our so-called strength comes from fear, not love; instead of having a strong back, many of us have a defended front shielding a weak spine. In other words, we walk around brittle and defensive, trying to conceal our lack of confidence. If we strengthen our backs, metaphorically speaking, and develop a spine that's flexible but sturdy, then we can risk having a front that's soft and open. . . . How can we give and accept care with strong-back, soft-front compassion, moving past fear into a place of genuine tenderness? I believe it comes about when we can be truly transparent, seeing the world clearly—and letting the world see into us.

For me, that strong back is grounded confidence and boundaries. The soft front is staying vulnerable and curious. The mark of a wild heart is living out these paradoxes in our lives and not giving into the either/or BS that reduces us. It's showing up in our vulnerability and our courage, and, above all else, being both fierce and kind.

5. Armored Leadership

Being a Knower and Being Right

Having to be the "knower" or always being right is heavy armor. It's defensiveness, it's posturing, and, worst of all, it's a huge driver of bullshit. It's also very common—most of us have some degree of knower in us. Too often we stereotype the knower as the irritating but lovable Cliff Clavin from the TV show *Cheers*. Unfortunately, needing to know everything is pretty miserable for the knowers and everyone around them. It leads to distrust, bad decisions, unnecessary rumbles, and unproductive conflict.

It sounds pretty easy to replace the armor of knowing with becoming a curious learner, but for many people the need to be a knower is driven by shame and for some even trauma. Being the knower can save people in hard situations, and it's easy to buy into the belief that being a knower is the only value we bring to relationships and work.

Knowing can also become a culture problem when only some people are valued as knowers. Others don't speak up because they're not "senior enough" or it's "not their place." One leader shared that he had been with his new company for six months and had never contributed in a meeting. He was brought in because of his twenty-plus years of experience, yet he was expected to be quiet in the meetings because of cultural norms that valued only the contributions of tenured leaders.

Daring Leadership

Being a Learner and Getting It Right

There are three strategies that I've seen work to transform *always knowing* into *always learning*. First, name the issue. It's a tough conversation, but clear is kind: *I'd like for you to work on your curiosity and critical thinking skills. You're often quick with answers, which can be helpful, but not as helpful as having the right questions, which is how you'll grow as a leader. We can work together on this.* Knowers often have a lot of people talking behind their backs, and that's unkind. Second, make learning curiosity skills a priority. Third, acknowledge and reward great questions and instances of "I don't know, but I'd like to find out" as daring leadership behaviors. The big shift here is from wanting to "be right" to wanting to "get it right." After these sections on rumbling with vulnerability, we're going to break down the skills and tools for curiosity and learning.

6. Armored Leadership

Hiding Behind Cynicism

Cynicism and sarcasm are first cousins who hang out in the cheap seats. But don't underestimate them—they often leave a trail of hurt feelings, anger, confusion, and resentment in their wake. I've seen them bring down relationships, teams, and cultures when modeled by people at the highest levels and/or left unchecked. Like most hurtful comments and passive-aggressiveness, cynicism and sarcasm are bad in person and even worse when they travel through email or text. And, in global teams, culture and language differences make them toxic. I mean, the word *sarcasm* is from the Greek word *sarkazein,* meaning "to tear flesh." *Tear. Flesh.*

In a world roiled by incessant and tumultuous change, swamped by boatloads of fear and anxiety and rampant feelings of scarcity, cynicism and sarcasm are easy and cheap. In fact, I'd say that they're worse than armor—we use cynicism and sarcasm as get-out-of-contributing-free cards.

Daring Leadership

Modeling Clarity, Kindness, and Hope

The antidote to sarcasm and cynicism is threefold:

1. Staying clear and kind.
2. Practicing the courage to say what you mean and mean what you say. Cynicism and sarcasm often mask anger, fear, feelings of inadequacy, and even despair. They're a safe way for us to send out an emotional trial balloon, and if it doesn't go over well, we make it a joke and make you feel stupid for thinking it was ever something different.
3. If what's under cynicism and sarcasm is despair, the antidote is cultivating hope. According to the research of C. R. Snyder, hope isn't a warm and fuzzy feeling; he actually defines it as a cognitive emotional process that has three parts. This is a process that most of us, if we're lucky, are taught growing up, though it can be learned at any time: The three parts are goal, pathway, and agency. We can identify a realistic goal (*I know where I want to go*), and then we can figure out the pathway to get there, even if it's not a straight line and involves a Plan B and scrappiness (*I know I can get there because I'm persistent and I will keep trying in the face of setbacks and disappointment*). Agency is belief in our ability to stay on that path until we've arrived (*I know I can do this*).

Again, while a cynic might argue that someone who clings to hope is a sucker, or ridiculously earnest, this type of armor typically comes from pain. Often, people's cynicism is related to despair. As the theologian Rob Bell explains, "Despair is the belief that tomorrow will be just like today." That is a devastating line. The problem with cynicism and sarcasm is that they are typically system- and culturewide—it's just so easy to take shots at other people. As brave leaders, it is essential not to reward or allow it. Reward clarity and kindness and real conversation, and teach hope instead.

7. Armored Leadership

Using Criticism as Self-Protection

As Roosevelt said, "It is not the critic who counts; not the man who points out how the strong man stumbles, or where the doer of deeds could have done them better." Open, honest discussion, in which everyone feels free to offer suggestions and contribute, stimulates creativity. But innovation is hindered by allowing criticism from the cheap seats—from those who aren't willing to get down into the arena.

There are two forms of criticism that can be a little harder to recognize: **nostalgia** and the **invisible army**. Sometimes when a new idea hits the table, the knee-jerk reaction is "That's not how we do it" or "We've never done it that way." People use history to criticize different thinking. We can also use the invisible army: "*We* don't want to change course," or "*We* don't like the direction you're taking the project." I hate the invisible army, and if you use it with me I will drill you down on exactly who makes up your *we*. On more than one occasion, Chaz has had to stop me from saying "What? You got a mouse in your pocket?" Voicing and owning our concern is brave. Pretending that we represent a lot of folks when we don't is cheap-seat behavior.

Criticism often arises from fear or feelings of unworthiness. Criticism shifts the spotlight off us and onto someone or something else. Suddenly we feel safer. And better than.

Daring Leadership

Making Contributions and Taking Risks

At the end of the day, at the end of the week, at the end of my life, I want to say I contributed more than I criticized. It's that simple. If you find yourself leading a team or culture in which criticism outweighs contribution, make a conscious and resolute decision to stop rewarding the former.

In fact, turn contribution into a rumble skill. In our company, you aren't allowed to criticize without offering a point of view in return—if you're going to tear something down, you have to offer a specific plan for how you would rebuild it to make it stronger and more substantial. In fact, even if there's nothing to criticize, we still require everyone who comes into any meeting to come with a prepared point of view and then share it. This supercharges contribution and puts everyone into the arena, where the stakes are high. Your point of view can shift as new data emerge, but you still have to participate and risk a little dirt and blood on your face. The people who count are the people who are putting themselves out there and making contributions, cheap seats be damned.

8. Armored Leadership

Using Power Over

In a 1968 speech given to striking sanitation workers in Memphis, Reverend Martin Luther King, Jr., defined power as the ability to achieve purpose and effect change. This is the most accurate and important definition of power that I've ever seen. The definition does not make the nature of power inherently good or bad, which aligns with what I've learned in my work. What makes power dangerous is how it's used.

Organizational life is inherently hierarchical, with very few exceptions. Those at the top hold a majority of the power, thanks to their proximity to the ultimate power holder (the CEO, founder, president, or board of directors)—the higher up you are, the more likely you are to have access to the meetings behind closed doors, the private spaces where the biggest decisions are discussed and made. Hierarchy can work, except when those in leadership positions hold *power over* others—when their decisions benefit the minority and oppress the majority.

What's perhaps most insidious in *power over* dynamics is that those who are powerless typically repeat the same behavior when the tables are turned and they are promoted into power. We see this in hazing rituals, and we see it in the perpetuation of policies that do not support the disenfranchised. *Why should I care about young working mothers when nobody cared about me?* The phrase *power over* is typically enough to send chills down spines: When someone holds power over us, the human spirit's instinct is to rise, resist, and rebel. As a construct it feels wrong; in the wider geopolitical context it can mean death and despotism.

Daring Leadership

Using Power With, Power To, and Power Within

In their publication *Making Change Happen: Power,* Just Associates, a global interdisciplinary network of activists, organizers, educators, and scholars, defines three variations of power within the context of social justice and activism. They are equally helpful in organizations, as they present pathways where team members can maintain their own agency and recognize their own sources of power, in a way that ladders up to the greatest good. In our culture, we often talk about "empowering" people, but it's a nebulous concept that's difficult to define. What does that actually mean? I think these three elements make clear the work we need to do.

Power with "has to do with finding common ground among different interests in order to build collective strength. Based on mutual support, solidarity, collaboration, and recognition and respect for differences, *power with* multiplies individual talents, knowledge, and resources to make a larger impact."

Power to translates to giving everyone on your team agency and acknowledging their unique potential. It is "based on the belief that each individual has the power to make a difference, which can be multiplied by new skills, knowledge, awareness, and confidence."

Power within is defined by an ability to recognize differences and respect others, grounded in a strong foundation of self-worth and self-knowledge. When we operate from a place of *power within,* we feel comfortable challenging assumptions and long-held beliefs, pushing against the status quo, and asking if there aren't other ways to achieve the highest common good.

9. Armored Leadership

Hustling for Your Worth

When people don't understand where they're strong and where they deliver value for the organization or even for a single effort, they hustle. And not the good kind of hustle. The kind that's hard to be around because we are jumping in everywhere, including where we're not strong or not needed, to prove we deserve a seat at the table.

When we do not understand our value, we often exaggerate our importance in ways that are not helpful, and we consciously or unconsciously seek attention and validation of importance. We put more value on being right than on getting it right. It creates franticness instead of calm cooperation.

Daring Leadership

Knowing Your Value

Daring leaders sit down with their team members and have real rumbles with them about the unique contributions they make, so that everyone knows where they're strong. Remember too that sometimes we overlook our own strengths because we take them for granted and forget that they're special. I'm a strong storyteller, the provenance of my upbringing—I sometimes forget that I'm uniquely equipped to do this because it's easy for me. Tuck your team members in around the areas where they quickly achieve flow—those are typically where they are particularly primed to contribute value. As Ken Blanchard, the author of the 1982 bestselling leadership guide *The One Minute Manager,* explains, "Catch people doing things right." It's much more powerful than collecting behaviors that are wrong.

Getting clear on our value and our team members' values will revolutionize our company and create lanes where none might have existed before—instead of a ten-person race, we start to develop a coordinated relay in which team members baton-toss to each other's strengths instead of vying to run the whole stretch alone. Once everyone understands their value, we stop hustling for worthiness and lean into our gifts.

10. Armored Leadership

Leading for Compliance and Control

Note: The compliance we're talking about is not legal, safety, or privacy compliance or organizational compliance (e.g., vetting partners, wearing a hairnet, setting the alarm code on your way out, or putting in a vacation request with two weeks' advance notice).

The armor of compliance and control is normally about fear and power. When we come from this place, we often engage in two armored behaviors:

1. We reduce work to tasks and to-dos, then spend our time ensuring that people are doing exactly what we want, how we want it—and then constantly calling them out when they're doing it wrong. The armor of compliance and control leads us to strip work of its nuance, context, and larger purpose, then push it down for task completion, all while using the fear of "getting caught" as motivation. Not only is this ineffective, it shuts down creative problem solving, the sharing of ideas, and the foundation of vulnerability. It also leaves people miserable, questioning their abilities, and even desperate to leave. The less people understand how their hard work adds value to bigger goals, the less engaged they are. It becomes a self-fulfilling prophecy of failure and frustration.

2. When we operate from compliance and control, we also have a tendency to hold on to power and authority, and push only responsibility down. This leads to huge alignment issues for people. They've been asked to do something that they don't actually have the authority to accomplish. They're not set up for success, so they fail. This just reinforces our power and resentment loop: *I knew I should have done it myself. I'll be responsible for this, you just do these small tasks that you can handle* versus *Let's dig into how we could have set you up for success. I know I have a part.*

Daring Leadership

Cultivating Commitment and Shared Purpose

Daring leaders, even in compliance-driven and highly structured industries like banking, healthcare, and the food industry, create and share context and color.

They take the time to explain the "why" behind strategies, and how tasks link to ongoing priorities and mission work. Rather than handing down black-and-white mandates stripped of story, they hold themselves responsible for adding texture and meaning to work and tying smaller tasks to the larger purpose.

We used to utilize the Apple DRI model, appointing someone as the "directly responsible individual" for a specific task and recording their duty in the meeting minutes. But what we learned is that despite the team member's willingness to own it and be held accountable for executing, they didn't always have the authority to be successful. We're currently switching to a TASC approach: the Accountability and Success Checklist:

1. T—Who owns the task?
2. A—Do they have the authority to be held accountable?
3. S—Do we agree that they are set up for success (time, resources, clarity)?
4. C—Do we have a checklist of what needs to happen to accomplish the task?

We also borrowed the Scrum technique of "What does 'done' look like?" when we assigned tasks, responsibilities, and deliverables. It was a *huge* improvement for us, but we needed to tweak it because it didn't address the need for tying deliverables to our purpose.

For example, I'm out of town with my colleagues Murdoch

and Barrett facilitating a daring leadership workshop. I ask them to collect one role-play scenario from everyone participating in our two-day training while I'm meeting with the CEO. I want to use these scenarios the next day. Later that evening, they slide a folder stuffed with handwritten scenarios under my hotel door. I wake up the next morning and panic. Now I have to sort through them and type them up. I'm frustrated with Murdoch and Barrett, and they have no idea why.

The next time, I ask for the same thing, but Murdoch replies with "Sure. What does done look like?"

I say, "Please type them up, and you and Barrett should pick three that are specific enough to be meaningful but general enough to apply across the group. It would be helpful if I could get them before eight P.M. so I can review them tonight."

Huge improvement. But wait . . .

Same scenario, but instead of saying "Sure. What does done look like?" Murdoch says "Sure. Let's paint done."

Rather than slinging directives *West Wing* walk-and-talk style, we find Barrett and talk for five minutes. I say, "Here's my plan. I want to collect scenarios from the participants today so we have new role-plays for the group tomorrow. I don't want to reuse the ones we brought and used today. They're really struggling with these hard conversations, and the more specific the scenarios are to their issues and culture, the more helpful the role-playing will be. My plan is to have you collect them and sort through them tonight, looking for ones that are specific but have broad appeal. I'd like y'all to type up three of them and make copies. Instead of breaking the group into pairs, I want to do triads with one person observing and supporting. So, if we have three role-plays for each group, they can each take a turn."

Murdoch and Barrett think about it for a minute, then Barrett says, "One issue is that everyone here today is from operations.

Tomorrow is the marketing team. Will that affect the relatability of the role-plays?"

Me: "Dammit. It totally changes what I'm thinking. Thank you."

Paint done. For us, it's significantly more helpful than "What does done look like?" because it unearths stealth expectations and unsaid intentions, and it gives the people who are charged with the task tons of color and context. It fosters curiosity, learning, collaboration, reality-checking, and ultimately success.

One more scenario:

Ben: Hey, Brené! Please pull all of the invoices together for me by four o'clock.
Brené: Okay.

Two hours later:

Brené: Here you go!
Ben: What is this?
Brené: It's your invoices.
Ben: I needed them back to 2005, and in date order. Now I'm not ready for my meeting with the CFO.
Brené: How was I supposed to know that?

BEN AND BRENÉ ARE VERY FRUSTRATED.
Paint done and TASC

Ben: Hey, Brené! Please pull all of the invoices together for me by four o'clock.
Brené: Okay. Paint done for me.
Ben: Pull everything back to 2005, and put them in date order.

BRENÉ: That's the whole picture?

BEN: Yeah. I need to track the expenses for two books.

BRENÉ: Wait. I don't understand. We didn't track expenses on invoices before 2007. You'll need separate receipts.

BEN: Can you get those too?

BRENÉ: Yes, but not by four. What specifically do you need for your meeting? Paint done.

BEN: I'm trying to make the point that the shift in how we format our invoices actually changed expense categorizations.

BRENÉ: I don't think you need to pull everything. There's a better way to do that. And I can get it done and put it in a graph for you by four.

BEN: Thanks so much. That would be awesome. What support do you need from me to get this done? Anything that you can think of that will get in your way?

BRENÉ: I'll need to clear my plate for the next two hours.

BEN: I'll take care of that if you'll jump on it.

BRENÉ: You got it.

BEN: I really appreciate it.

TASC: The Accountability and Success Checklist

1. **Task**—Brené owns the task.
2. **Accountability**—Ben has given Brené the necessary authority to be held accountable.
3. **Success**—Their conversation ensured that Brené is set up for success (in terms of time, resources, clarity).
4. **Checklist**—Check!

We want people to share our commitment to purpose and mission, not to comply because they're afraid not to. That's exhausting and unsustainable for everyone. Leaders who work from compliance constantly feel disappointed and resentful, and their teams feel scrutinized. Compliance leadership also kills trust, and, ironically, it can increase people's tendency to test what they can get away with.

We want people to police themselves and to deliver above and beyond expectations. Painting done and using a TASC approach cultivates commitment and contribution, giving team members the space and the trust to stretch and learn and allowing joy and creativity to be found in even the small tasks.

11. Armored Leadership

Weaponizing Fear and Uncertainty

In times of uncertainty, it is common for leaders to leverage fear and then weaponize it to their advantage. Unfortunately, it's been an easy formula throughout history—in politics, religion, and business—that if you can keep people afraid, and give them an enemy who is responsible for their fear, you can get people to do just about anything. This is the playbook for authoritarian leaders here and around the globe.

In the short term it's relatively easy for leaders to stir up scarcity and promise to deliver more certainty with easy answers and a common enemy to blame. But in the face of complex problems, that certainty is quite literally impossible to fulfill. Daring and ethical leaders fight against this brand of leadership.

Daring Leadership

Acknowledging, Naming, and Normalizing Collective Fear and Uncertainty

In the midst of uncertainty and fear, leaders have an ethical responsibility to hold their people in discomfort—to acknowledge the tumult but not fan it, to share information and not inflate or fake it. Daring leaders acknowledge, name, and normalize discord and difference without fueling divisiveness or benefiting from it.

When we are managing during a time of scarcity or deep uncertainty, it is imperative that we embrace the uncertainty. We need to tell our teams that we will share as much as we're able when we're able. We need to be available to fact-check the stories that our team members might be making up, because in scarcity we invent worst-case scenarios. We need to open up the room for rumbling around vulnerability.

There is incredible relief and power in naming and normalizing fear and uncertainty. We have to find the courage to look back at the people who are looking at us for leadership and say, "This is difficult. There are no simple answers. There is pain and fear that would be easy to unload on others—but that would be unfair and out of our integrity. We will walk through this in a way that makes us feel proud. It will be hard, but we will do it together."

12. Armored Leadership

Rewarding Exhaustion as a Status Symbol and Attaching Productivity to Self-Worth

I wrote about this armor in my 2010 book, *The Gifts of Imperfection,* at a time of cultural crisis around busyness and sleep deprivation. Things might be moderately better now—there's definitely a growing awareness that insufficient sleep contributes to diabetes, heart disease, depression, and even fatal accidents—but we still struggle as a society around pegging our self-worth to our net worth.

When worthiness is a function of productivity, we lose the ability to pump the brakes: The idea of doing something that doesn't add to the bottom line provokes stress and anxiety. It feels completely contrary to what we believe we want to achieve in life—we convince ourselves that downtime, like playing with our kids, hanging out with our partners, napping, tooling around in the garage, or going for a run, is a waste of precious time. Why sleep when you can work? And aren't treadmill desks supposed to be a replacement for a long Sunday run anyway? (I actually don't have anything against treadmill desks, as we all sit too much.)

Daring Leadership

Modeling and Supporting Rest, Play, and Recovery

The work of Dr. Stuart Brown, a psychiatrist, clinical researcher, and founder of the National Institute for Play, would argue that this lack of downtime, this lack of play, has a deleterious effect on our output in the office. In our desperate search for joy in our lives, we missed the memo: If we want to live a life of meaning and contribution, we have to become intentional about cultivating sleep and play. We have to let go of exhaustion, busyness, and productivity as status symbols and measures of self-worth. We are impressing no one.

What's more, according to Brown's research, play shapes our brain, fosters empathy, helps us navigate complex social groups, and is at the core of creativity and innovation. In some ways, it helps our overheated brain cool down. To weave this into office culture, leaders need to model appropriate boundaries by shutting off email at a reasonable time and focusing on themselves and their family. Do not celebrate people who work through the weekend, who brag that they were tethered to their computers over Christmas break. Ultimately, it's unsustainable behavior, and it has dangerous side effects, including burnout, depression, and anxiety—it also creates a culture of workaholic competitiveness that's detrimental for everyone.

As Stuart Brown says, "The opposite of play is not work—the opposite of play is depression."

13. Armored Leadership

Tolerating Discrimination, Echo Chambers, and a "Fitting-in" Culture

In my 2017 book, *Braving the Wilderness,* I share this definition of **true belonging:**

> True belonging is the spiritual practice of believing in and belonging to yourself so deeply that you can share your most authentic self with the world and find sacredness in both being a part of something and standing alone in the wilderness. True belonging doesn't require you to *change* who you are; it requires you to *be* who you are.

The greatest barrier to true belonging is fitting in or changing who we are so we can be accepted. When we create a culture of fitting in and seeking approval at work, we are not only stifling individuality, we are inhibiting people's sense of true belonging. People desperately want to be part of something, and they want to experience profound connection with others, but they don't want to sacrifice their authenticity, freedom, or power to do it.

Daring Leadership

Cultivating a Culture of Belonging, Inclusivity, and Diverse Perspectives

Only when diverse perspectives are included, respected, and valued can we start to get a full picture of the world: who we serve, what they need, and how to successfully meet people where they are. Daring leaders fight for the inclusion of all people, opinions, and perspectives because that makes us all better and stronger. That means having the courage to acknowledge our own privilege, and staying open to learning about our biases and blind spots.

We also have to watch for favoritism—the development of cliques or in/out groups. I often do focus groups with employees, and about half the time I hear people in their thirties, forties, fifties, and even sixties still talk about the "cool kids at work" and the "popular table in the cafeteria." Sometimes the quality that defines the "in group" is achievement or seniority, and sometimes it's identity.

Daring leaders work to make sure people can be themselves and feel a sense of belonging. Previously mentioned daring leadership strategies that promote this sense of belonging include recognizing achievement; validating contribution; developing a system that includes power with, power to, and power within; and knowing your value.

14. Armored Leadership

Collecting Gold Stars

It is natural to want to be recognized for our achievements. Early in our careers, when we're individual contributors, collecting gold stars is fine—particularly if it's driven by healthy striving rather than perfectionism. It can, in fact, be essential for figuring out where we add the most value when we're still at a stage where we're figuring out where we're strong (see "hustling" above). But once we transition into management or leadership roles, winning medals and stockpiling ribbons is no longer the goal, and it can be counterproductive to effective leadership.

Daring Leadership

Giving Gold Stars

It sounds counterintuitive, but what got us promoted in the first place, and what made us indispensable to the organization, can get in the way of good leadership skills. Rewarding others rather than seeking to be rewarded is the only way to continue to grow within an organization, and to fully embody the mantle of daring leadership.

In a daring leadership role, it's time to lift up our teams and help them shine. This is one of the most difficult hurdles of advancement, particularly for those of us who are used to hustling, or don't know exactly where we contribute value once the areas where we contributed value before are delegated to those coming up behind us. For this reason, **it is essential that leadership be one of the explicit priorities for anyone in a role with direct reports**—it cannot be a tacked-on assumption or done in our spare time.

Bill Gentry talks about the need to "flip the script" when we find ourselves in a new role as a leader. His book *Be the Boss Everyone Wants to Work For: A Guide for New Leaders* is smart, practical skill-building for those of us who are reluctant to give up our star collecting.

15. Armored Leadership

Zigzagging and Avoiding

When I was in third grade, we lived in New Orleans, and my parents took me and my brother fishing in a swamp. When we got there, the caretaker of the land said, "If a gator comes atcha, run a zigzag pattern—they're quick but they ain't good at makin' turns." Well, we were only there five minutes before a gator snapped off the end of my mom's fishing pole. Mercifully, it never tried to chase us; had it, I assure you that we would have all zigzagged back to the car like crazy.

Zigzagging is a metaphor for the energy we spend trying to dodge the bullets of vulnerability—whether it's conflict, discomfort, confrontation, or the potential for shame, hurt, or criticism.

I tend to zigzag in times of vulnerability—like when I need to make a difficult call, I'll write a script, then I'll convince myself that the following morning is definitely better, then I'll draft an email because that would clearly be superior to a call. I run back and forth until I'm wiped out. And I still need to make the call.

Daring Leadership

Talking Straight and Taking Action

We all know that it saves a tremendous amount of time and mental capacity to just turn around and face whatever is at our heels head-on. The other advantage of stepping into the discomfort? It's actually much less scary and intimidating to appraise the situation from a face-first position, rather than looking back over our shoulder while running.

In those moments, we need to stop and breathe—bring clarity and awareness to what we're trying to avoid—then get clear about what needs to be done to step into vulnerability.

When we find ourselves zigzagging—hiding out, pretending, avoiding, procrastinating, rationalizing, blaming, lying—we need to remind ourselves that running is a huge energy suck and probably way outside our values. At some point, we have to turn toward vulnerability and make that call.

A couple of years ago, I spoke at a global leadership event for

Costco. I was sitting at a table in the front row watching their CEO, Craig Jelinek, take questions from Costco leaders. The questions were tough, and 90 percent of the time, Craig's answers were as tough or tougher. I've seen a lot of CEOs take unvetted questions, and more often than not, when the questions have hard answers, the leader zigzags like there's a gator in hot pursuit. You hear a lot of non-answers:

"Great question. Let me give that some thought."

"Wow. Good idea. Someone write that down so we can do some discovery."

"Well, that's one way to frame the question . . ."

But on this cold morning in Seattle, there was no zigzagging, just straight talk:

"Yes. We did make that decision and here's why . . ."

"No. We're not going this direction and here's how we got to that decision . . ."

I started thinking, *Damn. I have to get onstage after this open question-and-answer session, and these people are going to be bristly.*

When Craig was done, the audience leapt to their feet, clapping and cheering. I was shocked. I turned to the woman sitting next to me and said, "That was really hard. He did not give them the answers they were looking for. Why is everyone cheering?"

She smiled and said, "At Costco, we clap for the truth."

We love the truth because it's increasingly rare. So let me give you a truth here: In case you find yourself in the swamp, you should know that humans can easily outrun alligators, which reach a max speed of 10 miles an hour and have no endurance. But they do have teeth. Lots of teeth.

16. Armored Leadership

Leading from Hurt

I've learned to live by the saying "You can never get enough of what you don't need." It's not easy, especially when it comes to BBC crime procedurals, chips and queso, and approval. One of the patterns that I've observed in working with leaders is that many people lead from a place of hurt and smallness, and they use their position of power to try to fill that self-worth gap. But we just can't fill a self-worth gap by leading and using power over people, because that's not exactly what we need.

To put it in simple terms, we work our shit out on other people, and we can never get enough of what it is we're after, because we're not addressing the real problem. In general, it's fair to say that we're all working our stuff out on people all day long. But when you add the leadership power differential, it gets dangerous.

"Leading from hurt" behaviors include feeling no value from our partner or our children, so we double down on being seen as "important" at work by taking credit for ideas that aren't ours, staying in comparison mode, and always knowing instead of learning. The most common driver of the hurt that I've observed is from our first families. The first-family stuff can look like seeking the approval and acceptance from colleagues that we never received from our parents. Also, if our parents' professional failures and disappointments shaped our upbringing, we can spend our careers trying to undo that pain. That often takes the shape of an insatiable appetite for recognition and success, of unproductive competition, and, on occasion, of having zero tolerance for risk.

Identifying the source of the pain that's driving how we lead and how we show up for other people is important, because returning to that place and doing that work is the only real fix. Projecting the pain onto others places it where it doesn't belong and leads to serious trust violations. Our long, hard search for whatever it is that we need never ends and leaves a wake of disconnection.

Daring Leadership

Leading from Heart

Let's go back to this sentence from section 2: "Leaders must either invest a reasonable amount of time attending to fears and feelings, or squander an unreasonable amount of time trying to manage ineffective and unproductive behavior." Well, leader, heal thyself.

We also have to invest time attending to our own fears, feelings, and history or we'll find ourselves managing our own unproductive behaviors. As daring leaders, we have to stay curious about our own blind spots and how to pull those issues into view, and we need to commit to helping the people we serve find their blind spots in a way that's safe and supportive.

Like all of us, most of the daring, transformational leaders I've worked with have overcome hurtful experiences—from childhood illness and painful family histories to violence and trauma. Many are in the middle of deep struggles like marriages that are failing, children in rehab, or health crises. The difference between leading from hurt and leading from heart is not what you've experienced or are currently experiencing, it's what you do with that pain and hurt.

One of the most powerful examples of leading from heart that I've witnessed was Tarana Burke's response to Harvey Weinstein's arrest. Tarana is the senior director at Girls for Gender Equity and founder of the Me Too movement—a movement to end sexual violence. In an interview with Trevor Noah, Tarana said, "This is not really a moment to, like, celebrate how the mighty have fallen." She explained that the focus should be on healing the survivors and recognizing their courage.

In a world full of rage and hate, Tarana, who is a survivor of sexual assault and has dedicated her career to helping other survivors, said, "It doesn't bring me personal joy, this is not really what it is about." She explained, "It's not about taking down powerful men, and it is not a woman's movement either—that's another sort of misconception. It's a movement for survivors."

Again, foreshadowing the work we will do together in the part on learning to rise, when we own our hard stories and rumble with them, we can write a new ending—an ending that includes how we're going to use what we've survived to be more compassionate and empathic. When we deny our stories of struggle, they own us. They own us, and they drive our behavior, emotions, thinking, and leading. Daring leadership is leading from heart, not hurt.

Putting Down the Armor

Roosevelt's speech makes no mention of armor or weaponry—there are no shields glinting in the afternoon sun, no sabers, swords, or rifles. It would appear that the unarmored person in the arena is fighting with wits, bravery, and bare hands. Roosevelt is talking about grappling, person to person.

That's where the credit goes: to the person "whose face is marred by dust and sweat and blood; who strives valiantly; who errs, who comes short again and again, who at the best knows in the end the triumph of high achievement, and who at the worst, if he fails, at least fails while daring greatly." The credit goes to the person in the arena—and the greatest arena in a world overrun with fear, criticism, and cynicism is vulnerability.

As long as I've studied vulnerability (which dates back to my dissertation research in 1998), I will always think that the very best example of vulnerability is saying "I love you" first. Talk about taking off the armor! Just thinking about that moment takes my breath away. Like many of you, I've taken that risk and had the indescribable experience of hearing "Oh, my God! I love you too!" And I've been on the shitty end of "Aww, thank you! But I think we're on different pages."

PEOPLE, PEOPLE, PEOPLE

In those moments, it's hard to remember that the brokenhearted are the bravest among us because they got past their egos and busted their hearts out of that prison so they could love. Yes, there's pain. And more dust and sweat and blood. It's hard. And when we don't understand that the willingness to risk hurt or failure is courage, or we don't have the skills to rumble and recover, it's easy to reach for the armor and weapons at the mere whiff of vulnerability.

As our work around the world has taught us, the fear of vulnerability and all that comes with taking off the armor—the fear of being judged or misunderstood, of making a mistake, being wrong, and experiencing shame—is universal. The leaders interviewed for this book represent organizations across the globe, from film studios, tech companies, and accounting firms to military commands, schools, and community-building organizations. How is it possible that the fear of taking off the armor is universal? *People, people, people everywhere are just people, people, people.*

A couple of years ago we held a training in London, and the participants came from more than forty countries. As we waded into the topics of vulnerability and shame, one of the participants stood up and said, "Our shared experiences of these emotions is so shocking. It's what we have in common more than anything else."

The cultural messages and expectations that fuel feelings of vulnerability and even shame may be different, but the experiences themselves, as well as their ability to alter who we are and how we show up, are universal. One powerful universal truth that has stood the test of global research: If *shame and blame* is our management style, or if it's a pervasive cultural norm, we can't ask people to be vulnerable or brave. Shame can only rise to a certain level before people have to armor up and sometimes disengage to stay safe.

Another learning about the universal applicability of the daring leadership findings came from the people we interviewed who lead distributed global teams. They talked about the importance of having ongoing difficult and vulnerable conversations about the different cultural messages and expectations that corrode trust and psychological safety in a team when they are not identified and discussed.

One participant, who is a champion of daring leadership in her company, leads a team of highly skilled analysts located all over the world who are diverse not only in terms of culture but also of age and gender identity.

She said, "One of the most important and most challenging parts of my job is surfacing what's getting in the way of our team's communication and performance. Last year, I noticed a pattern of our team in Hong Kong not participating in videoconference meetings. They're major contributors, so I couldn't figure out why they were holding back. I reached out to them without our other colleagues on the line and said, 'We need to hear from you in these meetings. Not participating is not working. What can I do to support your participation?' "

She told me there was a long pause before one man spoke up and said, "We've asked many times to receive the agenda in advance of the meetings. When we get the agenda ten minutes before the meeting starts, it feels disrespectful. If you really wanted our contribution, you would give us time to review and prepare."

She explained that this type of frank conversation was a norm. "These are almost always conversations about cultural norms and differences. No one wants to talk about these issues because they're awkward and uncomfortable. But I know it's critically important, and it's my job as a leader to push through the discomfort. It's never easy, but we're always grateful and stronger when we're done."

EMPATHY IS NOT CONNECTING TO AN EXPERIENCE.

Empathy is connecting to the emotions that underpin an experience.

section four SHAME AND EMPATHY

Digging into Shame

If you want to see the ego go to DEFCON 1, get anywhere close to shame. What makes embracing vulnerability feel the most terrifying is how taking off the armor and exposing our hearts can open us up to experiencing shame. Our egos are willing to keep our hearts encased in armor, no matter the cost, if we can avoid feeling "less than" or unworthy of love and belonging. What the ego doesn't understand is that stunting our emotional growth and shutting down our vulnerability doesn't protect us from shame, disconnection, and isolation, it guarantees them. Let's look at how shame works and why it can't survive a healthy dose of empathy.

Shame, which is often referred to as "the master emotion" by researchers, is the *never good enough* emotion. It can stalk us over time or wash over us in a second—either way, its power to make us feel we're not worthy of connection, belonging, or even love is unmatched in the realm of emotion. If we lean into vulnerability and resist the urge to armor up, and that leads to our feeling blamed, put down, ignored, or pushed away, shame can deal such a painful blow to our sense of self-worth that just the fear of it can send us running from the vulnerability rumble.

I've written extensively about shame in all of my books, so I've gathered the important pieces from other books to give you a primer here. Before we dissect shame, let me walk you through a recent example.

In July 2017, one month after I delivered the final manuscript for *Braving the Wilderness* to my publisher, I was three weeks into my pre-book-tour boot camp. The week after the *Rising Strong* tour ended, I had sworn to myself that I would never embark on another book tour without getting into physical, mental, and spiritual shape. The new book was set for release on September 12.

I love being on the road and spending time with our incredible, wholehearted community. It's truly one of the great unexpected gifts of my life. But if I'm not physically, mentally, and spiritually fit, the planes, hotels, and homesickness can crush me. Late night room service becomes my best friend, my coping skills start to wear thin, and, if I'm not careful, anxiety and loneliness can set in.

The worst part of this is that when I'm not in fighting shape, I collapse when I get home. I can't get out of bed for two or three days, and my kids come to my room and visit me like I'm in the hospital.

At first, I thought the problems were driven by my introversion. I'm a ten on a ten-point scale of introversion. I require a significant amount of alone time to function on all cylinders. But we started testing new travel strategies and I realized it's more than that. I've never been in a good place without working out and paying attention to my spiritual life. When I'm committed to these practices, it's magic. Well, magic, discipline, and a shit ton of hard work. But it's really, really solid.

Three weeks into running, working out, rocking my Keto plan, practicing my centering prayer, shopping for cute outfits to wear on the road, and setting master-class-level boundaries for the tour, things looked pretty good. On the tenth of July, I drove twenty minutes from my house to Wire Road Studios in the Houston Heights to record the audiobook for *Braving the Wilderness*. I love this studio and do all of my recording work there. I remember bouncing into the front office that morning and passing my favorite photo of Beyoncé hanging on the wall. I was in such a good mood, filled with possibility. I just wanted to give her photo a high-five. *H-town girls bringing it.*

We were ten minutes into the recording when the sound engineer's voice came over my headphones. "I can hear your earrings. Can you take those off, please?"

I said, "Sure! Sorry about that." I hustled out of the sound booth toward a bench in the hall where my purse was sitting. Walking fast and looking down to put the earring backing onto the hoop that I had just pulled off my ear, I plowed, forehead first, into a six-inch-thick glass wall.

I don't remember much after that, just waking up on the floor. And I remember the pain. I knocked myself unconscious for a full minute, and when I came to I was completely confused. I was crying and people were helping me, but I was out of it.

Karen, my audiobook producer, insisted that she should drive me home or to the doctor's office, but I wanted to go back to reading. We were on a super tight schedule. I read for thirty more minutes until I finally started crying again. I looked at Karen and said, "I just can't. I don't know what's wrong."

She offered to drive me home, but I assured her that I was fine. I drove to the office, but I don't remember a single minute of that drive. When I walked in, people gasped at the Ping-Pong-ball-sized lump protruding from my forehead.

Again, I assured everyone I was fine. I jumped on a Zoom call with my team. I was sitting next to Barrett and Suzanne in our office. Murdoch and Chaz were beaming in from New York and Austin. Apparently, a few minutes into the call, I said, "I don't understand what's happening. I don't understand."

Murdoch responded, "Brené, are you sure you're okay?"

They tell me that my mood shifted and I snapped back, "Leave me alone. I'm just tired."

Then I threw up in the trashcan under Suzanne's desk, wiped the throw-up off my chin, folded my arms on her desk, and went to sleep.

I woke up at home. My team had called my husband, and he had left his office to meet us at the house. He was asking me questions, and they tell me I was combative, frustrated, and crying. No matter how hard I tried, I couldn't line up my thoughts or my vision. Steve kept asking me to look at him, but I remember it being so much work that it hurt. I could only look through him or past him. My sister was standing out of sight, scared and fighting back tears.

I was diagnosed with a severe concussion. But, as familiar as that sounds, I would quickly learn that I had no idea what that meant.

The day after the injury, my team sprang into action. They started canceling upcoming speaking dates and shifting my calendar. I was pissed. I kept saying, "I'm going to be fine in a week, these are huge events with contracts that have been in place for over a year. There's no reason to cancel."

Murdoch was clear: "You don't get a vote on this."

I wouldn't relent. I couldn't. I was swallowed up by shame and fear.

Researchers Tamara Ferguson, Heidi Eyre, and Michael Ashbaker have found that "unwanted identity" is one of the primary elicitors of shame. They explain that unwanted identities are characteristics that undermine our vision of our ideal selves.

Sick, unreliable, and undependable are *huge* unwanted identities for me. As a fifth generation German American Texan, I grew up believing that illness is weakness. Not in other people—in other people it's human and okay and we should support and help. But in our family being sick is lazy, and if you're tough enough, you can walk off anything. Trust me when I tell you that no one who lives by this loves it, but the shame is so enveloping that it's hard to break free.

Unlearning this belief has been one of the hardest and most painful lessons of my life, and a battle I have to constantly refight, given the culture's reinforcement of it. But I will continue to fight and talk about it because I do not want to pass this belief down to my children. It's a terrible way to live.

Five days after I hit my head, I couldn't function. I had a black eye down to my cheek and a huge bruised forehead. I couldn't read, watch TV, look at a computer screen, or be in bright light. It hurt to think. And the harder I tried to get back to normal, the worse it got. Every time I pushed, I regressed. I had wrestled away the shame self-talk about canceling the events with some self-compassion and empathy from my team, but now I was feeling shame about losing control of what I believed made me *me*: my mind.

What about my plan to get stronger for my book tour? What if I don't get better? What if I don't heal? What if I've written my last book? What if I can never do research again?

Finally, Trey, a dear friend of our family, sat down with me and shared his nineteen-year-old wisdom. He laid it all out and held nothing back. He told me hard things that I didn't want to hear, but he did it with such tenderness and empathy that I just listened and cried. He was a rugby player in high school and had suffered his first concussion six months earlier, playing as a freshman in college.

He said, "I know this is scary and you can't even describe it to other people, but it's real. And the harder you fight it, the worse it's going to get and the longer it's going to take to heal. You can't win this fight by being tough. You can't fight your way back. You need time. This is real, and it's scary when your mind stops working. You're going to have to find a way to let go for the next few weeks."

After a month, I started slowly returning to work. Every time I pushed a little too hard, there was a setback. I still couldn't work out, but I could find my way to the pantry to comfort-eat. I gained ten pounds—just enough so that every outfit I bought for the tour no longer fit. Whatever good physical, mental, spiritual shape looked like, this was the opposite.

The fear that I would never get back to my old self, and that trying to come back was permanently damaging my brain, turned into serious anxiety. I made an appointment to see the neuropsychologist who works with the Houston Texans and Houston Rockets and specializes in concussion management.

Steve and I went together, and it was beyond helpful. I learned that the anticipatory anxiety I was experiencing about the fear that I would never feel like myself again was normal, and she gave me some strategies to deal with it. I also got the okay to go back to work and do some light exercise, and she gave me some tips on how to listen to what my body needed.

When I got home that day I felt hopeful. *I can do this. I've still got a little more than two weeks before the tour now, and I can start first thing tomorrow if this weather clears up.*

Hurricane Harvey hit Houston the next day. Our neighborhood was decimated. Team members lost their homes. It was heartbreaking.

The book tour launched on time, we moved in the middle of the hurricane cleanup, more hard things happened, more beautiful things happened, and connecting with my community was a healing balm. Somehow we all managed to love and lean on each other with so much empathy and kindness through those months that shame kept its distance.

Mercifully, I haven't had another injury or illness as serious as that concussion, but I did wrestle down a virus over Christmas and nurse both of my kids through mono over the past year. I'm happy to report that while I've never used "suck it up" and "push through" with anyone but myself, they are no longer in my vocabulary at all. It took fifty years to let go of those shame messages, but better late than never.

SHAME 101

I always start with the Shame 1-2-3's:

1. We all have it. Shame is universal and one of the most primitive human emotions that we experience. The only people who don't experience shame are those who lack the capacity for empathy and human connection. Here's your choice: 'Fess up to experiencing shame or admit that you're a sociopath. *Quick note: This is the only time that shame seems like a good option.*
2. We're all afraid to talk about shame. Just the word is uncomfortable.
3. The less we talk about shame, the more control it has over our lives.

First, shame is the fear of disconnection. As we talked about in the myths of vulnerability, we are physically, emotionally, cognitively, and spiritually hardwired for connection, love, and belonging. Connection, along with love and belonging, is why we are here, and it is what gives purpose and meaning to our lives. Shame is the fear of disconnection—it's the fear that something we've done or failed to do, an ideal that we've not lived up to, or a goal that we've not accomplished makes us unworthy of connection. Here's the definition of shame that emerged from my research:

Shame is the intensely painful feeling or experience of believing that we are flawed and therefore unworthy of love, belonging, and connection.

Shame drives two tapes:

Never good enough.

Who do you think you are?

These gremlinlike voices work as a terrible vise. Right when you overcome the "not good enough" whisper and muster up the courage to enter the arena, the shame gremlins hit you with "Wow. You think you have what it takes to pull this off? Good luck." The Texas gremlins would say, "Don't get too big for your britches, sister."

Retreating into our smallness becomes the most seductive and easiest way to stay safe in the midst of the shame squeeze. But, as we've talked about, when we armor and contort ourselves into smallness, things break and we suffocate.

Here are some of the responses we received when we asked people for an example of shame:

- Shame is getting laid off when we're expecting our first child.
- Shame is hiding my addiction.
- Shame is raging at my kids.
- Shame was my response to seeing my parents' shame when I came out.

- Shame is covering up a mistake at work and getting caught.
- Shame is failing at my business after my friends invested in it.
- Shame is getting a promotion, then getting demoted six months later because I wasn't succeeding.
- Shame is my boss calling me a loser in front of our colleagues.
- Shame is not making partner.
- Shame is my wife asking me for a divorce and telling me that she wants children, but not with me.
- Shame is getting sexually harassed at work but being too afraid to say anything because he's the guy everyone loves.
- Shame is constantly being asked to speak on behalf of all Latinos in marketing meetings. I'm from Kansas. I don't even speak Spanish.
- Shame is being proud of a completed project, then being told it wasn't at all what my boss wanted or expected.
- Shame is watching things change so fast and no longer knowing how and where I can contribute. The fear of being irrelevant is a huge shame trigger that we are not addressing at work.

We may not be able to relate to the exact examples, but if we know ourselves and are in touch with our vulnerability, we can recognize that unbearable pain in other people's experiences. Shame is universal.

Current neuroscience research shows that the pain and feelings of rejection that shame inflicts are as real as physical pain. Emotions can hurt. And just as we have to describe, name, and talk about physical pain to heal it, we have to recognize and talk about shame to get out from under it. This is even more difficult than talking about physical pain because shame derives its power from being unspoken. That's why even the word *shame* is tough to say.

SHAME, GUILT, HUMILIATION, AND EMBARRASSMENT

Another reason that shame is so difficult to talk about is vocabulary. We often use the terms *embarrassment, guilt, humiliation,* and *shame* interchangeably, when in reality these experiences are very different in terms of biology, biography, behavior, and self-talk, and they lead to radically different outcomes. Let's start with shame and guilt, because these are the two that we most often confuse, and the consequence of doing that is severe.

The majority of shame researchers and clinicians agree that the difference between shame and guilt is best understood as the difference between "I am bad" and "I did something bad."

Guilt = I did something bad.

Shame = I am bad.

When I was trying to decide how much I wanted to share with my team about how fear and anxiety were the real drivers behind my unreasonable timelines, it was shame that was holding me back. As I said in the previous section, the gremlin message was *You research leadership and you can't even lead. You're a joke.*

It wasn't guilt: *Man, I've been unfair to my team with these timelines. I've made the wrong choice for the wrong reasons.*

It was shame: *It's not that I've made bad choices. I am a bad leader.*

In our political chaos, people throw around the word *shameless* when they see someone make a self-serving or unethical decision, and attributing unconscionable behavior to a lack of shame. This is wrong and dangerous. Shame isn't the cure, it's the cause. Don't let what looks like a bloated ego and narcissism fool you into thinking there's a lack of shame. Shame and fear are almost always driving that unethical behavior. We're now seeing that shame often fuels narcissistic behavior. In fact, I define narcissism as the shame-based fear of being ordinary.

Grandiosity and bluster are easy to assign to an overinflated ego. It's tough to get a glimpse of the fear and lack of self-worth that are actually behind the posturing and selfishness because posturing leads to weaponizing hurt and turning it on other people. The last thing people like that need is more shame. More accountability for their behavior and lack of empathy? Yes. More shame just makes them more dangerous, gives them the opportunity to redirect attention to the shaming behavior, and, weirdly, can drum up support from others who are also looking for a way to discharge their pain and an enemy to blame.

Shame is not a compass for moral behavior. It's much more likely to drive destructive, hurtful, immoral, and self-aggrandizing behavior than it is to heal it. Why? Because where shame exists, empathy is almost always absent. That's what makes shame dangerous. The opposite of experiencing shame is experiencing empathy. The behavior that many of us find so egregious today is more about people being empathyless, not shameless.

While shame is highly correlated with addiction, violence, aggression, depression, eating disorders, and bullying, **guilt** is negatively correlated with these outcomes. Empathy and values live in the contours of guilt, which is why it's a powerful and socially adaptive emotion. When we apologize for something we've done, make amends, or change a behavior that doesn't align with our values, guilt—not shame—is most often the driving force.

We feel guilty when we hold up something we've done or failed to do against our values and find they don't match up. It's a psychologically uncomfortable feeling, but one that's helpful. The discomfort of cognitive dissonance is what drives meaningful change. Shame, however, corrodes the very part of us that believes we can change and do better.

Humiliation is another word that we often confuse with *shame*. Donald Klein captures the difference between shame and humiliation when he writes, "People believe they deserve their shame; they do not believe they deserve their humiliation." If Sonja is in a meeting with her colleagues and her principal, and her principal calls her a failure because of her class's test scores, Sonja will probably experience that as either shame or humiliation.

If Sonja's self-talk is *I am a failure*—that's shame. If her self-talk is "Man, my boss is so out of control, I don't deserve this"—that's humiliation. Humiliation feels terrible and makes for a miserable work or home environment—and if it's ongoing, it can certainly become shame if we start to buy into the messaging. It is, however, still less destructive than shame, where we internalize the "failure" comment. Sonja's humiliation self-talk is "This isn't about me." When we do that, it's less likely that we'll shut down, act out, or fight back. We stay aligned with our values while trying to solve the problem.

Embarrassment is normally fleeting and can usually eventually be funny. It's by far the least serious and detrimental of these emotions. The hallmark of embarrassment is that when we do something embarrassing, we don't feel alone. We know other folks have done the same thing and, like a blush, the feeling will pass rather than define us.

Getting clear on the language is an important start to understanding shame. Emotional literacy is the core of shame resilience, which means moving from shame to empathy—the real antidote to shame that we'll dig into more later in this section.

HOW SHAME SHOWS UP AT WORK

Looking for shame in organizations is like inspecting a home for termites. If you walk through a house and actually spot termites, you have an acute problem that's probably been going on for a while. If you walk through an office or school or place of worship and you actually see shame—you see a manager berating an employee or a teacher belittling a student or clergy using shame as a control mechanism or an activist using shame as a social justice tool—you're witnessing a full-blown threat to your culture. You have to figure out how and why it's happening and deal with it immediately (and without shame).

What's trickier is that in most cases, shame is hidden behind the walls of organizations. It's not dormant—it's slowly eating away at innovation, trust, connection, and culture—but it's tougher to spot. Here's what to look for:

Perfectionism
Favoritism
Gossiping
Back-channeling
Comparison
Self-worth tied to productivity
Harassment
Discrimination
Power over
Bullying
Blaming
Teasing
Cover-ups

These are all behavioral cues that shame has permeated a culture. A more obvious sign is if shame has become an outright management tool. Is there evidence of people in leadership roles bullying others, criticizing subordinates in front of colleagues, delivering public reprimands, or setting up reward systems that intentionally embarrass, shame, or humiliate people?

In one of our workshops, a woman leaned back in her chair with tears in her eyes and said, "My shame is so deep I don't even know how to go there." Her colleagues listened with care as she opened up about a boss who'd repeatedly criticized her in front of others.

Faith communities and schools are not exempt from shame. In our original research on shame, 85 percent of the people we interviewed could recall a school incident from their childhood that was so shaming, it changed how they thought of themselves as learners. What makes this worse is that approximately half of those recollections were what I refer to as *creativity scars*. The research participants could point to a specific incident in which they were told or shown that they weren't good writers, artists, musicians, dancers, or something else creative. The shame tool used in these situations was almost always comparison. This helps explain why the gremlins are so powerful when it comes to creativity and innovation, and why using comparison as a management tool stifles both.

On the flip side of that finding, the same data showed that more than 90 percent of the people we interviewed could name a teacher, coach, school administrator, or faculty member who reinforced their self-worth and helped them believe in themselves and their ability. What do these seemingly competing findings tell us? School leaders have enormous power and influence, and how they use that power and influence changes people. For better or worse.

I've met plenty of daring leaders who are committed to not using shame, but I've never been in a totally shame-free organization. Maybe they exist, but I'd be surprised to find one. The best-case scenario is that it's a limited or contained problem rather than a cultural norm.

One of the most common scenarios that come up in the research is the shame people feel when they're fired, and *how* they're fired.

Susan Mann has over three decades of senior leadership experience in banking, higher education, and philanthropy. Before starting her own coaching and consulting practice, Susan was the head of the global learning and development team at the Bill and Melinda Gates Foundation. Credentialed by the International Coach Federation, Susan is a founding member of the Daring Way senior faculty. (The Daring Way is our training and certification program for helping professionals offered through Daring Education, our nonprofit entity.)

Susan helps grow the leadership capacity of our company by coaching our emerging leaders. When I asked her about the very tough task of firing employees, she said this:

> Early in my human resources career one of my mentors taught me always to **give people a "way out with dignity."** Three decades later—after countless conversations advising leaders how to fire people—I feel like I have leaned into this advice hundreds of times.
>
> What does it mean to give someone a way out with dignity? Remember the human and pay attention to feelings. Of course, leaders must make the thoughtful business decisions that are right for the company: Lay people off, fire someone, reassign a person to a different role. Definitely do what makes sense to achieve the company's goals.
>
> *And,* while you're doing what you need to do, always hold the human in mind. Keep that person who will be impacted by your decision squarely in front of you. This person has a family, a career, and a life that will be affected.
>
> When you're delivering the news, be kind. Be clear. Be respectful. Be generous. Can you let the person resign rather than be fired? Can you provide severance pay? Ask the person how they want to let colleagues know about their departure and follow their lead on that if possible.

> Can you allow a graceful exit, so they retain their dignity? This isn't about avoiding hard decisions and hard conversations. It's about knowing that we all have hearts that can be hurt. Great leaders make tough "people decisions" and are tender in implementing them. That's giving people a way out with dignity.

I asked Susan what gets in the way of giving people a way out with dignity. Susan replied with these answers:

- Armoring up: I've seen a lot of leaders get defensive when they decide to fire someone. It's a weighty decision, and I see people stay in their heads and be super rational, citing all the reasons why the decision is correct and justifiable. It's a form of self-protection.
- Time and money: Giving people a way out with dignity is a bigger investment of time, money, heart, energy. It requires us to slow down, be more thoughtful, and have fuller conversations. That doesn't happen as often as it should.
- The fall guy: Sometimes a person takes the hit for a broken system or team. The leader is looking—often unconsciously—for someone to blame for what's not going well, rather than looking at herself in the mirror and wondering what she could do to fix the bigger issues.
- Lack of vulnerability and courage: an inability to hold the duality of head and heart and engage both at the same time. I see leaders express fear about the emotion the person being fired may show: "I'm afraid she's going to cry or get mad." Sometimes they're afraid they may show emotion themselves: "What if I'm so nervous I lose it?"

She concluded, "There is an art to giving people a way out with dignity. It's a huge skill to develop and it takes practice. Few companies and leaders make that skill a priority."

Perhaps the most devastating sign of a shame infestation is a cover-up. Cover-ups are perpetrated not only by the original actors, but by a culture of complicity and shame. Sometimes individuals are complicit because staying quiet or hiding the truth benefits them and/or doesn't jeopardize their influence or power. Other times, people are complicit because it's the norm—they work in a cover-up culture that uses shame to keep people quiet.

Either way, when the culture of a corporation, nonprofit, university, government, church, sports program, school, or family mandates that it is more important to protect the reputation of that system and those in power than it is to protect the basic human dignity of individuals or communities, you can be certain of the following problems:

Shame is systemic.
Complicity is part of the culture.
Money and power trump ethics.
Accountability is dead.
Control and fear are management tools.
And there's a trail of devastation and pain.

When it comes to real talk about shame, we have to set it up the right way so people feel safe. These are powerful conversations. Giving people permission to talk about shame is liberating. It shines a light in a dark corner. People realize they're not alone. Sharing their stories together normalizes shame, creates connection, and builds trust. These are the hard conversations that can point the way to desired new behaviors and culture shifts. And in some cases, a healing conversation about shame can change our lives.

SHAME RESILIENCE

The bad news is that shame *resistance* is not possible—as long as we care about connection, the fear of disconnection will always be a powerful force in our lives, and the pain caused by shame will always be real. But here's the great news: Shame *resilience* is possible, teachable, and within reach for all of us.

Shame resilience is the ability to practice authenticity when we experience shame, to move through the experience without sacrificing our values, and to come out on the other side of the shame experience with more courage, compassion, and connection than we had going into it. Ultimately, shame resilience is about moving from shame to empathy—the real antidote to shame.

In the next section, we're going to do a deep dive into empathy and self-compassion, but for now it's important to understand that if we share our story with someone who responds with empathy and understanding, shame can't survive. Self-compassion is also critically important, but because shame is a social concept—it happens between people—it also heals best between people. A social wound needs a social balm, and empathy is that balm. Self-compassion is key because when we're able to be gentle with ourselves in the midst of shame, we're more likely to reach out, connect, and experience empathy.

Empathy

Empathy is one of the linchpins of cultures built on connection and trust—it's also an essential ingredient for teams who take risks and show up for rumbles. There are five elements to empathy, and we will explore each one. Meanwhile, empathy is easily confused with sympathy, giving advice, and judgment disguised as concern. To add empathy to our courage toolbox, it's important that we be able to translate it into specific skills that we can learn and practice, readily distinguish empathy from sympathy, and understand the big barriers to empathy. Let's start with a story.

A couple of years ago, Suzanne—our president and COO—and I spent the day facilitating our daring leadership program at Fort Bragg. It was an amazing experience, and I had coordinated the logistics of the trip with military precision. The plan was to leave the base when we were done, drive 74.1 miles to the Raleigh-Durham International Airport, return our rental car, grab lunch, and get to the gate with ninety minutes to spare. After running several scenarios and checking on-time flight histories, I was confident I could make it home that night for the big game.

Ellen picked up a field hockey stick for the first time the summer before high school. With some encouragement from a coach she met at the open house for incoming freshmen and some grueling lessons in hundred-degree weather during the summer, she made the team her freshman year.

Sadly, when it comes to land sports, Steve and I have zero genetic gifts to pass down to our kids. We're swimmers and Steve is a water polo player, but we've got no turf speed. Ellen loved her coaches and her teammates. She worked hard, never missed games or practices, spent hours practicing her stick skills in our yard, and played with heart for all four years of high school.

Suzanne and I were scheduled to land back in Houston two hours before the big game, which gave me just enough time to change clothes, load twenty surprise fat heads in my car, and get to the fields for senior night. (Fat heads are photos of players' faces blown up to three feet tall and two feet wide, on sticks, to hold up in the stands.) This was the final field hockey game of Ellen's high school career, and during the halftime ceremony, parents give their senior daughters flowers and escort them across the field.

Everything was going according to plan, and I could barely contain my excitement when I got a text from Ellen: "I can't wait to see you tonight. I can't believe it's senior night!!! OMG! How did time go so fast???"

We were lining up to board when I texted back, "I'm so proud of you! I'll be home in a couple of hours. GO TIGERS!!!"

There had been no movement in the boarding line when the gate agent made an announcement that our flight was delayed ten minutes due to mechanical difficulties. *No sweat. I have built in sixty minutes of delays. If we hit ninety minutes of delays, I initiate Plan B: I go straight to the game and my friend Cookie picks up the fat heads.*

Twenty minutes later, I see the pilot talking to the gate agents, and I grab Suzanne by the arm. It startles her and she whispers, "What's wrong? What's going on? Are you okay?"

I'm trying to not make a scene so I whisper back, "They're going to cancel our flight. Get on your laptop right now and book the next flight."

Here's one of the many great things about Suzanne: She can get shit done like no one's business. Street fight? You want her on your side.

No questions asked, she starts working on flights, but the only way out of North Carolina is to fly to Atlanta, change airlines, and land in Houston at ten P.M. After she books it, she looks at me and says, "Why do you think they're canceling this flight?"

Before I can even answer her question, the gate agent announces that the flight is canceled for mechanical reasons, and there's an immediate stampede to the desk. Suzanne and I find a free space to sit down, and we call back to our office in Houston. Within minutes, three people are working on getting us home in time for the game. After forty-five minutes, Suzanne looked at me and said, "I'm so sorry. There's no way to get home in time for the game."

"But if we drive . . ."

She put her hand on my forearm. "We've tried everything. I'm sorry."

I said the one thing I tend to say and repeat when I'm desperately overwhelmed: "I don't understand. I don't understand."

Suzanne looked me right in the eyes. "We're not getting home before ten tonight."

I just started sobbing. I mean crying to the point that people were staring. It was a profound experience of empathy for me because Suzanne didn't care that I was losing it in public. And, more important, she didn't try to make the situation better. She just said, "This sucks. This is such bullshit. I'd walk back to Houston with you if it helped."

"I don't understand," I said again, trailing off.

"I know what a big deal this is for you. This just sucks. My heart is breaking too."

"But this is a big deal," I explained as if she hadn't just confirmed that in every way possible.

Suzanne looked at me and said, "Hell, yeah, it's a big deal. It is a super big deal. You did everything you could to be there. It's an important night."

So often, when someone is in pain, we're afraid to say, "Yes, this hurts. Yes, this is a big deal. Yes, this sucks." We think our job is to make things better, so we minimize the pain. But Suzanne didn't minimize my pain. She had the courage to reflect back to me the truth of how I was feeling, which was that I was destroyed that I couldn't be there for this big night for my daughter. She chose practicing empathy with me over her own comfort.

"I really do feel heartbroken." She had nailed what I was feeling when she said her heart was breaking too. Looking back, I see that it was the big game and the special ceremony, but it was also the fact that Ellen was months away from leaving home for college and this was the first of many formal goodbyes to high school. It was layers of grief.

I told Suzanne, "I know in the big scheme of things, it's not a big deal. When I see people crying at airports, I always think about what they might be going through, and I try to smile that *I see you and I'm sorry* smile. This is not a funeral or an accident or something really bad. I don't know what's happening to me."

Suzanne wouldn't have any of the **comparative suffering**. She wasn't going to minimize my hurt, and she wasn't going to watch me rank-order my misery: "No, it's not any of those things, but this is a big deal. This hurts."

I've learned a lot from research about the danger of comparative suffering and the race to misery. If we believe empathy is finite, like pizza, and practicing empathy with someone leaves fewer slices for others, then perhaps comparing levels of suffering would be necessary. Luckily, however, empathy is infinite and renewable. The more you give, the more we all have. That means all pain can be met with empathy—there's no reason to rank and ration.

This experience with Suzanne was empathy in practice. In those bad moments, it's not our job to make things better. It's just not. Our job is to connect. It's to take the perspective of someone else. **Empathy is not connecting to an experience, it's connecting to the emotions that underpin an experience.**

People often ask me how they can show empathy for someone who is going through something they've never experienced. Again, empathy is connecting to the feeling under the experience, not the experience itself. If you've ever felt grief, disappointment, shame, fear, loneliness, or anger, you're qualified. Now you just need the courage to practice and build your empathy skills.

Back at that airport, I was right on the verge of causing a scene with my crying, so I found a hiding spot at the Life Is Good airport shop. *Oh, the irony.* If you're the woman who was working there that day—thank you for seeing me and asking me if I was okay. But most of all, I'm so grateful that you let me sit on the floor and hide for thirty minutes. Your kindness mattered.

From behind the round rack of colorful T-shirts, I texted Ellen to let her know that I was going to miss the game. I considered calling but chose to text because I didn't want to lose it with her on the phone before the game. Of course, her text was the stuff that love is made of:

> I'm sorry about your flight. TBH, I know you're freaking out. But this is one night, and you've come to 100 games and practiced with me and made me go to camps when I didn't want to and hosted parties and took my entire team to Galveston. That's what counts. Love you so much. I'll tell Dad to take lots of pictures.

Steve, on the other hand, got the phone call from under the T-shirt rack. He just listened. When I swore that I was going to quit my job and never get on another flight, he said, "I don't blame you. You worked so hard on those giant heads and the flowers. You've been such a big support for Ellen. I'm just so sorry this is happening."

And thank God again for Suzanne. Several times on the flights home, I'd look at my watch and burst into tears. She would just squeeze my hand and say "I know."

Around 8:30 that night, I looked at her and said, "The game's over." She looked at me and said, "Did we get any pics yet?" She said *we*. She didn't say, "That was hard, but mercifully it's over."

She asked if *we* had any pictures yet. She was still in it because I was still in it. It was so hard. But I never felt alone.

Empathy is a choice. And it's a vulnerable choice, because if I were to choose to connect with you through empathy, I would have to connect with something in myself that knows that feeling. In the face of a difficult conversation, when we see that someone's hurt or in pain, it's our instinct as human beings to try to make things better. We want to fix, we want to give advice. But empathy isn't about fixing, it's the brave choice to be with someone in their darkness—not to race to turn on the light so we feel better.

If I share something with you that's difficult for me, I'd rather you say, "I don't even know what to say right now, I'm just so glad you told me." Because in truth, a response can rarely make something better. Connection is what heals.

If struggle is being down in a hole, empathy is not jumping into the hole with someone who is struggling and taking on their emotions, or owning their struggle as yours to fix. If their issues become yours, now you have two people stuck in a hole. Not helpful. Boundaries are important here. We have to know where we end and others begin if we really want to show up with empathy.

Theresa Wiseman, a nursing scholar in the UK, studied empathy across every profession that requires deep connection and relationship, and she identified four attributes of empathy. These attributes fully aligned with what emerged from my data, but they did not address the idea of "paying attention" to the degree that it emerged in my work. To solve for that, I added a fifth attribute from Kristin Neff's research. Dr. Neff is a self-compassion researcher at the University of Texas at Austin—we'll look at more of her work in a bit.

While each of these components is rich for study—you'll find hundreds of books in any research library on every one of the five—we're going to explore how these elements come together to create empathy, the rocket fuel for building trust and increasing connection.

Empathy Skill #1: To see the world as others see it, or perspective taking

We see the world through a set of unique lenses that bring together who we are, where we come from, and our vast experiences. Our lenses certainly include factors like age, race, ethnicity, ability, and spiritual beliefs, but we also have other lenses that shape how we see the world, including our knowledge, insights, and experience. Our take on the world is completely unique because our point of view is a product of our history and experiences. This is why ten people can witness the same incident and have ten different perspectives on what happened, how it happened, and why it happened.

Are there any observable, knowable, universal truths? Of course. Math and science have given us many examples. But when it comes to the swirl of human emotion, behavior, language, and cognition—there are many valid perspectives.

One of the signature mistakes with empathy is that we believe we can take our lenses off and look through the lenses of someone else. We can't. Our lenses are soldered to who we are. What we can do, however, is honor people's perspectives as truth even when they're different from ours. That's a challenge if you were raised in majority culture—white, straight, male, middle-class, Christian—and you were likely taught that your perspective is *the* correct perspective and everyone else needs to adjust their lens. Or, more accurately, you weren't taught anything about perspective taking, and the default—*My truth is* the *truth*—is reinforced by every system and situation you encounter.

Children are very receptive to learning perspective-taking

skills because they're naturally curious about the world and how others operate in it. Those of us who were taught perspective-taking skills as children owe our parents a huge debt of gratitude. Those of us who were not introduced to that skill set when we were younger will have to work harder and fight armoring up in order to acquire it as adults.

Perspective taking requires becoming the learner, not the knower. Let's say that I'm talking to a colleague on my team who is twenty-five, African American, gay, and grew up in an affluent neighborhood in Chicago. In our conversation we realize that we have completely different opinions about a new program we want to develop. As we're debating the issues, he says, "My experiences lead me to believe this approach will fall flat with the people we want to reach." I can't put down my straight, white, middle-aged, female lens and just snap on his lens to see what he sees, but I can ask, "Tell me more—what are you thinking?" and respect his truth as a full truth, not just an off version of my truth.

This is exactly why every study we see confirms the positive correlation between inclusivity, innovation, and performance. **Again, it's only when diverse perspectives are included, respected, and valued that we can start to get a full picture of the world, who we serve, what they need, and how to successfully meet people where they are.**

I love what Beyoncé said in her first-person essay in the September 2018 issue of *Vogue:*

> If people in powerful positions continue to hire and cast only people who look like them, sound like them, come from the same neighborhoods they grew up in, they will never have a greater understanding of experiences different from their own. They will hire the same models, curate

> the same art, cast the same actors over and over again, and we will all lose. The beauty of social media is it's completely democratic. Everyone has a say. Everyone's voice counts, and everyone has a chance to paint the world from their own perspective.

She was photographed for the magazine cover by Tyler Mitchell, making him the first African American photographer to shoot the cover of *Vogue* in its 126-year history.

As we push on these issues and discover our own blind spots (we all have them), we need to stay very aware of the armor assembly process here: We cannot practice empathy if we need to be knowers; if we can't be learners, we cannot be empathic. And, to be clear (and kind), if we need to be knowers, empathy isn't the only loss. Because curiosity is the key to rumbling with vulnerability, knowers struggle with all four of the building blocks of courage.

Empathy Skill #2: To be nonjudgmental

It is not easy to do this when you enjoy judging as much as most of us do. Based on research, there are two ways to predict when we are going to judge: We judge in areas where we're most susceptible to shame, and we judge people who are doing worse than we are in those areas. So if you find yourself feeling incredibly judgmental about appearance, and you can't figure out why, that's a clue that it's a hard issue for you.

It's important to examine where we feel judgment because it can quickly become a vicious shame cycle. The judgment of others leaves us feeling shame, so we offload the hurt by judging others. I see this happen often in organizations. Shit rolls downhill and ends up in the consumer's lap. I've yet to come across a company that has both a shaming, judgmental culture and wonderful customer service.

Staying out of judgment means being aware of where we are the most vulnerable to our own shame, our own struggle. The good news is that we don't judge in areas where we feel a strong sense of self-worth and grounded confidence, so the more of that we build, the more we let go of judgment.

Empathy Skill #3: To understand another person's feelings
Empathy Skill #4: To communicate your understanding of that person's feelings

I'm combining these two attributes because, when we break them down to skills, they're inextricably connected. Understanding emotions in others and communicating our understanding of these emotions require us to be in touch with our own feelings. Ideally, it also means that we are fluent in the language of feelings, or, at the very least, conversational and somewhat comfortable in the world of emotions. The vast majority of people I've interviewed are not comfortable in the world of emotions and nowhere close to fluent in the language of feelings.

Emotional literacy, in my opinion, is as critical as having language. When we can't name and articulate what's happening to us emotionally, we cannot move through it. Imagine going to the doctor with an excruciating pain in your right shoulder, a pain so great that every time you feel it you're left breathless and doubled over. But when you arrive at the doctor's office, you have duct tape over your mouth and your hands are tied behind your back.

The doctor is anxious to help you, but when she asks you what happened, you can only manage "Mmph. Mmph" through your tape. You're desperate to explain, but you're unable to speak, so you can't name it, you can't articulate it, you can't describe it. The doctor asks you to point to it, but your hands are tied, and all you can do is jump up and down with your eyes darting to the right. You mumble and jump until both you and the doctor are exhausted and give up. This is exactly what happens when we aren't fluent in feelings. It's almost impossible to process emotion when we can't identify, name, and talk about our experiences.

And if that's not enough of a reason to dig in and start learning, emotional literacy is also a prerequisite for empathy, shame resilience, and the ability to reset and rise after a fall. For example, how do we get back on our feet after a fall if we can't recognize the subtle but important differences between disappointment and anger, between shame and guilt, between fear and grief? And if we can't recognize these emotions in ourselves, it's almost impossible to do so with others.

We're finishing a study right now on **emotional literacy**, and I'll give you the movie trailer. Cue the music and pretend this is the dramatic announcer voice: *In a world of emotional literacy, we would be able to recognize and name between thirty and forty emotions in ourselves and others.* I'm hedging on the number because we're in the final stages of confirming the exact emotions, but it's safe to say that fluency in emotional conversation means being able to name at least thirty of them.

The last attribute, communicating our understanding of the emotions, can feel like the biggest risk because we can get it wrong. And not if but when we are off base, we need the courage to circle back. In fact, as long as we show up with our whole hearts, pay attention, and stay curious, we can course-correct. This is why therapists are frequently stereotyped as saying "What I hear you saying is . . ." It's a check-in that allows someone to say, "Nope. That's not what I'm saying. I'm not sad. I'm pissed off."

For example, in non-therapisty language, you could say: "I'm sorry about the project assignment. That sucks and must be so frustrating. Want to talk about it?" This question tells your colleague that you're willing to "go there" and rumble openly about what they're feeling.

Because you were willing to put emotion on the table, it gives them the opportunity to come back and say, "I don't know about frustrated. I think I'm actually really embarrassed and disappointed. I mean, everyone talked about me being the perfect person for it. I never imagined not getting it. Now I have to explain why I didn't get it and I don't even understand." This exchange alone builds the connection and alignment that we need to have a meaningful, trust-building, and even healing conversation.

NAVIGATING THE ICEBERG

One reason emotion is difficult to identify and name is the iceberg effect. Think about an iceberg for a minute. There's the part that you can see above the water, and then it potentially goes on for miles beneath the surface. Many of the emotions that we experience show up as pissed off or shut down on the surface. Below the surface, there's much more nuance and depth. Shame and grief are two examples of emotions that are hard to fully express, so we turn to anger or silence.

This is an easy concept to understand, for one reason: The vast majority of us find it easier to be mad than hurt. Not only is it easier to express anger than it is to express pain, our culture is more accepting of anger. So the next time you're shutting down or angry, ask yourself what lies beneath.

To review, empathy is first: I take the perspective of another person, meaning I become the listener and the student, not the knower. Second: I stay out of judgment. And third and fourth: I try to understand what emotion they're articulating and communicate my understanding of that emotion.

Empathy Skill #5: Mindfulness

I borrowed the fifth element, mindfulness, from Kristin Neff. Neff describes mindfulness as "taking a balanced approach to negative emotions so that feelings are neither suppressed nor exaggerated. . . . We cannot ignore our pain and feel compassion for it at the same time. . . . Mindfulness requires that we not be 'overidentified' with thoughts and feelings, so that we are caught up and swept away by negative reactivity."

The word *mindfulness* can get on my nerves sometimes, so I opt for *paying attention*. Neff's findings on mindfulness, especially the piece on not overidentifying with or exaggerating our feelings, are completely aligned with what we found in our work. Ruminating and getting stuck is as unhelpful as not noticing at all. In short, I try to practice mindfulness by paying attention to what's happening in these conversations, to the feelings they're bringing up in me, to my body language, and to the body language of the person I'm talking to. Minimizing and exaggerating emotions lead to empathic misses in equal measure.

WHAT EMPATHY LOOKS LIKE

Whenever I'm teaching empathy, people want more certainty. Early in my teaching career, a social work student asked if I could develop an empathy decision tree: *If they say this, I respond with this. If they take that turn, I turn with them and say that.* No such luck. Empathy is about connection, and being connected is the best navigation system. If we make a wrong turn in our attempt to be with someone in their struggle, connection is not only forgiving, it's quick to reroute.

The empathy decision tree doesn't work because we're all different. For example, if you're sharing something difficult with someone, do you want that person to:

Make eye contact?
Look away?
Reach out and hug you?

Give you space?
Respond right away?
Stay quiet and listen?

If you ask a hundred people these questions, you'll get a hundred different answers. The only solution is to connect and pay attention.

After I looked at Suzanne in the airport and said "I don't understand," and she made it clear that I was going to miss Ellen's game, she pulled back a bit but stayed right with me. Coming in for a hug would have been a bad idea. I wouldn't have actually punched her or put her in a headlock, but I would have wanted to. She was locked in, engaged, and could read me well enough to know that she should look me straight in the eye, tell me that I wasn't going to make Ellen's game, and then lean back and give me some space.

Suzanne and I were connected after spending the day together at Fort Bragg, but this also works if you're practicing empathy with someone you don't know that well. Engage, stay curious, stay connected. Let go of the fear of saying the wrong thing, the need to fix it, and the desire to offer the perfect response that cures everything (that's not going to happen). You don't have to do it perfectly. Just do it.

I had the great pleasure of working with leaders at the Bill and Melinda Gates Foundation a couple of years ago and getting to know Melinda, who is a champion of courage-building across the foundation and is doing tremendous work modeling how empathy and vulnerability work together to create a more connected culture.

A little history on Melinda: After joining Microsoft in 1987, Melinda distinguished herself as a leader in the development of multimedia products and was later appointed Microsoft's general manager of information products. In 1996, Melinda left Microsoft to focus on her philanthropic work and family.

Today, along with Bill, she shapes and approves the foundation's strategies, reviews results, and sets the overall direction of the organization. Together, they meet with grantees and partners to further the foundation's goal of improving equity in the United States and around the world. Melinda has seen firsthand that empowering women and girls can bring transformational improvements in the health and prosperity of families, communities, and societies. Her current work focuses on gender equity as a path to meaningful change.

On her experiences with vulnerability, Melinda writes:

> I started experimenting with vulnerability, and honestly I have been shocked at the response. Bill and I meet with all foundation employees several times a year, and these meetings are important opportunities for us to build a connection with our team. Recently, I admitted during one of these sessions that Bill and I keep a list of dos and don'ts for ourselves—basically the things we need to work on to make sure we're setting the right example. So many people came up to me later and said knowing I am clear about my need to improve helped them feel OK about the things they could do better.
>
> I also started talking a little bit more about my children in these meetings. I'd always shied away from the subject, just because it felt so personal. But it's turned out to resonate with a lot of employees who are also trying to balance work and home life—and who are also living their values every day at the foundation and through their parenting. I feel more connected to the individuals and the collective

culture of the foundation because I've taken steps to let myself be vulnerable.

EMPATHY IN PRACTICE

When we're struggling and in need of connection and empathy, we need to share with someone who embraces us for our strengths and struggles—someone who has earned the right to hear our story. Finding that right someone takes practice. And so does *being* that right person. When it comes to empathy, it's a matter of the right person, at the right time, on the right issues.

There are six known barriers to empathy, where the practice can go sideways or you can experience an empathic miss. Everyone knows what that feels like—when you share something with someone that is personal and vulnerable, like a struggle—or even something exciting or happy—and you don't feel heard, seen, or understood. It's a sinking feeling, where you feel exposed and sometimes right on the edge of shame. The clinical term for that is *empathic failure,* though I prefer *empathic miss,* because it's not quite as shaming.

Let's look at the six big ways we tend to miss, so that we can recognize them when we experience them, and be better when we have the opportunity to connect with people in struggle.

Empathy Miss #1: Sympathy vs. Empathy

Want to know what would have made me feel alone and worse at the airport? Sympathy. If Suzanne had said, "I'm so sorry. You poor thing." Or "I can't imagine how hard this must be for you." She didn't feel bad *for* me. She felt pain *with* me.

Empathy is feeling with people. Sympathy is feeling for them. Empathy fuels connection. Sympathy drives disconnection. I always think of empathy as this sacred space where someone's in a deep well, and they shout out from the bottom, "It's dark and scary down here. I'm overwhelmed."

We peer over the edge and say "I see you," then we climb down with the confidence that we can get back out. "I know what it's like down here. And you're not alone." Of course, you don't climb down without your own way out. Jumping into the hole with no way out is **enmeshment**—jumping into struggle with someone while maintaining clear lines about what belongs to whom is empathy.

Sympathy, on the other hand, is looking over the edge of that hole and saying: "Oh, it's bad, that looks terrible. So sorry." And you keep walking. There's a fun animated short on the difference between empathy and sympathy that the Royal Society for the Encouragement of Arts, Manufactures and Commerce developed from a short snippet of a lecture I gave in London on empathy. It's illustrated and animated by the talented Katy Davis. You can watch it at brenebrown.com/videos/.

The two most powerful words when someone's in struggle are "Me too." So powerful, in fact, that Tarana Burke started one of the most important movements of our time, the Me Too movement, with these two words, backing them up with action. The movement addresses the widespread prevalence of sexual harassment and assault, especially in the workplace, and is a great example of how empathy builds courage and can facilitate deep change.

"Me too" says *I may not have had the exact same experience as you, but I know this struggle, and you are not alone.*

Sympathy says *Wow, that's bad, I feel so sorry for you. I don't know or understand what your experience is like, but I'll grant you that it looks pretty bad and I don't want to know.*

Again, the difference between empathy and sympathy: feeling *with* and feeling *for*. The empathic response: *I get it, I feel with you, and I've been there.* The sympathetic response: *I feel sorry for you.*

If you want to see a shame cyclone turn extra deadly, throw one of these at it: "Oh, you poor thing." It's the equivalent of the Southern saying "Aww, bless your poor heart." When someone feels sorry for us, it magnifies our feelings of being alone. When someone feels with us, it magnifies our feeling of connection and normalcy.

Empathy Miss #2: The Gasp and Awe

In this scenario, your colleague hears your story and feels shame on your behalf—they might gasp, and then they will likely confirm how horrified you should be. They're appalled. They're upset. There's awkward silence, and then you have to make your colleague feel better. Here's an example: "I finally turned in that report yesterday and I was so excited. I felt so good about it and then my principal called me and told me the last two pages of it were missing. I forgot to attach them."

You're hoping your co-worker is going to say, "Oh, man, I've done that. It just sucks." But instead, this person gasps and says, "Oh, God, I'd just die." And then you're rushing in to say, "No, it's okay." Suddenly, you need to make that person feel better.

Empathy Miss #3: The Mighty Fall

In this scenario, your friend needs to think of you as a pillar of worthiness and authenticity. This person can't help you because they're so let down by your imperfections. They're disappointed. This is the person you confide in and say, "My performance evaluation did not go how I thought it was going to go and it kind of . . . I don't know if I'm in a shame storm, or . . . I'm just almost numb right now. I cannot believe that my rating was so low this quarter."

This person's response is: "I just never expected that from you. When I think of you I don't think of you as the kind of person that gets that rating, I mean what happened?" Then all of a sudden, you're not experiencing connection in an empathic way. You're defending yourself to someone because they're disappointed. (Hint: This happens frequently in childhood and is a huge driver of perfectionism.)

Empathy Miss #4: The Block and Tackle

Let's bring that performance review to this scenario, where your friend is so uncomfortable with vulnerability that he or she scolds you: "How did you let this happen? What were you thinking?" Or the friend looks for someone else to blame. "Who is that guy? We'll kick his ass. Or report him!" That's a huge empathic miss. I came to you because I'm in struggle about something, and you're making it easy on yourself by refusing to sit in discomfort—you're choosing instead to be pissed off at someone else or stand in judgment of me. It's not helpful.

Empathy Miss #5: The Boots and Shovel

This is a co-worker who desperately needs to make it better so that they can get out of their own discomfort. This person refuses to acknowledge that you can actually make mistakes or bad choices. This is the person who says, "You know, it's not that bad. It cannot be that bad. You know you're awesome. You're amazing." He's hustling to make you feel better, not hearing anything you feel, and not connecting to any emotion that you're describing. It is pretty disconcerting and reeks of bullshit.

Empathy Miss #6: If You Think That's Bad . . .

This person confuses connection with the opportunity to one-up. "That's nothing. Let me tell you about my performance evaluation in 1994, fourth quarter." Here's what gets dicey with comparing or competing. The most important words you can say to someone or you can hear from someone when you're in struggle are "Me too. You're not alone." That is different from "Oh, yeah? Me too.

Listen to this." The primary distinction is that the latter response shifts the focus to the other person.

THIS IS US

So here's the bad news: When it comes to empathy, we all know people who come up short, and we've all been the person who comes up short. Empathy is a skill. Here's the ~~good~~ amazing news: With some skill-building, we can all learn how to practice empathy. That's a huge gift.

There are a couple of questions that we should think about as part of our skill-building:

1. When you think about those six types of empathy misses, are there one or two that shut you down?
2. What emotion comes up for you when your sharing meets one of these barriers, and how does that affect your connection with the person?
3. On the flip side, how do you rate your own empathic skill?
4. Are there one or two responses that you typically use that you need to change?

Again, we all have friends and colleagues who do this. And we all *are* friends and colleagues who do this. This is not about us and them. This is all of us. Including me, and I've taught this skill for two decades.

I hawkishly watch myself when someone's story stirs up my own perfectionistic fear—especially if I think their situation impacts me. When that happens, I'm very susceptible to this big empathy miss: "Oh, my God, how could you have done that?"

I'm pretty good at avoiding sympathy, because I've studied empathy and sympathy for so long. I don't do a lot of "I feel bad for you" or "I'm so sorry for you," just because it's probably the one that I'm most affected by on the receiving end. I also get a lot of disappointment masquerading as empathy.

In a lecture I once said, "I just want to punch somebody." During the Q&A, someone raised their hand and said "You know, the need to punch someone does not feel very wholehearted to me. And you are my wholehearted icon."

I jumped right in. "I should not be your wholehearted icon. Wholeheartedness is something I'm striving for, but don't make me your role model. I'm on the journey with you trying to get there, but I don't have it mastered." Any assumption of perfection is an empathic miss.

Empathy is a hard skill to learn because mastery requires practice, and practice means you'll screw it up big-time more than once. But that's how practice works. If you're not willing to miss 3,759 shots from the free throw line, you'll never be consistently good at making those shots.

In many of our empathy workshops, we ask the participants to sign a poster that says:

I agree to practice empathy, screw it up, circle back, clean it up, and try again.

Make that commitment to yourself, your team, your friends, and your family. You have no idea how much it means to someone when you circle back and say, "You shared something hard with me, and I wish I had shown up in a different way. I really care about you and what you shared. Can I try again?" That's daring leadership.

HOW TO PRACTICE SELF-COMPASSION

The trickiest barrier to empathy? Take a look in the mirror. Being kind and extending the hypothesis of generosity to ourselves when we mess up is the first step. Resisting the urge to punish or shame ourselves when we make mistakes is true mastery.

Dr. Kristin Neff of the University of Texas at Austin, mentioned earlier in this section, runs the Self-Compassion Research Lab and is the author of *Self-Compassion: Stop Beating Yourself Up and Leave Insecurity Behind.* She writes about the three elements that make up the practice: self-kindness, humanity, and mindfulness. You'll remember mindfulness as empathy skill #5 from above, which I tweaked slightly to "paying attention."

While mindfulness has applications for empathy as well as self-compassion, with regard to self-compassion, she writes that it requires that we not take on thoughts and emotions as our own that might not belong to us. Put plainly: Do not take responsibility and ownership for the words of other people—just own your part. So in practice, change "She was so irritated with me" to simply "She was so irritated." Don't fixate, don't ruminate, don't get stuck.

Neff's definition of self-kindness is contained and self-explanatory: "being warm and understanding toward ourselves when we suffer, fail, or feel inadequate, rather than ignoring our pain or flagellating ourselves with self-criticism." In my own life, this translates to one simple mandate: **Talk to yourself the way you'd talk to someone you love.** Most of us shame, belittle, and criticize ourselves in ways we'd never think of doing to others. I would never look at Ellen or Charlie and say, "God, you're so stupid!" Yet I can whisper that to myself in a heartbeat.

I'll give you a real example from my life. I recently did an interview with a journalist for a magazine article. I always feel extremely vulnerable during media interviews because I'm not good at filtering, staying on script, and watching everything that I say. The "on the record" scenario is exactly the opposite of the type of interviewing I've done thousands of times for over twenty years, where the goal is to uncover real experiences by connecting, being open, and mutually sharing without any fear or filters. I'm never going to use anything in the research that you ask me not to, and you're never going to be identified unless we talk about it first, you agree, and you sign off on how I capture your words.

Well, in the middle of this two-hour interview (which is way too long), the interviewer asks a question about juggling multiple priorities and I respond with "Oh, that's so [effing] hard." But the real word. I immediately say, "Sorry! Scratch that!"

But it was too late. I was "on the record." That was fair. I was careless.

Now, don't get me wrong—I'm a cusser from a long matriarchal line of cussers. I'm super comfortable with that; I just try to limit it in my writing. I think it has to do with my belief that in conversation, a well-placed cuss word or three seems really good, but in writing, it seems more intentional and less organic. And if it's on a T-shirt or something worn in public, I'll go Texas Baptist church lady on you.

According to Steve, my language is way worse now than when I started my work, and it gets worse with every year of research. People share the toughest, most wrenching moments of their lives with me, and they don't sugarcoat their language, thankfully. Their words are as real, gritty, and rough as their stories.

To make matters worse, Steve has nicknamed me "the Borg" from *Star Trek*. Just like the fictional drones that copy and replicate other aliens, I have the tendency to pick up the accents and mannerisms of other people if I'm around them for any length of time. I interviewed a guy a few months ago who constantly talked about his bosses being "total pricks." Not a week later, Steve and I were in his truck when someone cut us off, and I pushed my face against the closed window and said, "What a total prick. Don't be such a total prick, dude!" Steve, having never heard me use that particular term in thirty years, just shook his head and laughed.

Anyway, once I realized that my f-bomb was on the record, the very first thing I said to myself was, "You're such an idiot, Brené.

Can't you hold it together for two hours?" Again, I would never talk that way to my family members or my colleagues. I would say, "You're exhausted, on a crushing book deadline, and overwhelmed. Give yourself a break. And don't be so hard on yourself—you're human and a lot of people relate to your messiness."

But I beat myself up for two days until Steve grabbed me by the shoulders and said those exact words. Self-kindness is self-empathy. And even when I talk to myself like someone I love and it feels weird, it works.

I also love Neff's definition of common humanity as uniting us in our discomfort rather than pushing an "it's just me" worldview. Common humanity recognizes, she writes, "that suffering and personal inadequacy is part of the shared human experience—something that we all go through rather than being something that happens to 'me' alone." This is one of the foundations of empathy and one of the linchpins of the Me Too movement. The more we practice these conversations of connection, the more we learn that we are all connected—in both the good things and the bad.

Remember, empathy is the most powerful connecting and trust-building tool that we have, and it's the antidote to shame. If you put shame in a petri dish and cover it with judgment, silence, and secrecy, you've created the perfect environment for shame to grow until it makes its way into every corner and crevice of your life. If, on the other hand, you put shame in a petri dish and douse it with empathy, shame loses its power and begins to wither. Empathy creates a hostile environment for shame—an environment it can't survive in, because shame needs you to believe you're alone and it's just you.

That's why there's so much power in:

- Oh, man. I feel you.
- I know that feeling and it sucks.
- Me too.

- I see you. You're not alone.
- I've been in a similar place and it's really hard.
- I think a lot of us experience that. Either we're all normal or we're all weird. Either way, it's not just you.
- I understand what that's like.

EMPATHY AND SHAME RESILIENCE

Now that we're building some understanding and skills around empathy, let's examine the four elements of shame resilience. When we're in shame and we can share our story with someone who responds with empathy and understanding, shame can't survive.

1. Recognizing Shame and Understanding Its Triggers

Can you physically recognize when you're in the grip of shame, feel your way through it, and figure out what messages and expectations triggered it? Research participants with the highest levels of shame resilience can recognize the physical symptoms of shame—they know the physiology of it, and that's a huge cue to pay attention. My saying is, "When in shame, I don't talk, text, or type—I'm not fit for human consumption" until I get back on my emotional feet.

When we have understanding and awareness around shame, we're less likely to default to our **shame shields,** or what Linda Hartling and her fellow researchers at the Stone Center at Wellesley call *strategies of disconnection:*

> **Moving away:** Withdrawing, hiding, silencing ourselves, and keeping secrets.
> **Moving toward:** Seeking to appease and please.
> **Moving against:** Trying to gain power over others by being aggressive, and by using shame to fight shame.

Like all armor, these are appealing forms of self-protection, but they move us away from our authenticity and wholeheartedness.

2. Practicing Critical Awareness

Shame works like the zoom lens on a camera. When we are feeling shame, the camera is zoomed in tight, and all we see is our flawed self, alone and struggling. We think, "I'm the only one. Something is wrong with me. I am alone."

When we zoom out, we start to see a different picture. We see many people in the same struggle. Rather than thinking "I'm the only one," we start thinking "I can't believe it! You too? I'm normal? I thought it was just me!" Once we start to see the big picture, we are better able to reality-check our shame triggers and the social expectations that fuel shame.

3. Reaching Out

One of the most important benefits of reaching out to others is learning that the experiences that make us feel the most alone are actually universal. Regardless of who we are, how we were raised, or what we believe, all of us fight hidden, silent battles against not being good enough and not belonging enough. When we find the courage to share our experiences and the compassion to hear others tell their stories, we force shame out of hiding and end the silence. When we don't reach out, we often end up in fear, blame, and disconnection.

4. Speaking Shame

Shame derives its power from being unspeakable. That's why it loves perfectionists—it's so easy to keep us quiet. If we cultivate enough awareness about shame to name it and speak it, we've basically cut it off at the knees. Shame hates having words wrapped around it. If we speak shame, it begins to wither. Language and story bring light to shame and destroy it. When we don't talk about how we feel and ask for what we need, we often shut down, act out, or do both.

Learning to speak shame also allows you to pick up on some of the subtle and even gaslighting language of shame. This is language that is used to shame and to defend shaming when we're trying to explain how we feel and what we need. I'm now very cautious when I hear things like:

- You're so sensitive.
- I didn't realize you were so fragile.
- I didn't realize that was such an issue for you.
- You're so defensive.
- I guess I'll have to watch what I say around you.
- It's all in your head.
- You seem really hostile.

And I've totally banned words like *loser, lame,* and *weak.*

I'm also not a fan of anything that's brutal, including honesty. Honesty is the best policy, but honesty that's motivated by shame, anger, fear, or hurt is not "honesty." It's shame, anger, fear, or hurt disguised as honesty.

Just because something is accurate or factual doesn't mean it can't be used in a destructive manner: "Sorry. I'm just telling you the truth. These are just the facts."

The big takeaway from this section is that empathy is at the heart of connection—it is the circuit board for leaning into the feelings of others, reflecting back a shared experience of the world, and reminding them that they are not alone. To be able to stand in discomfort with people who are processing shame, or hurt, or disappointment, or hardship, and to be able to say to them "I see you, and I can hold space for this" is the epitome of courage. The best part is that empathy is not hardwired into our genetic code: We can learn it. And we need to, because as the poet June Jordan wrote, "We are the ones we have been waiting for."

SELF-AWARENESS AND
SELF-LOVE MATTER.

Who we are is how we lead.

section five CURIOSITY AND GROUNDED CONFIDENCE

Grounded confidence is the messy process of learning and unlearning, practicing and failing, and surviving a few misses. This brand of confidence is not blustery arrogance or posturing or built on bullshit; it's real, solid, and built on self-awareness and practice. Once we witness how courage can transform the way we lead, we can trade the heavy, suffocating armor that keeps us small for grounded confidence that lifts us up and supports our efforts to be brave.

It's unreasonable to believe that we can just rip off our self-protection mechanisms and streak through the office. Most of us armor up early in our lives because, as children, we needed to. In some instances, the armor protected us from being hurt or disappointed, from feeling invisible or unlovable. In some situations we had to self-protect to stay physically or emotionally safe. Vulnerability is the greatest casualty of trauma. When we're raised in unsafe environments, confronted with racism, violence, poverty, sexism, homophobia, and pervasive shaming, vulnerability can be life-threatening and armor is safety.

And when we think about how millennials and Gen Zers were raised, many of their parents swaddled them in armor out of their own lack of confidence as parents and people. The more grounded confidence parents have, the more likely they are to *prepare their child for the path* by teaching courage, praising effort, and modeling grit, versus trying to *prepare a perfect path for their child* by fixing, praising only results, and intervening.

We've spent a disproportionately large amount of time on rumbling with vulnerability for a simple reason: It's *the* fundamental skill of courage-building. Building the grounded confidence to rumble with vulnerability and discomfort rather than armoring up, running away, shutting down, or tapping out, completely prepares you for living into your values, building trust, and learning to rise.

Understanding rumbling with vulnerability as the fundamental skill of daring leadership is absolutely essential. Skill-building in sports provides a great analogy.

All sports rely on key fundamentals, those skills that are drilled into players from the first day you sign up for a class or join a team. When I reflect on my experiences playing tennis and swimming, I remember always thinking "Let's race! I'm tired of doing fifty flip turns in a row" or "I don't want to sashay across this dang tennis court holding my racket in volley position one more time, let's play!" But developing fundamental skills through disciplined practice is what gives players the grounded confidence to dare greatly.

The same is true for leaders—developing a disciplined practice of rumbling with vulnerability gives leaders the strength and emotional stamina to dare greatly.

In sports, when you're in the heat of play and under pressure, you have to be able to rely on the skills you've built to be able to execute, deliver, and perform. If you've flip-turned and sashayed enough times, the mechanics of those moves enter muscle memory. Having the grounded confidence to rely on the skills we've developed over time allows us to focus on higher-order objectives, challenges, and goals. My pool playing efforts are a good example.

I always thought playing pool looked pretty easy and attributed my poor performance in college to trying to juggle a beer in one hand and a cigarette in the other while lining up a shot. But Chaz, whom you met earlier, plays competitively and has disabused me of the notion that it was the partying that got in the way of my running a table. It turns out that I suck at pool because I've done it only a handful of times, and the players who make it look easy are deeply skilled in the fundamentals of billiards.

When pool players design their shots, they always consider three elements: angles, speed, and spin. The success of executing their designed shot is dependent on the fundamental skill of being able to reliably and constantly deliver the cue stick to the spot on the cue ball that will set the shot in motion. That means good pool players spend hundreds of hours building that foundational skill of consistent cue delivery. Not to mention the equally tedious work of building a steady bridge, mastering a pendulum arm stroke, and developing a stable stance. One fundamental exercise that's commonly practiced is the empty bottle drill. Players set an empty glass soda bottle on its side and practice stroking their cue stick into the neck of the bottle without moving the bottle. There's little margin for error.

Of course, you never see a glass bottle on a pool table during a tournament, but you can bet that the best players have spent hours practicing their strokes, their breaks, and their shots. When the pressure is on, they've built the necessary strength and stamina to make it through ten hours of play, and they are confident enough in their fundamentals to focus on strategy and shot selection.

Lauren, our director of facilitator community engagement and research, is an ex–professional soccer player from Scotland and a former graduate student of mine. She explained that the fundamental skill in soccer is ball control. She told me that from the time she was little, coaches would run drills that had players touching the ball a million times with different parts of the foot. Even as a professional athlete, she spent countless hours passing the ball with a partner using different parts of her foot.

She told me, "We had a four-foot brick wall that went around the perimeter of our garden at our house in Scotland. I would stand in front of one section of the wall and I would pick a brick and try and hit it with the ball. I would do this for hours, picking another brick, then another. The entire time I was just working on my ball control."

As in Chaz's story about solid fundamentals allowing you to focus on higher-order challenges, Lauren said, "You have to master the fundamentals of ball control so you can pick your head up in a game and see what is going on around you. You have to read the field and strategize your next move before you even have possession of the ball. You have to have complete confidence about your mastery of that skill so you can focus on other things."

In tough conversations, hard meetings, and emotionally charged decision making, leaders need the grounded confidence to stay tethered to their values, respond rather than react emotionally, and operate from self-awareness, not self-protection. Having the rumbling skills to hold the tension and discomfort allows us to give care and attention to others, stay open and curious, and meet the challenges.

Earlier this year, I had the opportunity to work with Nutanix, an enterprise cloud software company in Silicon Valley. In my conversations with their founder, chairman, and CEO, Dheeraj Pandey, I was struck not only by his belief in the importance of vulnerability in leadership, but the *why* behind that belief. Dheeraj explained to me that when leaders don't have the skills to lean into vulnerability, they're not able to successfully hold the tension of the paradoxes that are inherent in entrepreneurship. His examples of the paradoxes that elicit vulnerability in leaders align with what we heard from the research participants:

- Optimism and paranoia
- Letting chaos reign (the act of building) and reining in chaos (the act of scaling)
- Big heart and tough decision making
- Humility and fierce resolve
- Velocity and quality when building new things
- Left brain and right brain
- Simplicity and choice
- Thinking global, acting local
- Ambition and attention to detail
- Thinking big but starting small
- Short-term and long-term
- Marathons and sprints, or marathon of sprints in business-building

Dheeraj told me, "Leaders must learn the skills to hold these tensions and get adept at balancing on the 'tightrope' of life. Ultimately, leadership is the ability to thrive in the ambiguity of paradoxes and opposites."

Building rumbling skills is not easy, but easy is overrated. An increasing number of studies are confirming what most of us have always known but hated: **Easy learning doesn't build strong skills.** In an article in *Fast Company* magazine, Mary Slaughter and David Rock with the NeuroLeadership Institute write:

> Unfortunately, the trend in many organizations is to design learning to be as easy as possible. Aiming to respect their employees' busy lives, companies build training programs that can be done at any time, with no prerequisites, and often on a mobile device. The result is fun and easy training programs that employees rave about (making them easier for developers to sell) but don't actually instill lasting learning.
>
> Worse still, programs like these may lead employers to optimize for misleading metrics, like maximizing for "likes" or "shares" or high "net promoter scores," which are easy to earn when programs are fun and fluent but not when they're demanding. Instead of designing for recall or behavior change, we risk designing for popularity.
>
> The reality is that to be effective, learning needs to be *effortful.* That's not to say that anything that makes learning easier is counterproductive—or that all unpleasant learning is effective. The key here is **desirable difficulty.** The same way you feel a muscle "burn" when it's being strengthened, the brain needs to feel some discomfort when it's learning. Your mind might hurt for a while—but that's a good thing.

Learning how to rumble with vulnerability is work. And vulnerability never becomes comfortable, but practicing means that when vulnerability is washing over us, we can hear grounded confidence whisper in our ear, "This is hard and awkward, and uncomfortable. You may not know how it's going to turn out, but you are strong and you have practiced what it takes to create and hold the space for this."

Grounded Confidence = Rumble Skills + Curiosity + Practice

We've covered a lot of new language, skills, and tools, and as you can probably tell, they all share the same DNA: **curiosity.**

Curiosity is an act of vulnerability and courage. Researchers are finding evidence that curiosity is correlated with creativity, intelligence, improved learning and memory, and problem solving. A study published in the October 22, 2014, issue of the journal *Neuron* suggests that the brain's chemistry changes when we become curious, helping us better learn and retain information. But curiosity is uncomfortable because it involves uncertainty and vulnerability.

In his book *Curious: The Desire to Know and Why Your Future Depends on It,* Ian Leslie writes, "Curiosity is unruly. It doesn't like rules, or, at least, it assumes that all rules are provisional, subject to the laceration of a smart question nobody has yet thought to ask. It disdains the approved pathways, preferring diversions, unplanned excursions, impulsive left turns. In short, curiosity is deviant."

This is exactly why curiosity leads to grounded confidence in rumble skills. We're scared to have hard conversations because we can't control the path or outcome, and we start coming out of our skin when we don't get to resolution fast enough. It's as if we'd rather have a bad solution that leads to action than stay in the uncertainty of problem identification.

• • •

Einstein is one of our best curiosity and confidence mentors. I love two of his sayings:

"If I had an hour to solve a problem, I'd spend fifty-five minutes thinking about the problem and five minutes thinking about solutions."

He also reportedly said, "It's not that I'm so smart, it's just that I stay with problems longer."

The knower in us (our ego) either races to beat everyone in the room with an answer that may or may not address the real issues, or thinks: *I don't want to talk about this because I'm not sure how it's going to go or how people are going to react. I might not say the right thing or have the right answers.*

Curiosity says: *No worries. I love a wild ride. I'm up for wherever this goes. And I'm in for however long it takes to get to the heart of the problem. I don't have to know the answers or say the right thing, I just have to keep listening and keep questioning.*

Here are some specific **rumble starters and questions** that we use:

1. The story I make up . . . (This is by far one of the most powerful rumble tools in the free world. It's changed every facet of my life. We'll walk through it in the part "Learning to Rise.")
2. I'm curious about . . .
3. Tell me more.
4. That's not my experience (instead of "You're wrong about her, him, them, it, this . . .").
5. I'm wondering . . .
6. Help me understand . . .

7. Walk me through . . .
8. We're both dug in. Tell me about your passion around this.
9. Tell me why this doesn't fit/work for you.
10. I'm working from these assumptions—what about you?
11. What problem are we trying to solve? Sometimes we'll be an hour into a difficult rumble when someone will bravely say, "Wait. I'm confused. What problem are we trying to solve?" Ninety percent of the time we'll realize that we're not on the same page because we skipped the problem identification process and set a meeting intention of finding a solution to a problem that we had yet to define.

Sometimes the best rumbles start with a thirty-minute fact-finding conversation and an agreement to circle back in a few hours or the next day (but don't wait too long). I recently had a conversation with two colleagues about a training we're planning. As soon as we sat down and they presented the plan, I knew it was going to get hard. We were on totally different pages. I simply said, "We're in very different places. Why don't we spend twenty minutes rumbling on how we got here, then circle back tomorrow and land on an approach?

"Walk me through all of the assumptions you are working off.

"How did y'all come up with the schedule?

"What are y'all seeing as the goal of the training?

"Help me understand what you see as the benefit of this approach."

It took only ten minutes before we realized that we were working toward different goals, we had different priorities, and we were working off different data.

My colleague said, "Wow. This is really helpful. Let's come back with some of the information we're both missing and get on the same page about the goals and priorities tomorrow." *Great!*

Another helpful curiosity tool is staying on the lookout for **horizon conflict.** Our role dictates where we should set our lens in terms of the organizational horizon. As a founder and CEO, I'm expected to plot a long-term course for the company. I try to bounce back and forth from a ten-year horizon to the current state of affairs. Other leaders on my team have responsibility for different horizons. An operations leader may be focused on a six-month horizon because of a huge launch schedule.

To lead effectively, we're responsible for respecting and leveraging the different views and staying curious about how they can often conflict. When rumbles start to get tough, we know to check in on horizon issues. And while we may have different perspectives and may not share the same level of knowledge about every detail of the organization, we must have a shared reality of the current state of the organization. Horizon conflict doesn't give us permission to lose focus on the organization as a whole. I can't be so concerned with the five-year goal that I don't know about a culture issue that we need to address.

DRIVING GREATNESS FROM CURIOSITY AND LEARNING

When I was researching and writing *Rising Strong,* I learned that the most common barrier to getting curious is having "a dry well." In his 1994 article "The Psychology of Curiosity," George Loewenstein introduced his information gap perspective on curiosity. Loewenstein, a professor of economics and psychology at Carnegie Mellon University, proposed that curiosity is the feeling of deprivation we experience when we identify and focus on a gap in our knowledge.

What's important about this perspective is that it means we have to have some level of knowledge or awareness before we can get curious. We aren't curious about something we are unaware of or know nothing about. Loewenstein explains that simply encouraging people to ask questions doesn't go very far toward stimulating curiosity. He writes, "To induce curiosity about a particular topic, it may be necessary to 'prime the pump' "—to use intriguing information to get folks interested so they become more curious.

And here's the good news: If you've read up to this point in the book, you're primed and ready to go. We may not know enough or have enough practice nailing every rumble, but we know enough to get curious. And there's even more good news: A growing number of researchers believe that curiosity and knowledge-building grow together—the more we know, the more we want to know.

I want to share two case examples with you that demonstrate how the combination of rumbling skills and the grounded confidence to take off the armor and get curious can transform an organization. The first is from Stefan Larsson and the second is from Dr. Sanée Bell.

Stefan Larsson is a seasoned retail leader who was most recently chief executive officer of the Ralph Lauren Corporation. He is credited with turning around the iconic American apparel brand Old Navy, where he and his team delivered twelve straight quarters of growth and added $1 billion in sales in three years. He also spent fourteen years as a key part of the leadership team that built the Swedish-based fashion giant H&M into one of the three most valued fashion brands in the world, with global operations in forty-four countries and sales that grew from $3 billion to $17 billion.

As you read through this case study, you will see the role vulnerability plays as the foundation for the next three skill sets: living into our values, braving trust, and learning to rise.

Stefan writes:

> When I took the helm of Old Navy, the brand had faltered for a number of years, and we had to find our way back to the

original vision. After a few days in the archives, we uncovered the original vision statement, which was about making aspirational American style accessible to every family. Now we just had to deliver on it! The most crucial component to unlock and the biggest driver of success turned out to be transforming the organizational culture. What was once an entrepreneurial, fast-moving, and empowering culture had over the course of several years of struggling performance become hierarchal, siloed, political, and filled with fear.

Most team members understood our collective challenges; they saw clearly what we needed to do and what stood in the way. However, very few dared to share their insights or voice their concerns in larger settings or take action on them, because of the fear of looking bad or making someone else look bad. To turn the brand around, our main job was to build a culture of trust.

To do this we set out with a few goals that turned out to be key drivers of our success:

- We started with weekly learnings sessions for our top sixty leaders: two hours every week together as one team, with the premise that we would no longer judge outcomes as good or bad, we would just read the outcomes as outcomes, learn from them, and quickly improve. The goal was to outlearn our competitors. We would stop the shaming and blaming and the judging of outcomes as good or bad, and instead continuously ask ourselves, "What did we set out to do, what happened, what did we learn, and how fast can we improve on it?"
- We launched quarterly town halls and companywide calls where we, in connection to our vision and the plan we had

set out, shared the outcomes, learnings, and improvements on a regular basis.

- As a management team we physically moved in together into one big room with glass walls (where we intentionally unlocked the doors) in the middle of our headquarters to further enable openness, trust, and teamwork by using the space to visually mirror our approach and attitude. We also encouraged all team members, regardless of their position in the organization, to come by and reach out with ideas and thoughts around anything that could improve what we were doing (or not doing).

It didn't take long until everyone started to come up with more and more ideas of how to improve the business. At first, people were hesitant to believe that we were really serious about the no shaming and blaming, but over time they started to speak up in meetings, whether it was asking a question without knowing the answer or sharing the outcomes from an initiative that had underdelivered (formerly talked about as "failures," now reframed as "learnings").

We all started to show more vulnerability in front of each other. We started to trust each other more since we were all in it together. As a management team, we focused on asking questions, experimenting and driving continuous improvement until we started to get traction. Instead of thinking about outcomes as good and bad, we set up a "failure proof" way of working. This allowed us to overcome setbacks and put the focus on learning instead of blaming. Once we removed the fear of failure and the fear of being judged, we started to outlearn and outperform our best competitors.

> As a result, we delivered twelve consecutive quarters of growth in a very challenging market and added $1 billion in sales in three years. But what I'm most proud of as a leader was being able to empower my team to take vulnerability and make it into a strength, to foster a culture of trust, openness, and collaboration, and to shift our mentality to one of continuous learning. Today, over two years after I moved on to lead another company, I still get emails from team members who want to share what they've learned and how they continue to drive greatness from their learnings. Those emails make all the difference.

I love the idea of driving greatness from our learnings. I've seen it work in organizations across the globe where people are willing to be vulnerable. Another great example is this next case study, from Dr. Sanée Bell. She is the principal of Morton Ranch Junior High in Katy, Texas. She has served as an administrator since 2005 at both the elementary and secondary levels. She taught middle school and high school English and also coached girls' basketball. Sanée was named the 2015 Katy ISD Elementary Principal of the Year.

Sanée writes:

> Leading others is hard. Being the leader of adults, children, and a school community is even harder. The role of a principal is complex, challenging, rewarding, and lonely all at the same time. When I began my daring leadership journey, I was a successful school leader. During my second principalship, I did a deep dive into this daring leadership work and realized that I had only scratched the surface of what it means to dare to lead.
>
> This personal and professional journey has changed

my practice as a leader in three specific ways: teaching me how to practice vulnerability, increasing my self-awareness, and giving me the tools to have tough conversations. Today, these three areas of focus are foundational components of my leadership approach.

PRACTICING VULNERABILITY

There's an old saying that I lead by now: "People don't care how much you know until they know how much you care." I've learned one way to help people understand how much you care is to share your story. Practicing vulnerability has given me the courage to share my personal story, of growing up in situational poverty and a broken home, with my staff. When they hear about my journey to overcome huge obstacles, they better understand my commitment to building a supportive school environment.

As a leader, I no longer check my personal life at the door. In fact, sharing stories and leading through the lens of multiple perspectives and experiences has made me more approachable and relatable to my students, staff, and community. By sharing my story and my *why* for leading, I helped my staff understand my purpose, passion, and commitment to courage. It also gave others permission to practice vulnerability and to be brave in sharing and owning their life journey.

BECOMING SELF-AWARE

When I lack self-awareness as a leader and when I'm not connected with the intentions driving my thoughts, feelings, and actions, I limit the perspective and insights that I can share with the people I lead. Today, through journaling and seeking feedback from others, I have been able to grow and refine my leadership skills in a way that is more responsive to the needs of my staff, students, and community. Spending time in quiet reflection has become part of my weekly practice.

ENGAGING IN TOUGH CONVERSATIONS

Doing this work made me realize that there is no way to address the academic disparities between the different student groups without leaning into tough conversations on an ongoing basis.

I knew there was a critical and urgent need to move past the "This is the way we have always done it" attitude held by many people on our campus. To make this happen, I would have to lead these potentially emotionally charged discussions and I would need support. *If not me, then who? If not now, then when?*

My strategy was to be intentional about building enough trust and connection to talk about equity issues, and to commit to helping those who are normally silenced acquire the skills and grounded confidence to participate in these tough conversations. I invested in building high-performing, connected teams by using strengths-based and work-personality assessments, and I developed structured protocols for hard conversations, including progress checks.

I'm committed to tackling problems that threaten our mission, vision, and values, and I challenge others to call out the culture killers in our organization. We celebrate what works, and we change things that don't add value to the organization.

I changed the narrative of our school by growing power *with* people through distributive and collaborative leadership, and by empowering others to lead. Ultimately, being true to who I am as a person, respecting my journey, and owning my story have given me the opportunity to lead in a deeper, more meaningful way.

More Rumble Tools

Just a reminder that you can find more resources for rumbling with vulnerability on the *Dare to Lead* hub on brenebrown.com. You'll find a downloadable workbook, a glossary, and images, as well as role-play videos that you can watch as part of building your own rumble skills.

And, whether or not you choose to download the workbook or watch the videos, never underestimate the value of role-playing, practicing, and writing down notes and bringing them with you into important meetings or conversations. I do all three every day.

I once worked for a boss who said "Are you referring to notes?" when he saw me looking at my journal during a very tough resignation conversation.

I said, "Yes. I've given this conversation a lot of thought. It's important to me, and I want to make sure to share all of what I've prepared with you."

He shifted in his chair as I prepared to defend my notes.

He said, "That's a really cool idea. Do you just use bullet points, or do you write paragraphs?"

People, people, people are just people, people, people.

part two

LIVING INTO OUR VALUES

Daring leaders who live into their values are never silent about hard things.

The arena, particularly during dark and hard moments when we're trying to be really brave, can be confusing and overwhelming: distractions, noise, a rapidly blinking Exit sign that promises immediate relief from the discomfort, and the cynics in the stands. In those tough matches, when the critics are being extra loud and rowdy, it's easy to start hustling—to try to prove, perfect, perform, and please. God knows these are my four big *p*'s. We can either hustle to show the crowd that we deserve to be there, or we can let them scare us off. Either way, it's easy to let them get in our head and hijack our efforts.

In those moments when we start putting other voices in front of our own, we forget what made us go into the arena in the first place, the reason we're there. We forget our values. Or, frequently, we don't even know what they are or how to name them. If we do not have clarity of values, if we don't have anywhere else to look or focus, if we don't have that light up above to remind us why we're there, the cynics and the critics can bring us to our knees.

More often than not, our values are what lead us to the arena door—we're willing to do something uncomfortable and daring because of our beliefs. And when we get in there and stumble or fall, we need our values to remind us why we went in, especially when we are facedown, covered in dust and sweat and blood.

Here's the thing about values: While courage requires checking our armor and weapons at the arena door, we do not have to enter every tough conversation and difficult rumble completely empty-handed.

The daring leaders we interviewed were never empty-handed in the arena. In addition to rumble skills and tools, they always carried with them clarity of values. This clarity is an essential support, a North Star in times of darkness.

According to the *Oxford English Dictionary,* values are "principles or standards of behaviour; one's judgment of what is important in life." In our work, I simplify the definition: **A *value* is a way of being or believing that we hold most important.**

Living into our values means that we do more than profess our values, we practice them. We walk our talk—we are clear about what we believe and hold important, and we take care that our intentions, words, thoughts, and behaviors align with those beliefs.

Living into our values requires some upfront work—contemplation that most of us have never taken the time to do. And, as much as I don't want to make this part feel like a workbook, it's going to be work-in-a-book. I'll take you through the three steps and share some of my experiences (good and bad), so if you hang with me, after a few short pages, I bet you'll know more about yourself and how to live into your values than you do right now.

Step One: We Can't Live into Values That We Can't Name

The first step of living into our values is divining what's most important to us. What is our North Star? What values do we hold most sacred? We can't work to stay aligned with values when we haven't spent any time getting curious about, or naming, what we care about most.

When I facilitate this work in organizations, I always get this question: "Do you want me to identify my professional values or my personal values?" Here's the rub: **We have only one set of values.** We don't shift our values based on context. We are called to live in a way that is aligned with what we hold most important regardless of the setting or situation. This, of course, is the challenge of living into our values: those moments when our values are in conflict with the values of our organization, our friends, a stranger in line at the grocery store or polling station, or even our family.

Below is the list of values that we use in our work. As you can see, there are blank spaces for you to write in values that we may not have included. The task is to pick the two that you hold most important. I know this is tough, because almost everyone we've done this work with (including me) wants to pick somewhere between ten and fifteen. I can soften the blow by suggesting that you start by circling those fifteen. But you can't stop until you're down to two core values.

Here's why: The research participants who demonstrated the most willingness to rumble with vulnerability and practice courage tethered their behavior to one or two values, not ten. This makes sense for a couple of reasons. First, I see it the same way that I see Jim Collins's mandate "If you have more than three priorities, you have no priorities." At some point, if everything on the list is important, then nothing is truly a driver for you. It's just a gauzy list of feel-good words.

list of values

Accountability
Achievement
Adaptability
Adventure
Altruism
Ambition
Authenticity
Balance
Beauty
Being the best
Belonging
Career
Caring
Collaboration
Commitment
Community
Compassion
Competence
Confidence
Connection
Contentment
Contribution
Cooperation
Courage
Creativity
Curiosity
Dignity
Diversity
Environment
Efficiency
Equality
Ethics
Excellence
Fairness
Faith
Family
Financial stability
Forgiveness
Freedom
Friendship
Fun
Future generations
Generosity
Giving back
Grace
Gratitude
Growth
Harmony
Health
Home
Honesty
Hope
Humility
Humor
Inclusion
Independence
Initiative
Integrity
Intuition
Job security
Joy
Justice
Kindness
Knowledge
Leadership
Learning
Legacy
Leisure
Love
Loyalty
Making a difference
Nature
Openness
Optimism
Order
Parenting
Patience
Patriotism
Peace
Perseverance
Personal fulfillment
Power
Pride
Recognition
Reliability
Resourcefulness
Respect
Responsibility
Risk taking
Safety
Security
Self-discipline
Self-expression
Self-respect
Serenity
Service
Simplicity
Spirituality
Sportsmanship
Stewardship
Success
Teamwork
Thrift
Time
Tradition
Travel
Trust
Truth
Understanding
Uniqueness
Usefulness
Vision
Vulnerability
Wealth
Well-being
Wholeheartedness
Wisdom

Write your own:

____

____

Second, I've taken more than ten thousand people through this work, and when people are willing to stay with the process long enough to whittle their big list down to two, they always come to the same conclusion that I did with my own values process: My two core values are where all of the "second tier" circled values are tested.

Here's how that works in my life: My two central values are faith and courage. I hated not circling "family." But as I dug in, I realized that while my family is the most important thing in my life, my commitment to them is fueled by my faith and my courage.

For example, when I say no to an exciting work opportunity because I don't want to miss driving carpool, I lean into my courage and faith. It may be different for you, but I have to be brave enough to say no and not let the fear that someone might think I'm being ungrateful for not taking the opportunity get the best of me. I also need the strength of my faith to remind me that if I do what's right for me, there will be other opportunities. Sometimes my prayer is simply *If I miss the boat, it wasn't my boat.*

Our values should be so crystallized in our minds, so infallible, so precise and clear and unassailable, that they don't feel like a choice—they are simply a definition of who we are in our lives. In those hard moments, we know that we are going to pick what's right, right now, over what is easy. Because that is **integrity—choosing courage over comfort; it's choosing what's right over what's fun, fast, or easy; and it's practicing your values, not just professing them.**

Choose one or two values—the beliefs that are most important and dear to you, that help you find your way in the dark, that fill you with a feeling of purpose. As you read them, you should feel a deep resonance of self-identification. Resist holding on to words that resemble something you've been coached to be, words that have never felt true for you.

Ask yourself:
Does this define me?
Is this who I am at my best?
Is this a filter that I use to make hard decisions?

Step Two: Taking Values from BS to Behavior

The reason we roll our eyes when people start talking about values is that everyone talks a big values game but *very* few people actually practice one. It can be infuriating, and it's not just individuals who fall short of the talk. In our experience, only about 10 percent of organizations have operationalized their values into teachable and observable behaviors that are used to train their employees and hold them accountable. *Ten percent.* (And yes, I've taken to the occasional "izing" of words.)

If you're not going to take the time to translate values from ideals to behaviors—if you're not going to teach people the skills they need to show up in a way that's aligned with those values and then create a culture in which you hold one another accountable for staying aligned with the values—it's better not to profess any values at all. They become a joke. A cat poster. Total BS.

In this second step of the Living into Our Values process, we need to define three or four behaviors that support our values and three or four "slippery behaviors"—actions we find ourselves tempted to do even though they are counter to our values. And get explicit. There's no magic in three or four behaviors—it's just enough to force us to think beyond what's easy and not so many that we're just making a list.

The best way to do this is to think through some arena moments when you either did or did not show up in a way that felt aligned with your values. For example, I often find myself in dust-ups on social media around social justice issues. People will leave comments like "Stick to the writing—immigration isn't your issue," or "Stop talking about race so much." These sentiments even show up at my public events during the Q&A sessions.

My value of courage calls on me to stand up and speak out for my beliefs. If you say something to me, or in front of me, that I find racist, or sexist, or homophobic, even if other people are laughing, I'm not going to laugh. I'm going to ask you not to say that stuff around me. I don't do this out of self-righteousness or being "better than"—trust me, there are times when I'd rather just shoot you a dirty look and walk away. I say something because courage is one of my key values, and for me to feel physically, emotionally, and spiritually okay, courage *insists* that I honor it by choosing my voice over my comfort.

If there's an issue that I feel passionate about, I'm going to write about it and post about it on social media. If you leave a shaming comment or you're hateful toward me or anyone in my community, I'm going to delete it and ban you from my page. One of my courage behaviors is *Don't choose silence over what is right. It's not my job to make others more comfortable or to be liked by everyone.*

Faith has been so tough for me over the past year because one of my faith behaviors is to *find the face of God in everyone*. Ugh. That means rather than hating people, I have to hate only their ideas. Rather than shaming and blaming people, I have to hold them accountable. *Blame is so easy and accountability is such a time-suck. And no fun at all.* I tried reworking faith to be finding God in the face of people I like and with whom I agree, but that didn't last more than a day. I quickly turned into someone I didn't like—I couldn't find God in myself.

Another one of my faith behaviors is *no dehumanizing language*. I've been living into this value for close to twenty years, and now I cringe when I hear anything dehumanizing from either side of the aisle. I cringe a lot and I have to take regular social media sabbaticals. It's the most difficult when I have to say something to someone who shares my politics and justifies dehumanizing language because "we're the good guys."

We all know what it feels like to walk outside our values. We all know what it feels like to stay silent and comfortable instead of voicing what we believe. I test my values all the time. I see how far I can push and cajole them before they break. I'm imperfect and scared a lot. We all are.

But think about those moments when something really hard has happened to someone in our lives—maybe a friend or a colleague has a partner or parent or child who has been hurt or killed. And we know that we need to make a call to check in and see how we can support. But rather than doing that, we zigzag; we walk past the phone so many times that we eventually convince ourselves that it's too embarrassingly late to make the call.

It starts with "Okay, I should call, but they're probably eating dinner, I'll call later." Several hours go by. "You know what, it's bedtime, I'm going to call tomorrow." You wake up the next morning: "I bet they still have a lot of family over. I'll call in a few days when it's quieter." And what do we feel when we never make that call, and we run into that colleague or friend two or three weeks later at the grocery store? Most of us feel shame, and we feel completely outside our integrity. On my list of courage behaviors is something my mom taught us growing up: *Show up for people in pain and don't look away.*

From my experience and from what I've learned from the daring leaders I've interviewed, I will pick those five to ten seconds of discomfort any day over pulling in to my driveway and turning off the car while thinking about what I did, or didn't do, and how missing the opportunity to do or say something was a betrayal of what I value most. Another courage behavior for me: *Choose courage over comfort.*

And I'll share a little hack with you about those seconds of discomfort. I did an experiment several years ago to see how long the intense, in-the-moment discomfort lasts. After a couple of months of tracking it, I landed on eight seconds. In most situations, there are eight seconds of intense discomfort. I told Steve, "Oh, my God! It's like riding a bull! You have to make it eight seconds!" So now, when I know something hard is "fixin' to happen," I always think of George Strait's "Amarillo by Morning":

But I'll be looking for eight
When they pull that gate.

I mean, c'mon. We can do anything for eight seconds, right? The discomfort may linger long after, but the hardest part of the ride has settled down. Below are some questions and prompts to help you think through operationalizing your values.

Value #1 ________________________________

1. What are three behaviors that support your value?
2. What are three slippery behaviors that are outside your value?
3. What's an example of a time when you were fully living into this value?

Value #2 ________________________________

1. What are three behaviors that support your value?
2. What are three slippery behaviors that are outside your value?
3. What's an example of a time when you were fully living into this value?

Step Three: Empathy and Self-Compassion: The Two Most Important Seats in the Arena

One of the greatest challenges during our arena moments is the people in the stands, specifically the hardened season ticket holders who show up whether it's rain, shine, or sleet. The arena is full of seats, but these are the seats we choose to focus on. Shame has two of those season tickets. Gremlins travel in pairs so they can squeeze you from both sides: *Not good enough* and *Who do you think you are?* Scarcity and comparison are also in seats close by. Scarcity is the voice of "Never enough time, money, love, attention . . . ," and comparison brings "Look how other people are doing it so much better than you."

The box seats are the privileged seats. They are filled with the people who built the arena. And they built that arena to benefit the people who look like them in terms of race, class, sexual orientation, ability, and status. These people have already determined your odds based on stereotypes, misinformation, and fear. And we have to acknowledge this and talk about it. **Regardless of the values you pick, daring leaders who live into their values are never silent about hard things.**

There is an incredibly important, uncomfortable, and brave discussion that every single leader and every organization in the world should be having about privilege. The truth is, when I walk into the arena, I do not have the same experience as other people walking into the same arena. I'm white, I'm straight, I'm educated. There are a lot of people in those stands who are expecting me to do well and are cheering me on. Do I have something to overcome around gender? Absolutely. But there is no doubt that I operate from a place that is far more privileged than others. When we think about the arena, we have to think about factors like race, age, gender, class, sexual orientation, physical ability, and cognitive ability, to name just a few.

I haven't been in a company in five years where people aren't whispering, "This is great, but, um, how do we talk about race?" My response: "You first *listen* about race. You will make a lot of mistakes. It will be super uncomfortable. And there's no way to talk about it without getting some criticism. But you can't be silent." To opt out of conversations about privilege and oppression because they make you uncomfortable is the epitome of privilege.

Silence is not brave leadership, and silence is not a component of brave cultures. Showing up and being courageous around these difficult conversations is not a path you can predetermine. A brave leader is not someone who is armed with all the answers. A brave leader is not someone who can facilitate a flawless discussion on hard topics. A brave leader is someone who says *I see you. I hear you. I don't have all the answers, but I'm going to keep listening and asking questions.* We all have the capacity to do that. We all have the ability to foster empathy. If we want to do good work, it's imperative that we continue to flesh out these harder conversations, to push against secrecy, silence, and judgment. It's the only way to eradicate shame from the workplace, to clear the way for a performance in the arena that correlates with our highest values and not the fearmongers from the stands.

The most important seats in the arena, the ones we need to be able to focus on, especially in difficult times, are reserved for empathy and self-compassion. In the empathy seat, or seats, we just need one or two people who know our values and support our efforts to put them into action. And the self-compassion seat is for us. It's a reminder that if we can't cheer ourselves on, we shouldn't expect others to do it. If we don't make our values priorities, we can't ask others to do it for us.

1. Who is someone who knows your values and supports your efforts to live into them?

2. What does support from this person look like?
3. What can you do as an act of self-compassion to support yourself in the hard work of living into your values?
4. What are the early warning indicators or signs that you're living outside your values?
5. What does it feel like when you're living into your values?
6. How does living into your two key values shape the way you give and receive feedback?

I'm lucky because I feel I have an empathy section behind my empathy seat. The empathy seat belongs to Steve. Even when he knows that my taking on an issue will bring stress to our house, he will say, "This is what you have to do. It's who you are and why I love you. Now let's batten down the hatches and do this thing." My sisters, and even my kids, now that they're older, are often in that empathy hot seat. It's not always easy to support someone who has a public presence. They know that the backlash from speaking up can be cruel and even threatening at times. My work team is also a huge part of my empathy section. I couldn't do the work I do without them.

Support looks like love, encouragement, straight talk, boundary setting, and the occasional "No—I don't support this, and here's why."

Self-compassion is an easy list to write, and a hard list to live. For me, it's all about sleep, healthy food, exercise, and connection. It's what I mentioned in the concussion story—the best predictor of living into my values is being in physical, spiritual, and emotional shape.

I know I'm living outside my values when I am . . . *drum roll . . . this is a huge issue for me* . . . resentful. Resentment is my barometer and my early warning system. It's the canary in the coal mine. It shows up when I stay quiet in order not to piss off someone.

It shows up when I put work before my well-being, and it blows the doors off the hinges when I'm not setting good boundaries.

Faith and courage take a lot of work. You are far enough into this book that you know how much effort and skill it takes to be brave. Faith is the same. My favorite definition of spirituality is from my friend and mentor Pittman McGehee. Pittman is a Jungian analyst, Episcopal priest, and author whose work has been a tremendous help to me. Pittman says, "Spirituality is the deep human longing to experience the transcendent in our ordinary life—it's the expectation to experience the extraordinary in the ordinary, the miraculous in the mundane, and the sacred camouflaged in the profane."

My faith requires serious daily practice. I don't have time to get caught up in some bullshit beef on Twitter with a stranger. I'm busy trying to find the miraculous in the mundane (I feel a new out-of-office automated email reply coming on). When it hits me that I'm squandering precious time, I get resentful and mad at myself. If you're thinking "Maybe your Twitter fight is the sacred camouflaged in the profane?"—I'm not quite there yet.

What it feels like when I'm living into my values: How I think about this question has changed over the years. I used to believe that we would always know we're in our values when the decision comes easily, but I've learned as a leader that it's actually the opposite: I know I'm in my values when a decision is somewhere between tough and really tough. I wish doing the right thing was the easy thing, but it rarely is. I no longer expect wonderful moments. Instead, I look for quiet moments when I feel strong and solid. And, usually, tired. To quote Leonard Cohen, as I often do about the tough arena moments, "Love is not a victory march. It's a cold and it's a broken hallelujah."

Living into Our Values and Feedback

One of the biggest challenges we face, especially at work, is staying aligned with our values when giving and receiving feedback.

I put together the engaged feedback checklist for *Daring Greatly,* which is worth revisiting here. I wrote it based on the research we did for that book, and I'm happy to report that it stands the test of the new leadership data as well.

This is a guideline for readiness. Are you in the right headspace to sit down and give someone feedback?

1. I know I'm ready to give feedback when I'm ready to sit next to you rather than across from you.

Often, sitting across from someone is not just about logistics. It reflects that we think about relationships as inherently adversarial. Maybe it's okay to occasionally sit across from someone, but if there's something huge between you, then a massive desk is only going to create more distance. It is also a representation of a power differential.

2. I know I'm ready to give feedback when I'm willing to put the problem in front of us rather than between us (or sliding it toward you).

A big lumbering issue between two people is very different than sitting next to someone and putting the issue in front of both of you, so that you can look at the problem from the same perspective. Often, this requires a shift in language from "You are wrong here" to "There's something that needs to change." It is a completely different physical, cognitive, emotional, and spiritual experience when someone is on your side and helping you through the hurdle rather than pointing out your participation in the problem.

3. I know I'm ready to give feedback when I'm ready to listen, ask questions, and accept that I may not fully understand the issue.

Often, in the midst of a feedback session, we forget that we're supposed to be facilitating and fact finding from a place of curiosity, not lecturing. When we lecture, we're typically focused on getting it over with, on shoveling one lesson into one session. We want to get this difficult feedback or hard conversation over with, and we certainly don't want to string it along over multiple sessions. Instead, we must lean into our grounded confidence: "Here's what I'm seeing; here's what I'm making up about what I see. I have a lot of questions. Can you help me understand?" Then dig in, take notes, and ask questions, followed by: "I need some time to think about this. Can we circle back tomorrow? I'll come to you if more questions come up, and if you have questions, please come to me."

4. I know I'm ready to give feedback when I'm ready to acknowledge what you do well instead of just picking apart your mistakes.

Now, this can be tricky. Sometimes there's a crisis, and sometimes there is a work product or a deliverable that has a tight timeline and is not coming along according to expectations. In those moments, it doesn't always feel authentic to sit down and say "Hey, thanks for your time. Here are three things you do well" when you're dying to cut to the chase with "This is not right, and it's due at five o'clock." But the latter doesn't serve. I think back to Ken Blanchard's wisdom and how catching people doing things right is so much more powerful than just angrily listing the mistakes. It takes two minutes to say "I know this is due at five o'clock, and the executive summary looks pitch perfect. The tables need some serious work, though. What does support look like?"

5. I know I'm ready to give feedback when I recognize your strengths and how you can use them to address your challenges.

I believe a strengths-based feedback style is the best approach, in which you explain some of the strengths or things that they do really well that have not been applied to the current situation. "One of your great strengths is attention to detail. You do sweat the small stuff and it makes a big difference in our team. As I look at this, I don't see you applying that skill here, and we need it." If you are in such a state of anger that you cannot come up with a single positive quality that this person possesses, then you are not in the right headspace to give good feedback until you can be less emotionally reactive.

6. I know I'm ready to give feedback when I can hold you accountable without shaming or blaming.

Unfortunately, many of us were raised in families where feedback came in only one of two packages—shame or blame. Giving productive and respectful feedback is a skill set that most of us have never learned. It can be helpful to think through a conversation and make note of where it might get shaming. When you acknowledge your potential to go to that place, you're in a safer mindset to avoid it.

7. I know I'm ready to give feedback when I'm open to owning my part.

If you're not ready to own anything, if you're convinced that you did nothing to contribute to the issue, you're not ready to meet. As I mentioned in "The Call to Courage," I've never seen a situation that required feedback where the person delivering the feedback didn't own some part.

8. I know I'm ready to give feedback when I can genuinely thank someone for their efforts rather than just criticizing them for their failings.

Look for opportunities to call out the good: "I want to share some feedback with you about that phone call. I think you did a really good job putting a time fence around this project with our clients. I know that was very difficult, and I think you kicked ass on that."

9. I know I'm ready to give feedback when I can talk about how resolving these challenges will lead to growth and opportunity.

Be prepared to discuss what needs to change within the context of productive feedback and career tracking. "What I'm asking you to change ties directly to what we've talked about as one of your personal growth areas or one of your personal challenges." It's essential to tie what you're observing to what's important for the people you're talking to.

10. I know I'm ready to give feedback when I can model the vulnerability and openness that I expect to see from you.

If you're expecting someone to operate from a place of receptivity, then you had better show up open, curious, vulnerable, and full of questions. You have to model the behavior. You can't hold yourself to a different set of expectations and standards. If you come in defensive, guarded, and ready to kick some ass with hard feedback, that feedback will bounce right off someone sitting across from you who is also defensive, guarded, and ready to kick some ass.

In addition to this readiness checklist, we have to think about how we're going to live into our values while giving and receiving feedback. Before I deliver feedback, whether it's to direct reports, other leaders, or partners outside the business, I think carefully about how I want to show up in the conversation. One of the most painful things we experience in difficult interactions is coming out of our values and stepping out of our integrity.

I always bring my core values to feedback conversations. I specifically bring courage, which means that I don't choose comfort over being respectful and honest—choosing politeness over respect is not respectful. Second, I allow people to have feelings without taking responsibility for those feelings. If I'm sharing something that's difficult, I need to make space for people to feel the way they feel—in contrast to either punishing them for having those feelings because I'm uncomfortable, or trying to caretake and rescue them from their feelings, because that's not courageous, and that's not my job. And it gets in the way of good feedback.

GETTING GOOD AT RECEIVING FEEDBACK

Our core values are relevant here as well, but in a different way. The primary question here is *How do we stay aligned with our values while we're receiving feedback, regardless of the skill of the person delivering it?*

One of the most difficult through-lines of our lives is that we are on the receiving end of feedback starting at birth: parents, teachers, clergy, coaches, college professors, and then those thirty or forty years of bosses, managers, and colleagues. Giving good feedback is a skill and some do it well. Others do not.

We have to be able to take feedback—regardless of how it's delivered—and apply it productively. We have to do this for a simple reason: Mastery requires feedback. I don't care what we're trying to master—and whether we're trying to develop greatness or proficiency—it always requires feedback.

Receiving feedback is tricky for several reasons. One, we might be receiving feedback from someone who lacks delivery skills. Two, we might be at the hands of a skilled person, but we don't know their intentions. Three, unlike when we're giving feedback and we schedule it and know precisely what we're going to say or do, when we're receiving feedback, we can sometimes be taken off guard. Someone calls us into their office, or we pick up the phone and it's a client, and they say, "Hey, we're looking at the pitch you all submitted. We think it sucks, and it's so far off brief, and we can't believe you think we're going to spend this much money with you." And that's feedback. Does it feel productive? Is it easy to stay open and receptive to it? Not so much after we hear the word *sucks*.

But there are several tactics that can help. When receiving feedback, we can identify a value-supporting behavior or a piece of self-talk to help in the moment. Here's mine: When I'm receiving feedback, and I want to stay aligned with my value of courage, I say to myself, "I'm brave enough to listen." I actually put it on repeat: "I'm brave enough to listen. I don't have to take it all in or add it to my load, but I'm brave enough to listen."

Another thing I repeat to myself, particularly when I'm sitting across from, or with, someone who does not have great feedback delivery skills, is "There's something valuable here, there's something valuable here. Take what works and leave the rest."

The third thing I repeat to myself, even if the person who is offering feedback is skilled and it's a productive conversation, but I'm still reeling because it's hard to hear, is "This is the path to mastery, this is the path to mastery," or "These people care about this as much as I do." I get feedback all the time about my speaking style, or what I'm wearing onstage, or how I'm coming across in a video. I have to remind myself that the person who is offering it has in mind the best interest of what we're trying to create. I stay embedded in my value of courage by the way I talk to myself when the hard things are happening.

A man who took one of our courses and cites knowledge as a core value explained that feedback is an essential lever for understanding himself better: "I always stay curious about what I'm hearing, because I know I can take this feedback and turn it into a learning, or use the knowledge I already have to improve or better understand." I asked a woman whose core value is family how she shows up when receiving feedback, and her response moved me: "I show up how I would want my niece to watch me showing up; be calm, respectful, listen, don't get discouraged, keep asking questions."

It also takes practice to stay present and avoid being defensive. Achieving this is a huge success in and of itself because everything in you is likely wanting to shut down in a strategy of disconnection. If my body is saying, "This doesn't feel safe or good, you'd better shut down," I'm not going to hear anything you're telling me, I'm just going to mutter, "Mm-hmm, mm-hmm, got it."

Think back to a recent feedback conversation in which you became defensive. Physical signs: arms folded over chest (or hands in pockets), dry mouth. Thought patterns: listening for what you don't agree with ("They haven't heard my side of the story," "They aren't seeing the big picture"). Emotional signs: feeling anxious, frustrated, overwhelmed.

If we find ourselves in this position frequently, it is important that we work to develop behaviors and self-talk phrases that reposition how we show up so that we can lean into curiosity, ask questions, learn the other person's perspective, and slow down the conversation. If we're truly overwhelmed, we need to be able to suggest making time to talk about the issue later.

The ultimate goal in receiving feedback: a skillful blend of listening, integrating feedback, and reflecting it back with accountability. Being able to fully acknowledge and hold the discomfort gives us power in both the giving and receiving of feedback. If I'm sitting there getting hard feedback, feeling overwhelmed by all these things I'm not doing well, or all the ways in which I've failed, it's okay to say: "You know what, I'm overloaded right now. If we can pick one of these and dig into it, and then make time to come back and talk through the other issues, I'm willing to do that, but I can only hear so much right now." That is productive and respectful and brave.

Because of my core value of courage, I give myself permission to say "I need a break" or "The way you're acting is keeping me from hearing what you're saying. I get that you're pissed, that's okay, but we're going to have to find a different way to do this because I'm just defending myself." For me, that aligns with courage. Ask for more time; ask to circle back; ask them to say more. When you can walk out of a difficult feedback session and say "I stayed connected, I stayed courageous, I stayed authentic, I stayed curious," then that itself is daring, and that in itself is a win.

To close this section on feedback, I want to share a story from Natalie Dumond, the chief culture officer at Miovision, a smart city technology company that provides cities with the data, tools, and insights they need to reduce traffic congestion, make intelligent urban planning decisions, and improve safety on their roads. It's a powerful example of how it's possible to create a feedback culture that works.

Natalie writes:

> Like many organizations, Miovision has struggled for years to find a way to make performance management—more specifically, performance feedback—have meaning and offer valuable perspectives for each employee. When we started on this journey we implemented long-winded

performance forms with star rating systems and lists of competencies. After the form was established we eventually incorporated 360 reviews, which seemed to promote passive-aggressive behaviors and make employees anxious about what was being said about them.

Human resources and team leaders were having to police the program to ensure everyone was participating. To make it worse, leaders weren't equipped to have hard conversations. As a result, they were avoiding the conversations entirely or executing them poorly. Overall, the program wasn't working, and it wasn't adding meaning or value for the employees. The program also wasn't cultivating or promoting the behaviors we wanted to see throughout the organization. Behaviors like trust, vulnerability, curiosity, positive intent, and self-awareness.

After years of trying to find a meaningful performance management system, we decided to strip it all away and do something radical and vulnerable. We put the employees in the driver's seat, with their leads riding shotgun, and feedback and growth became everyone's responsibility. Our goal was to create a culture of trust built through courageous feedback, where employees leaned into their vulnerability and sought out feedback from their colleagues one-on-one. We envisioned a culture where employees have the courage and skills to say the hard things to their peers, and where leaders see the value in candor and how difficult conversations lead to growth.

We were successful in implementing this approach, and it's now a part of our culture. A lot of the vision and inspiration behind this program came from Brené's Daring Leadership program, especially our focus on courageous feedback. That work taught us that meaningful feedback requires getting to the heart of issues, with heart, and that we had to teach and encourage appropriate vulnerability skills. We continue to train employees and leaders to lead with courage and heart, and we teach them how to give and receive daring feedback. This is how we build a culture of trust, curiosity, positive intent, and self-awareness, a culture that thrives.

Today, what you will see at Miovision is a performance management program where employees share feedback with their colleagues on a continual basis; where nothing is anonymous, hard conversations are the norm, and this whole process is run by the employee, including how they want to integrate the feedback they receive. We encourage them to lean into the feedback and share what they have learned from their peers with their leaders, so the leaders can coach them. We truly want employees to own their performance, and create authentic relationships with their colleagues while cultivating a growth mindset.

A major key to the success of our program is training leaders and employees on what courageous feedback looks and feels like. We offer workshops to employees where they practice giving feedback to each other in real time to help strengthen their "feedback muscle." As an organization, it's incredibly liberating to have employees own their own performance and feedback, and it's incredibly powerful when you set your leaders up to be strong coaches who are equipped to have hard conversations. We've found that this approach builds and promotes the right behaviors for all employees, and encourages everyone to lean into their courage.

KNOW MY VALUES = KNOW ME. NO VALUES = NO ME. Sharing values is a massive trust and connection builder for teams. I pride myself on being connected to the people I lead. But after we spent a morning sharing our two values and some of the answers to the questions from the last section with one another, I realized that you don't really know people until you take the time to understand their values. One of my direct reports was relatively new and had been struggling with a sense of belonging in our culture. I tried various things but nothing seemed to really move the needle.

During our values-sharing exercise, I learned that one of her values is connection. She identified one of the behaviors that supports that value as taking the time to make small, human connections, not just connecting on work issues as colleagues. For example, checking in and saying hello in the morning, or catching up on our lives outside work. So easy. I love these small connections too, but I didn't do them on a regular basis. Now I do, and I enjoy it as much as she does. It made a big difference for her and in our relationship.

Another example of how value sharing strengthened a relationship was with my friend Chaz. To be honest, we've known each other for so long, I wasn't sure that any more connecting was possible. But when he left his job as CFO at a very successful ad agency to come work with me, there were some difficult shifts. During our values exercise, I learned that one of his values is financial stability. Now, you're probably thinking, *That makes sense—he's your CFO and one of your closest confidants.* But honestly, I had no idea. And when I wanted to take big risks or make large investments in new businesses, I made up the story that he was pushing back and asking a million questions because he didn't trust me, or because he thought his job was to talk me out of stuff. When I learned that it was his value—not just his job—I wanted to cry. In that moment it became one of my favorite things about him. I trust him so much I could cry just writing about this. We don't fully see people until we know their values.

I've done this exercise with leadership groups all over the world, some of whom have worked together for twenty-plus years and were shocked to learn their colleagues', or in many cases friends', values. Last year we did a really great exercise to close out the year. We did a companywide read and asked every team to do a twenty-minute presentation on the year-end state of their team, incorporating two to three learnings from the book. It was a very university-professor move—integrating and teaching others is the best way to embed learning from a book. At the beginning of the two-day event, every person wrote their two values on a large poster. Over the course of the two days, we all wrote down on each poster one reason we appreciated that person and how they live into their values. It was beautiful. I still have mine. It's hanging in my study as a reminder.

THE VALUES OPERATIONALIZINATOR

My all-time favorite innovator is Dr. Heinz Doofenshmirtz. Born in Drusselstein, he's the founder of Doofenshmirtz Evil Incorporated, a company committed to wreaking havoc and asserting his rule across the entire tri-state area.

If you or your kids are fans of the Disney cartoon *Phineas and Ferb* (2007–2015, RIP), you know who I'm talking about. If you don't watch this cartoon, you should. Heinz Doofenshmirtz is one of many awesome characters. My favorite thing about Doofenshmirtz is that all of his inventions are suffixed with *-inator*. Here are a few examples or a little catch-up-inator for the uninitiated:

Pop-Up-inator—trying to place his own evil pop-up ads virtually everywhere in the tri-state area.
Dodo-Bird-Incubator-inator—trying to create a fierce bird-monster that can help him take over the tri-state area.
Salt-Water-Taffy-inator—trying to give all kids in the tri-state area cavities.
Chicken-Soup-inator—trying to put a deli out of business that refused to serve him.

While I would never try to compete with Doofenshmirtz, my team and I have created a values operationalizinator. Many of the companies that we work with have asked us to help them operationalize their values into skills-based behaviors that can be taught, observed, and evaluated. We don't have a machine with a giant funnel or even a cool algorithm (yet), but we do have a bank of several hundred behaviors that ladder up to some of the most widely adopted organizational values.

Let me give you an example from our own organization. At Brené Brown Education and Research Group, we are called to live into the following values:

Be brave.
Serve the work.
Take good care.

Each of these has been operationalized into behaviors that we are all held accountable for demonstrating. Each behavior is evaluated on a Likert scale (5–1, always to never) by the employee and their manager separately, and then compared in a series of one-on-one conversations throughout the year. In these conversations we identify strengths and opportunities for growth, areas where people need coaching, and places where they might offer mentoring or help to others.

"Be brave" is tied to the courage-building work presented in this book. Here is an example of three behaviors that support that value:

- I set clear boundaries with others.
- I lean into difficult conversations, meetings, and decisions.
- I talk to people, not about them.

"Serve the work" is about stewardship. Three of these behaviors are:

- I take responsibility for our community's and consumers' experience.
- I am responsible for the energy I bring to situations, so I work to stay positive.
- I take ownership of adapting to the fast pace of this environment.

"Take good care" has to do with how we take care of ourselves and each other:

- I treat my colleagues with respect and compassion by responding when appropriate in a timely and professional manner.
- I practice gratitude with my team and colleagues.
- I am mindful of other people's time.

You can see how this process takes lofty and subjective values and makes them real and actionable. *Clear is kind. Unclear is unkind.*

In addition to setting clear expectations, the process gives us shared language and a well-defined culture. It helps us determine cultural fit during hiring, and offers us very straightforward standards of behavior when there are non-performance-related issues.

Operationalized values also drive productive decision making. When values aren't clear, we can easily become paralyzed—or, just as dangerous, we become too impulsive. Operationalized values drive what I think of as the sweet spot of decision making: thoughtful and decisive.

Melinda Gates, who has shared some of her daring leadership experiences with us throughout the book, writes:

> It's much easier to deal with conflicts when you are able to engage your team in a values conversation. People, and I include Bill and myself, can get attached to specific tactics. But when you're forced to tie those tactics to core values and then explain them to others, you are better able to question your own assumptions and help others question theirs. At the foundation, our guiding principle is equity. So when we disagree about, say, whether we should spend more on delivering imperfect tools to save lives now or discovering better tools to save more lives later, we can always go back to how each of those tactics aligns with the core value of equity.
>
> The thing is, there's not a correct answer to any of these debates. Each side has merit. But making my case through the lens of equity gives me a sense of solidity about what I feel and why I feel it. Sometimes we go in a different direction from what I initially suggested, but it's usually okay because I understand how other people see their preferences advancing equity. A values focus just leads to a much more

productive conversation—and a feeling of satisfaction, of being heard, no matter what decisions those conversations lead to.

Operationalizing values also forces us to get clear on the skills or combination of skills that undergird values. A great example of this is the value of "assumption of positive intent." This is a very popular value that we see adopted across diverse organizations. It basically means that we will extend the most generous interpretation possible to the intentions, words, and actions of others.

Well, it sounds straightforward enough, but I've studied positive intent for years, and I can tell you that it's a skill set that is not easy to learn and practice. I can also tell you that I've never once seen the actual skill set that supports an assumption of positive intent explicated or taught in an organization that holds this as a value. What's the foundational skill of assuming the best in people? Setting and maintaining boundaries. What's the fundamental belief underpinning the assumption of positive intent? That people are doing the best they can. We're going to take these one at a time, but from the get-go you should know that most people don't have the skills to set boundaries, and only about 50 percent of the people we've interviewed believe that people are doing the best they can. So, as you can see, it's easy to have the value on the company poster, but way more difficult to practice it. Let's look at boundary setting first.

The people who are the most generous in their assumptions of others have the clearest boundaries. The most compassionate and generous people I've interviewed in my career are the most boundaried. It turns out that we assume the worst about people's intentions when they're not respectful of our boundaries: It is easy to believe that they are trying to disappoint us on purpose.

However, we can be very compassionate toward people who acknowledge and respect what's okay and what's not.

This is why we actually call this value **Living BIG** (boundaries, integrity, and generosity). The assumption of positive intent is only sustainable when people ask themselves this question:

What boundaries need to be in place for me to be in my integrity and generous with my assumptions about the intentions, words, and actions of others?

When you have a value printed on posters hanging in the halls but you don't dig into the behaviors that support it and teach people those behaviors, you're in BS territory. It starts to corrode trust.

In addition to boundaries, an assumption of positive intent relies on the core belief that people are doing the best they can with what they've got, versus that people are lazy, disengaged, and maybe even trying to piss us off on purpose. Sure, we're all capable of change and growth, but assuming positive intent requires the belief that people are really trying in that moment.

I've spent years researching this idea. When you ask people if they believe that everyone is doing the best they can, you get either an emphatic "Hell no," from people who are as tough on themselves as they are on other people, or a quasi-apologetic "Well, I actually do believe that," from people who are stronger practitioners of self-compassion and empathy. I think the apologetic tone comes from knowing that theirs is not a popular sentiment in the world today. There is very little between those answers, and as a former "Hell no" person, I hate to report that in the early studies, the people we categorized as practicing wholeheartedness were constantly in the "Yes, people are doing the best they can" camp and those who actively struggled with perfectionism, like me, were in the "No, they are not" camp. With our new focus on daring leadership, the pattern holds. Daring leaders work from the assumption that people are doing the best they can; leaders struggling with ego, armor, and/or a lack of skills do not make that assumption.

Ultimately, Steve's response moved me from my staunch "Hell no" position. When I asked him if he believed that people are doing the best they can with what they have, he said, "I don't think you can ever know for certain. But I do know that my life is better when I work from the assumption that everyone is doing the best they can."

In *Rising Strong,* I shared the outcome of an exercise I sometimes do with people. I want to share it with you here because it really drives home the point. For the exercise, we ask folks to write down the name of someone who fills them with frustration, disappointment, and/or resentment, and then we propose the idea that that person is doing the best they can. The responses have been wide-ranging. "Crap," one man said. "If he's really doing the best he can, I'm a total jerk, and I need to stop harassing him and start helping him." One woman said, "If this was true and my mother was doing the best she can, I would be grief-stricken. I'd rather be angry than sad, so it's easier to believe she's letting me down on purpose than to grieve the fact that my mother is never going to be who I need her to be."

Asking leaders to answer this question is almost always difficult because they quickly move to believing that if people are doing the best they can, they don't know how to lead them. Their strategies of pushing and grinding on the same issues must give way to the difficult tasks of teaching their team, reassessing their skill gaps, reassigning them, or letting them go.

As crazy as it sounds, many of us will choose to stay in the resentment, disappointment, and frustration that come with believing people aren't trying rather than face a difficult conversation about real deficits. One of the most profound responses to this exercise came out of a focus group I did with a group of leaders at West Point. One officer pushed me a little on "the accuracy of the intel" and kept asking, "You are 100 percent certain that this person is doing the best he can?"

After I answered yes two or three times, the officer took a deep breath and said, "Then move the rock."

I was confused. "What do you mean by 'move the rock'?"

He shook his head. "I have to stop kicking the rock. I need to move it. It's hurting both of us. He's not the right person for this position, and there's no amount of pushing or getting on him that's going to change that. He needs to be reassigned to a position where he can make a contribution."

Assuming positive intent does *not* mean that we stop helping people set goals or that we stop expecting people to grow and change. It's a commitment to stop respecting and evaluating people based solely on what we think they should accomplish, and start respecting them for who they are and holding them accountable for what they're actually doing. And when we're overwhelmed and struggling, it also means turning those positive assumptions toward ourselves: *I'm doing the very best I can right now.*

The behaviors and skills that support seemingly simple values are not always as complex as those that undergird the assumption of positive intent; however, they are almost always more complex than what we assume. If we want to be values-driven, we have to operationalize our values into behaviors and skills that are teachable and observable. And we have to do the difficult work of holding ourselves and others accountable for showing up in a way aligned with those values.

In the next part, you'll see more work from the operationalizinator as we break down the concept of trust. For now, it's important to remember that there are no guarantees in the arena. We will struggle. We will even fail. There will be darkness. But if we are clear about the values that guide us in our efforts to show up and be seen, we will always be able to find the light. We will know what it means to live brave.

part three

BRAVING TRUST

Integrity is choosing courage over comfort;

IT'S CHOOSING WHAT'S RIGHT OVER WHAT'S FUN, FAST, OR EASY; AND IT'S PRACTICING YOUR VALUES, NOT JUST PROFESSING THEM.

I've seen the word *trust* turn an openhearted person into a Transformer in a matter of seconds. Just the slightest inkling that someone is questioning our trustworthiness is enough to set total vulnerability lockdown in motion. You can almost see it happening: *Shields engaged? Check. Armor up? Check. Heart closed? Check. Defenses activated? Check.*

Once we're in lockdown, we can't really hear or process anything that's being said because we've been hijacked by the limbic system and we're in emotional survival mode. We all want to believe that we are trustworthy, even though, ironically, many of us struggle to trust others. Most people believe they're completely trustworthy, yet they trust only a handful of their colleagues. The math just doesn't work, because believing we're trustworthy and being perceived as trustworthy by others are two different things.

Charles Feltman's definitions of trust and distrust are completely aligned with how our research participants talked about trust. In *The Thin Book of Trust,* Feltman defines trust as "choosing to risk making something you value vulnerable to another person's actions." He describes distrust as deciding that "what is important to me is not safe with this person in this situation (or any situation)."

Just reading those definitions helps us understand why we can go full-on Transformer when we talk about trust. How terrible would it be to hear someone say, "Brené, what is important to me is not safe with you in this situation, or really in any situation." It would be awful because, true or not, it threatens how I see myself on one of the most important dimensions of a social species. No trust, no connection.

Because talking about trust is tough, and because these conversations have the potential to go sideways fast, we often avoid the rumble. And that's even more dangerous. First, when we're struggling with trust and don't have the tools or skills to talk about it directly with the person involved, it leads us to talk *about* people instead of *to* them. It also leads to lots of energy-wasting zigzagging. Both are major values violations in our organization, and I bet they conflict with most of our personal values too.

Second, trust is the glue that holds teams and organizations together. We ignore trust issues at the expense of our own performance, and the expense of our team's and organization's success. And there's plenty of research to back up that statement.

In a *Harvard Business Review* article by Stephen M. R. Covey and Doug R. Conant—two leaders who have shaped how I try to show up in my own leadership—they described how "Inspiring Trust" was Doug's number one mission in his remarkable ten-year turnaround of Campbell Soup Company. They quote information from the annual list of the "100 Best Companies to Work For," where *Fortune*'s research showed that "trust between managers and employees is the primary defining characteristic of the very best workplaces," and that companies with high levels of trust "beat the average annualized returns of the S&P 500 by a factor of three."

My favorite part of this article is this quote:

> While few leaders would argue against the idea that trust is necessary for building elite performance, not nearly enough realize the height of its importance, and far too many disregard trust-building as a "soft" or "secondary" competency. But in our joint experience, we've learned that trust is the one thing that changes everything. It's not a nice-to-have; it's a must-have. Without it, every part of your organization can fall, literally, into disrepair. With trust, all things are possible—most importantly: continuous improvement and sustainable, measurable, tangible results in the marketplace.

Trust Talk We Can Actually Hear

So, if trust is a "must-have" and many leaders experience the trust conversation as a "must-avoid," what's the solve?

Get specific. Rather than rumbling generally about trustworthiness and using the word *trust,* we need to point to specific behaviors. We need to be able to identify exactly where the breach lies and then speak to it. The more exact we can be, the more likely it is that people can hear us, that we can give feedback on behavior and stay away from character, and that we can support real change.

Let's imagine that my boss, Javier, pulls me into his office and says: "I know you're really disappointed that you didn't get that promotion. There are some trust issues that are getting in the way of putting you in a more senior position."

A statement like that has the real potential to spike fear, defensiveness, and probably shame in me. It would more than likely blow to bits any container we've built. *How and why am I only hearing about what feels like a character issue after I lost the promotion?* I use this as an example because it happens every day. We're so afraid to talk about trust that our team members don't even know it's an issue until there are irreversible consequences. It's totally demoralizing.

In our trust research, we started with a very interesting question that we wanted to answer: *What are we really talking about when we talk about trust?* What if we could determine the anatomy of this big triggering word—the elements that define it—so that when Javier calls me in to tell me about why I'm not getting the promotion, he could give me some actionable strategies for changing what's problematic? And, better yet, he could call me in before the decision and say, "Here are some specific behaviors that need to change if you want to be considered for this senior position. Let's make a plan."

To get specific, our team dug into *trust* and identified seven behaviors that make up the anatomy of trust. *Thankful again for that operationalizinator.* I came up with an acronym—BRAVING—for the behaviors that define trust. I think it's a good name for the inventory because it reminds us that trust is a vulnerable and courageous process.

The BRAVING Inventory

There's a saying from the Asaro tribe in Papua New Guinea that I love: "Knowledge is only rumor until it lives in the bones." The only way I know to get knowledge into our bones is to practice it, screw it up, learn more, repeat. The **BRAVING Inventory** is first and foremost a rumble tool—a conversation guide to use with colleagues that walks us through the conversation from a place of curiosity, learning, and ultimately trust-building. We're in the process of developing a trust assessment for teams and an instrument that allows you to measure your individual level of trustworthiness based on the seven behaviors. You can visit the Dare to Lead hub at brenebrown.com for more information.

We use the inventory with our colleagues in a similar way to how we talk about values. Each person fills out the BRAVING Inventory independently, then meets one-on-one to discuss where experiences align and where they differ. It's a relational process that, when practiced well and within a safe container, transforms relationships.

Let's look at the seven elements. Some are very straightforward and some require unpacking, which I'll do after the list.

Boundaries: You respect my boundaries, and when you're not clear about what's okay and not okay, you ask. You're willing to say no.

Reliability: You do what you say you'll do. At work, this means staying aware of your competencies and limitations so you don't overpromise and are able to deliver on commitments and balance competing priorities.

Accountability: You own your mistakes, apologize, and make amends.

Vault: You don't share information or experiences that are not yours to share. I need to know that my confidences are kept, and that you're not sharing with me any information about other people that should be confidential.

Integrity: You choose courage over comfort. You choose

what is right over what is fun, fast, or easy. And you choose to practice your values rather than simply professing them.

Nonjudgment: I can ask for what I need, and you can ask for what you need. We can talk about how we feel without judgment. We can ask each other for help without judgment.

Generosity: You extend the most generous interpretation possible to the intentions, words, and actions of others.

Unpacking *vault*: The subtleties of confidentiality have been one of my biggest learnings. Let's go back to the trust conversation with Javier, who has turned me down for the promotion. Instead of saying "There are some trust issues," he says "There are some vault, or confidentiality, issues."

I'm shocked. I look at Javier and say, "We share a lot of proprietary stuff in here, and I have never once shared a single thing outside this office that you have shared with me."

He nods and responds: "I believe that, but you frequently come into this office and share things with me that are not yours to share."

People forget about that side of confidentiality. How many of you have had that experience where someone doesn't betray your confidence but constantly tells you things they shouldn't? When they walk out of your office, do you trust them less? Even though I have no proof that they've broken a confidence with me, I am skeptical of their ability to hold information that does not belong to them without feeling compelled to share it.

When it comes to secrets, it's easy to understand our impulsivity—a lot of us have bought in to the myth that gossiping or secret sharing hotwires connection. But it doesn't. When I walk into a co-worker's office and spill, there might be a moment of connection, but it's counterfeit connection. The second I walk out, that colleague is likely thinking, "I should be careful about what I tell Brené; she's got no boundaries."

Unpacking *integrity*: The word *integrity* may be overused, watered down, and written on way too many inspirational eagle posters from the '90s, but that doesn't make the concept any less important. When I was doing the research for *Rising Strong,* I looked all over for a definition of integrity that reflected what we were seeing in the data. Nothing captured all three of the properties that were emerging from the data, so I developed this definition:

Integrity is choosing courage over comfort; it's choosing what's right over what's fun, fast, or easy; and it's practicing your values, not just professing them.

In today's culture of fun, fast, and easy, that's the biggest stumbling block to integrity. It is easy to justify shortcuts based on expediency or cost. But integrity does not work that way. I can safely say that I've never done anything meaningful in my life that wasn't hard and that did not take time. Integrity is a big one—the perception of a lack of it, or even of a tendency to cut corners, creates instant wariness.

One of the best tools for putting these new skills and tools into practice is finding an **integrity partner**—someone at work who we can check in with to make sure we're acting in our integrity. This should be someone we can talk to when we're questioning how we showed up in a recent exchange or if we want to role-play a hard conversation. I have two integrity partners at work and we role-play, circle back, and practice together on a daily basis. Building courage with a partner or in a team is more powerful than doing it alone.

• • •

Unpacking *nonjudgment*: This element is a tough one. The desire to judge is strong in most of us. What's interesting is that from a research perspective, we can quantify it: There are two variables that predict when we judge and whom we judge. Typically, we pick someone doing worse than we're doing in an area where we're the most susceptible to shame: *Look at him. I may suck, but he sucks worse.* This is also why parenting is a judgment minefield. In our parenting, we're all screwing up, all the time—it's such a relief to catch someone in worse struggle, even if it's just for five minutes.

Going back to that filter of susceptibility to shame—when it comes to work, we're afraid of being judged for a lack of knowledge or lack of understanding. We hate asking for help. But that's where it gets wild. We asked a thousand leaders to list marble-earning behaviors—what do your team members do that earns your trust? The most common answer: asking for help. When it comes to people who do not habitually ask for help, the leaders we polled explained that they would not delegate important work to them because the leaders did not trust that they would raise their hands and ask for help. Mind. Blown.

When we refuse to ask for help, we will find that we keep getting the same projects that leaders know we can do. We will not be given anything that might stretch our capacity or skill set because they don't believe we will ask for help if we find ourselves in over our heads. Within my own team, I see this play out all the time: To the team members I trust the most, I will hand over important projects simply because I know that if they're stuck, if they don't understand, if it's too much work or it doesn't make sense, they will come back to me—that makes me feel safe in delegation. Not only will things not get too far down the wrong path, but the team member who is acknowledging a need for assistance also leaves space for me to come in and help guide. It has nothing to do with intelligence or competency or raw talent; it has everything to do with a relationship of trust.

When you are operating in a space of nonjudgment—I can ask for what I need, and you can ask for what you need—then we can talk about how we feel without fear of judgment. When I start to feel that smugness of judgment welling up, I immediately think, "What's the insecurity, Brené?"

Asking for help is a power move. It's a sign of strength to ask and a sign of strength to fight off judgment when other people raise their hands. It reflects a self-awareness that is an essential element in braving trust.

An example of *generosity*: In the previous part we talked about Living BIG and why generosity requires boundaries:

What boundaries need to be in place for me to be in my integrity and generous with my assumptions about the intentions, words, and actions of others?

To add some color to this concept, I want to share a story from Dara Schmidt, the director of the Cedar Rapids Library.

Dara writes:

> Daring Leadership has changed the way I work with my team. It's made me a better listener and given me the tools to be brave enough to deal with the stuff that's always easier to avoid. Choosing what's right over what's easy has become my mantra.
>
> All of the work leads back to self-awareness and personal accountability. Knowing who I am and what I'm about makes me brave enough to do "what's right," includ-

ing confronting unproductive patterns that I developed in response to long-term institutional issues. In the end, it was embracing personal accountability that gave me the courage to change.

My biggest problem as a leader was that sometimes people made me crazy. It was as if they were purposefully ignoring me. So I'd respond by getting bigger and louder so I could make myself heard. When I learned what it means to assume positive intent and set boundaries, everything changed.

I had to accept the fact that when I assumed negativity, it was my fault, not theirs. When I examined the times I assumed negative intent, I could see those were times where either I or my organization failed to provide appropriate boundaries or guidelines. I learned to recognize "making me crazy" or "feeling frustrated" as huge red flags for my own behaviors. Now when I start to go negative, I stop. I breathe and think and stay in my integrity. When I'm ready to respond rather than react emotionally, I first ask myself if I'm the problem.

When I provide clear expectations and set boundaries, people perform admirably. It's not difficult to assume positive intent when I do my part to set people up for success. I'm a better leader and a better person for it.

PUTTING THE BRAVING INVENTORY INTO PRACTICE

Let's start with a real example from a leader who uses the inventory with his team:

I recently sat down with my direct report to go through the BRAVING Inventory and talk about the strengths and areas for growth in our working relationship. When we got to *R*—

> reliability—an issue surfaced about how I was often late to our meetings or needed to postpone them due to meetings with our executive team running late or being called at the last minute. It made my teammate think that I didn't prioritize our time together. We came up with a plan together to address this issue by building in more time between meetings so I can be on time, and by getting clearer in our communication about how we address meeting changes when my schedule shifts. We left feeling committed to a new way of working together that has led to deeper trust. I'm not sure this issue would have surfaced if we didn't have the BRAVING Inventory to walk us through the issues and didn't make the time to engage in the process. Without a tool and an investment of time, things fester and go bad in teams before you know it.

We also encourage teams to work together to develop one or two observable behaviors for each of the seven elements. These behaviors can be specific to your work style and your culture. They should reflect how your team wants to operationalize the specific element, and each behavior should be something that you're willing to do, be held accountable for doing, and hold others accountable for doing.

We tell teams that they can each fill out the BRAVING Inventory worksheet (available online) individually, then share their answers as you build the team expectation worksheet, or the team can jump straight to building the team worksheet. Both ways work. This is a great example of building trust at the same time you're operationalizing it.

Also—returning to the marble jar story and the research finding that trust is earned in small moments—getting specific with the seven elements of BRAVING helps us identify how and what small trust-building moments ladder up to the different elements of trust.

There's a terrible pattern in organizations in which leaders turn to their teams, or their investors, or their board, and say "You need to trust me." Typically, that happens in a moment of crisis, when it is far too late. Trust is the stacking of small moments over time, something that cannot be summoned with a command—there are either marbles in the jar or there are not.

We don't earn trust by demanding it with "Trust me!" We earn it when we say "How is your mom's chemotherapy going?" or "I've been thinking a lot about what you asked, and I want to dig in deeper and figure this out with you." Even when you've put in the legwork to build a sturdy foundation of trust, and you've checked in with your folks using BRAVING, trust is a living process that requires ongoing attention. And if you haven't made the investment and there's nothing substantial there, there's no way to duct-tape it together. You cannot establish trust in two days when you find yourself in an organizational crisis; it's either already there or it's not.

I love what Melinda Gates shares about the marble jar and the BRAVING process:

> After you taught me your metaphor about marbles in a jar, I adopted it as my entire framework for thinking about trust. Every small gesture I make in support of a colleague puts one marble in the jar. But any time I undercut a colleague—any time I betray trust—a huge handful of marbles goes out of the jar. Thinking in this way makes me more aware of the seemingly small things that lead to building trust, and also the small things that might break trust.
>
> The seven elements of BRAVING have helped me think more clearly about what those small things are.

> For example, I focus on integrity, on matching actions to words. The foundation is a values-driven organization. If I am behaving in ways that are consistent with what we say we're all about—if I treat people equally, if I welcome open dialogue—then I am putting marbles in the jar. But if I act counter to those values—if I resist innovative approaches because I'm worried about the risk, for example—I take a lot of marbles out. I also concentrate on accountability. As the leader of the organization, there aren't as many structures to hold me accountable. I don't have regular meetings with my boss. So I have to be very careful about being my own boss, about asking myself how I'm doing and owning up to what I'm doing wrong.

Again, the intention behind the BRAVING Inventory is a tool for creating the time, space, and intention to talk about trust in a way that's productive and actionable. It's a rumble tool, a guide, and a touchstone.

The Basics of Self-Trust

While trust is inherently relational and most pronounced in practice with other people, the foundation of trust with others is really based on our ability to trust ourselves. Unfortunately, self-trust is one of the first casualties when we fail or experience disappointment or setbacks. Whether it's conscious or not, when we're wondering how we ended up facedown in the arena, we often reach for the blanket statement "I don't trust myself anymore." We assume that we must have made a bad decision and therefore it is a fallacy to count on ourselves to deliver.

Think about a time where you experienced a setback or a disappointment—a small thing, not a big glaring failure where there might be extra baggage to unpack. Instead, focus on a time where you hit a bump, and that stumbling block made you call into question your ability to depend on yourself to follow through on what you know is important. We all have those moments. As you hold that memory in your mind, go back through BRAVING quickly and recontextualize the elements for self-trust.

Boundaries: Did I respect my own boundaries in the situation? Was I clear with myself and then others about what's okay and what's not okay?

Reliability: Could I count on myself? Or was my self-talk: "Brené, you know, you set these intentions at seven A.M. when you wake up. I need the exhausted four P.M. Brené to follow through on all that stuff with the same passion that you had when you popped up in the morning."

Accountability: Did I hold myself accountable or did I blame others? And did I hold others accountable when I should have?

Vault: Did I honor the vault, and did I share, or not share, appropriately? Did I stop other people who were sharing inappropriately?

Integrity: Did I choose courage over comfort? Did I practice my values? Did I do what I thought was right, or did I opt for fast and easy?

Nonjudgment: Did I ask for help when I needed it? Was I judgmental about needing help? Did I practice nonjudgment with myself?

Generosity: Was I generous toward myself? Did I have self-compassion? Did I talk to myself with kindness and respect and like someone I love? When I screwed up, did I turn to myself and say "You gave it the best shot you could. You did what you could do with the data you had at that time. Let's clean it up, it's going to be okay," or did I skip the self-love and go straight into berating myself?

You are in control of your relationship with self-trust, and you can hold yourself accountable where you might be falling short. This isn't always possible when you are working through BRAVING in relationship with someone else, where the absence of trust might be muddied by ambiguity of intention. When you're on the mat with yourself, it's much easier to put a spotlight on where you need to work.

As you begin to address those areas that need improvement, remember one of the founding concepts of this part: Trust is built in small moments. If you struggle with reliability, make small and doable promises to yourself that are easy to fulfill, until you get a flywheel of reliability going again. If you struggle with boundaries, set small ones with your partner—like you will not be responsible for both cooking and cleaning up dinner—until you are adept at putting boundaries into action in a more meaningful way. That's how you fill your own marble jar. And never forget—we can't give people what we don't have.

I'll close this part with a story from Brent Ladd, who is the director of education at Purdue University for a National Science Foundation project. It's a powerful story that lives at the intersection of braving trust with others and with ourselves.

Brent writes:

> I work at a large research university as a professional staff member. I often feel I'm in "no-man's-land" as my efforts overlap with many categories of people from researchers to instructors to administrators. Although I've "worn many hats" in my work, I have tended to work independently—almost like a solo contractor. I'm an introvert with a big dose of Puritan work ethic and a rural cultural background that taught me a successful man doesn't ask for help, he does it himself.

During the daring leadership work, all of this was thrown into stark relief, as I became self-aware that I had not been doing much to build positive relationships at my workplace. I started to see that the way I went about achieving results was likely telling others in my group that I didn't really trust them. I also have a perfectionistic vibe, and I was realizing that I judged others' work harshly—even if I kept that mostly to myself, it came through loud and clear anyway. I had even overstepped my role quite a bit at times, without even realizing it, by "helping" others do their job better—major facepalm. This all was a big wakeup call for me.

I made a commitment to start building trust and connection with the people I worked with each day by simply engaging with them for a few minutes on a personal level: asking them about this or that, and genuinely being interested in their personal lives or details they wanted to share. I am a good listener and usually am able to engage well one on one. This initially felt a little weird for me and was not easy for me to do. I tend to avoid personal encounters—and have tended to divide the work world from the "rest of my life" world. Over time these interactions became easier. I made it a priority each day to engage each person in the office for however long was naturally appropriate. I started to "show up" as a colleague. I saw my co-workers less as competition, or inept. I started to see everyone as people who were doing the best they could, just like I was doing. Over the last several months, trust and connection have grown. I feel more of a sense of being part of a team, and have engaged in more sharing of professional efforts as a result.

Running parallel with these co-worker relationship-building efforts was becoming aware that I had a fear I had held on to for quite a few years—a "cave I didn't want to enter" but now knew I needed to. My backstory on this—years ago I had started my Ph.D. It was a dream to accomplish this, but unfortunately, everything went wrong that could go wrong. I ended up dropping my program, getting a divorce, withdrawing from the world for a period, returning home, and eventually remarrying and starting a family. I tried to return to my Ph.D. work at one point but ultimately dropped it again in order to focus on my children and wife, and my full-time job.

I have carried around this sense of "I'm not enough" due to the absence of achieving my doctorate. Fast-forward to a time period a few months ago when I had been tracking and analyzing data from a seven-year education project that I had designed and implemented. I had discovered some very interesting patterns and outcomes. Some of these results are scant or nonexistent in the literature. I had hesitated for several years to submit this type of work to a professional conference and present it to the scientific community. The old voice saying "You don't belong in that group—you don't have your Ph.D.—they won't take you seriously" kept me down. But I made a decision to submit the research work I had painstakingly conducted. My abstract was selected, and I joined a conference where I knew not a single soul. I was an outsider. However, I experienced a sense of belonging—that these might be "my people," "my tribe." What resulted is that my work was taken seriously, and I received genuine interest from others in this science community.

Another positive outcome of that decision is that in order for me to travel and participate in that science conference, I had to let go of something that I had held on to

> with a very tight grip for the past seven years: I had organized and run a successful annual workshop from top to bottom. Every tiny aspect of it was "under my control." The workshop had originally been planned for the same week as the conference where I wanted to present my results. I reached out to my co-workers, one in particular, and asked her if she would consider co-chairing the workshop with me. I said we could open up a larger chunk of the workshop to integrate some of her ideas. Though we'd been competitive, we worked together very well, and I learned a lot from her efforts, and she learned a lot from running the workshop in my absence. We both gained each other's respect, and we felt like a team after that. Trust was built.
>
> Through all of this experience the last six months I have come to realize some important things. I had shown up, put myself out there, and entered the cave. Only by showing up and being vulnerable was any of this possible. I couldn't have done it as a lone wolf. I presented myself authentically. I reached out and made connections. I shared. I realized that I am a part of the larger science community, and that I am enough. I don't need to attach my personal worth to what I produce. I bring a unique set of experiences and wisdom, and I can contribute as part of a team.

We can never overestimate the relationship between self-trust and trusting others. Maya Angelou said, "I don't trust people who don't love themselves and tell me, 'I love you.' There is an African saying which is: Be careful when a naked person offers you a shirt."

part four

LEARNING TO RISE

When we have the courage to walk into our story and own it, we get to write the ending.

AND WHEN WE DON'T OWN OUR STORIES OF FAILURE, SETBACKS, AND HURT—THEY OWN US.

We have to teach people how to land before they jump. When you go skydiving, you spend a lot of upfront time jumping off a ladder and learning how to hit the ground without hurting yourself. I haven't experienced this personally, but I've watched. The same is true in leadership—we can't expect people to be brave and risk failure if they're not prepped for hard landings.

One of the most unexpected findings that emerged from the leadership research is about the timing of teaching skills for rising or resilience. Often, leaders and executive coaches gather people together and try to teach resilience skills *after* there's been a setback or failure. It turns out that's like teaching first-time skydivers how to land after they hit the ground. Or, maybe worse, as they're free-falling.

Our research shows that leaders who are trained in rising skills as part of a courage-building program are more likely to engage in courageous behaviors because they know how to get back up. Not having those skills in place is a deterrent to braver leadership, and teaching people how to get up once they're already on the ground is much more difficult. This is why we teach falling and failing upfront. In fact, in our organization, we teach falling as part of courage-building during onboarding. It's our way of saying, "We expect you to be brave. That means that you should expect to fall. We've got a plan."

While the merits of failing and falling have received some global attention in the last couple of years, I seldom see the "fall forward" or "fail fast" slogans put into practice alongside actual reset skills and honest rumbles about the shame that almost always accompanies failure. Mere slogans, without teaching skills and putting systems in place, are a half-assed attempt at normalizing that leaves people thinking, "God, this is painful, but I think I'm supposed to feel innovative. Now I have shame about feeling shame. Better keep that a secret."

Today, with millennials making up 35 percent of the American labor force (the largest represented generation), teaching how to embrace failure as a learning opportunity is even more important. I've been in the university classroom for twenty years, and I've observed that the resilience and bounce of some students have decreased while the exposure to trauma for other students has increased. On the one hand, we were (and are) constantly intervening, constantly fixing, constantly helping some kids. As the head of my son's school said, "Many parents have gone from helicopter parents to lawnmower parents. Instead of preparing the child for the path, we prepared the path for the child." That's definitely not courage-building.

On the other hand, we've raised our kids on a steady stream of pervasive and systemic violence against marginalized communities, a vitriolic social media environment, and monthly active shooter drills at school. Today, some young adults are overprotected while others are grossly underprotected. Some are paralyzed by perfectionism and what other people think, while others have found it physically and emotionally safer to shut down and/or armor up. Either way, it feels like we're failing young adults, and it's easy to understand why many of them are entering the workforce without grounded confidence and rumbling skills.

Millennials make up 48 percent of our staff, and including interns it's 56 percent. They are all very different people, but as a group I experience them as curious, hopeful, always learning, painfully attuned to the suffering in the world, and anxious to do something about it. Because perspective is a function of experience, as a group they can struggle with patience and understanding how long it takes to cultivate meaningful change. It's our job to help give them the experiences that broaden their perspectives.

When they complete our Daring Leadership program as part of their onboarding, almost every millennial who works with us has told me some version of "I never learned how to have these kinds of conversations. I never learned about emotions or how to talk so openly about failure, and I've never seen it modeled. When you're used to using technology for everything, these hard face-to-face conversations are awkward and so intense." The only exceptions are employees who have had experience in therapy, which is one reason we have a special reimbursement program for mental health visits on top of our regular health insurance.

My experience is that millennials and Gen Zers lean in and learn hard. They're starving for the ability to put courage into practice. I'm a pretty typical Gen Xer, and I'm starving for it too. I think we all are. But I do think some of us got more of it growing up than we've modeled and taught today's young adults.

Here's the bottom line: If we don't have the skills to get back up, we may not risk falling. And if we're brave enough often enough, we are definitely going to fall. The research participants who have the highest levels of resilience can get back up after a disappointment or a fall, and they are more courageous and tenacious as a result of it. They do that with a process that I call Learning to Rise. It has three parts: the reckoning, the rumble, and the revolution.

My goal for this part is to give you the language, tools, and skills that make up the essentials of this process so you can immediately start putting this work into practice. The research is profound in its potential impact: It's almost a neurobiological hack for your brain. I'm going to walk you through this process with a story, because I don't think there's a better way to introduce the reckoning, the rumble, and the revolution.

The Ham Fold-over Debacle

A few years ago, in the midst of growing my companies, I decided that within a three-week period in September, I would launch a new company, go on a book tour, and skill up fifteen hundred people who were trained in my work. I decided in February that this was a great idea. As we've discussed, the part of my brain that accounts for timing is missing, which seems to be a scientific fact. When I made this announcement to my team and Steve, they all pushed back, but I had a secret weapon that I was keeping to myself: *By September, I'm going to be an instructor-level Pilates person and ready to run some half-marathons. That way I'll have ten times the energy I have now, and this will be easy peasy, lemon squeezy.*

August arrived. Difficult, difficult, lemon difficult.

The wheels had completely fallen off my life, both at home and at work. I'd been to one Pilates class that I hated. And I was still run/walking the same three-mile route I had for years. I commandeered the dining room of my house, which looked like a crime scene. Things were taped up all over the wall; piles of loose paper and boxes covered every inch of our table. I had stacks of stock photos and font sheets to sift through for a new website, and training materials everywhere. It was pure chaos.

I was sitting in the dining room, on the brink of collapsing in tears, when I heard the back door open and Steve come in. He walked down the hall, headed into the kitchen, set his bag down on the breakfast room table, and opened the refrigerator. The first thing I heard him say was "We don't even have any damn lunch meat in this house."

In the past, when telling this story to an audience, I've asked them for their reaction to his "damn lunch meat" comment. Without fail, women in the audience shout out comments that range from "Get your own lunch meat!" and "It's always our fault!" to "Give her a break!" One woman shouted, "Leave him!" That felt like a strong choice.

In reality, my first thought was *What did he just say?* I clenched my jaws and tightened my fists. *I can't believe he would be so shitty.*

I walked into the kitchen and said, "Hey, babe?" But not in the nice way. I did it with the voice and tone that have launched a thousand fights in kitchens across the globe.

He responded, with a little wariness and a little hopefulness, "Hey. What's up?"

"You know the big ol' truck you drive?" I asked.

"Yeah . . ." he responded, wariness overtaking hopefulness.

"I bet if you point it west and you go about a mile and a half, you're going to run into a big-ass HEB grocery store. I bet if you go in there and you give them your credit card, they'll give you a bag of ham."

At this point, I was very pleased with myself.

He looked less impressed and more worried. "Did you leave your credit card at HEB again?"

Dammit. You're killing my jam here.

"No, I did not lose my credit card. I'm just saying that you can get your own lunch meat."

He looked at me with genuine worry. "Geez. Are you okay?"

"Yes, I'm okay. I understand that it's six thirty, and you're pissed off that there's no dinner on the table. I get it."

"Wait, wait, wait, what?"

"I understand it's six thirty. You're hungry. Dinner is not on the table. I get it."

"Okay, Brené, what's thirty times three hundred sixty-five?"

Oh, my God. On top of everything else, he's math-shaming me! This is a total takedown.

I looked at him with that look that you get when you feel just a little bit unhinged.

You wanna dance? Let's dance.

In my most sarcastic voice, I answered, "I don't know, Steve, what *is* thirty times three hundred sixty-five?"

Completely refusing to engage, he said, "I don't know either, but it's the number of days we've been together, and in that number of days, not once, not whatever that big number is, have I ever come home and seen dinner on the table. Not once."

He went on. "Number one: If I came home and dinner was on the table, I would think one of two things was happening: You're leaving me, or someone in our family is really sick. Number two: When we cook dinner, we normally do it together. Number three: Who has done the grocery shopping in this family for like the last five years?"

Dammit to hell. This is not following the script for the movie in my head.

I shrugged and kicked at the ground like a toddler. "You, I guess. You buy the groceries."

Still calm and more curious than pissed, he said, "Right. I get the groceries. So what's going on?"

There's a sentence that hovered over my data for about ten years, but I never investigated it because it didn't saturate across all of the interviews. However, when I was interviewing and coding data for *Rising Strong,* the research participants who demonstrated the highest level of resilience used some form of these sentences:

The story I'm telling myself . . .
The story I make up . . .
I make up that . . .

If you put one rising skill into practice, start with this one. It's a game changer. In fact, I'm so sure of it that I'll risk the possibility of overpromising by saying it has the power to transform the way you live, love, parent, and lead. Just watch how it works.

Back in my kitchen in Houston, I looked at Steve and said, "Look, the story I'm telling myself right now is this: I am a half-ass leader, a half-ass mom, a half-ass wife, and a half-ass daughter. I am currently disappointing every single person in my life. Not because I'm not good at what I do, but because I'm doing so many different things that I cannot do a single one of them well. What I'm making up in my head right now is that you want to make sure that I know that you know how bad things suck right now. It's like you need to announce how sucky things are in our house on the off chance that I—the purveyor of everything that's currently sucking—happen not to know."

Steve looked at me and said: "You know what? I get it. I know you're making that up because that is your go-to story when you're in a hard place, and you are in a harder place than I have seen you in years. The work you have in front of you is beyond human scale.

You are so far under the water, you can't even find your way up right now. So here's what we're going to do. I'm diving down. I'm going to find you, and I'm going to pull you to the surface, because when I'm that lost, you always find me and you pull me to the surface. And then we'll feed the kids Chick-fil-A for day number four. Maybe we'll add some spinach just to make our way into parenting purgatory. And then we will sort this out. We will sort this out together."

By this point I was crying. "Thank you, I'm just so overwhelmed, and I don't know what to do next. I can't dig myself out of this. It's so much. People are depending on me."

Steve gave me a long bear hug, and when I pulled away to wipe the snot off my face, I looked up at him and said, "Can I ask you an honest question, though?"

He said "Yeah. Of course" as he pushed the hair off my face.

"Why the big proclamation at the refrigerator? Why the 'We don't even have any damn lunch meat in this house' announcement? Was that a jab? It's okay if it was. I get it. But was it a little dig at me, or maybe just the situation?"

"Let me think about it." Steve is a very sincere guy, and I thought he'd come back with "Yeah, I'm kind of sick of the stress. It was a little passive-aggressive." But instead he said: "I am so hungry."

"What do you mean?" I asked, totally confused.

"I'm just hungry. I said it because I'm hungry. I got stuck with a patient at lunch, and on the way home today I thought to myself, we probably won't eat until seven. I'm gonna make a ham fold-over."

"And . . . ?" I asked, still confused.

"And nothing. That's it. I'm hungry for a ham fold-over."

Ah, the ham fold-over debacle. I'm guessing every person with this book in their hand or everyone who is listening on audio has experienced the equivalent of a ham fold-over debacle. You make yourself the center of something that has nothing to do with you out of your own fear or scarcity, only to be reminded that you're not the axis on which the world turns. That's not just one of the oldest maneuvers in history, it's our brain at work. Ironically, trying to keep us safe.

Holding this story in mind, let's break down the three-step process for Learning to Rise.

The Reckoning, the Rumble, and the Revolution

The Learning to Rise process is about getting up from our falls, overcoming our mistakes, and facing hurt in a way that brings more wisdom and wholeheartedness into our lives. As tough as it is, the payoff is huge: **When we have the courage to walk into our story and own it, we get to write the ending. And when we don't own our stories of failure, setbacks, and hurt—they own us.**

I call the research participants who had the highest level of resilience and reset *the risers*. It just fits, plus I always think about "the arena" when I hear the chorus to the song "Riser" by Dierks Bentley:

> *I'm a riser*
> *I'm a get up off the ground, don't run and hider*
> *Pushin' comes to shove*
> *And hey, I'm a fighter*

THE RECKONING

We are emotional beings, and when something hard happens to us, emotion drives. Cognition or thinking is not sitting shotgun next to behavior in the cab of the truck. Thinking and behavior are hog-tied in the back, and emotion is driving like a bat out of hell. *Picture me at the dining room table when Steve makes the damn ham announcement.*

Risers immediately recognize when they're emotionally hooked by something: *Hey, something's got me.* And then they get curious about it. We don't have to pinpoint the emotion accurately—we just need to recognize that we're feeling something. There will be time to sort out exactly what we're feeling later.

Some of the ways risers talked about knowing they were hooked include:

- I don't know what's happening, but I'm coming out of my skin.
- I can't stop playing that conversation over and over in my head.
- How did I end up in the pantry?
- I feel ________________________ (disappointed, regretful, pissed, hurt, angry, heartbroken, confused, scared, worried, etc.).
- I am __________________________ (in a lot of pain, feeling really vulnerable, in a shame storm, embarrassed, overwhelmed, in a world of hurt).
- My stomach is in knots.
- I wanna punch someone.

The reckoning is as simple as that: knowing that we're emotionally hooked and then getting curious about it.

The challenge is that very few of us were raised to get emotionally curious about what we are feeling. Whether it is a failure, a sideways comment from a colleague, a meeting that is full of disconnection and frustration, or a feeling of rising resentment when asked to do more than someone else, we're hooked, and we weren't taught the skill that the most resilient among us share: Slow down, take a deep breath, and get curious about what's happening. Instead, we bust out the armor.

While most of us get busy sucking it up, ignoring our feelings, or taking out our emotions sideways on other people (marching into the kitchen loaded for bear), the risers are getting curious about what's really going on so they can dig in, figure out what they are feeling, and why. It's kinda like thinking before you talk, but it's feeling before you swing or hide.

How do we recognize that we've been snagged by emotion? From the wisest part of us—our body. We call emotions *feelings* because we feel them in our bodies—we have a physiological response to emotions.

Risers are connected to their bodies, and when emotion knocks, they feel it and they pay attention. For example, since putting this work into practice, I learned that when I'm emotionally hooked, time slows down, my armpits tingle, my mouth gets dry, and I immediately start playing whatever has happened on a continuous loop in my head. Now when any of those things happens, I try to pay attention and take it as a cue. My cue is personalized just for me: *Something's going on. Get curious or get crazy.* If I think back to the ham fold-over debacle, the clenched jaw and balled-up fists were probably a good sign. *Sigh.*

Here's the hard news about this process. Very few people make it through the reckoning, for one reason: Instead of feeling our emotions and getting curious, we offload them onto others. We literally take that ball of emotional energy welling up inside us and hurl it toward other people. I'm going to share the six most common offloading strategies from *Rising Strong*. As you read through them, ask yourself two questions: *Do I do this?* and *How does it feel to be on the receiving end of this?*

Offloading Strategy #1: Chandeliering

We think we've packed the hurt so far down that it can't possibly resurface, yet all of a sudden, a seemingly innocuous comment sends us into a rage or sparks a crying fit. Or maybe a small mistake at work triggers a huge shame attack. Perhaps a colleague's constructive feedback hits that exquisitely tender place, and we jump out of our skin.

I learned the term *chandelier* from Steve. It's used within the medical community to describe a patient's pain that is so severe that if you touch that tender place, their response is involuntary. No matter how hard they try to hide the hurt or how distracted they are by other things, they jump up to the ceiling, or chandelier.

The chandeliering I'm describing is the emotional equivalent, and it's especially common and dangerous in "power-over" situations: in environments where, because of power differentials, people with a higher position or status are less likely to be held accountable for flipping out or overreacting. This type of volatility creates distrust and disengagement.

For example, someone might maintain their prized stoicism in front of customers or other people they want to impress or influence, but the second they're around people over whom they have emotional, financial, or physical power, they explode. And because it's not a behavior seen by many of the higher-ups, their version of the story is usually perceived as truth. We see power-over chandeliering in families, churches, schools, communities, and offices. And when you mix in issues like gender, class, race, sexual orientation, or age, the combination can be toxic.

Most of us have been on the receiving end of such outbursts. Even if we have the insight to know that our boss, friend, colleague, or partner blew up at us because something tender was triggered, and even when we know it's not actually about us, it still shatters trust and respect. **Living, growing up, working, or worshipping on eggshells creates huge cracks in our sense of safety and self-worth. Over time, these cracks can be experienced as trauma, whether this happens at work or at home.**

Offloading Strategy #2: Bouncing Hurt

Pain is hard, and it's easier to be angry or pissed off than to acknowledge hurt, so our ego intervenes and does the dirty work. The ego doesn't own stories or want to write new endings; it denies emotion and hates curiosity. Instead, the ego uses stories as armor and alibi. The ego says "Feelings are for losers and weaklings."

Like all good hustlers, our ego employs crews of ruffians in case we don't comply with its demands. Anger, blame, and avoidance are the ego's bouncers. When we get too close to recognizing an experience as an emotional one, these three spring into action. It's much easier to say "I don't give a damn" than it is to say "I'm hurt."

The ego likes blaming, finding fault, making excuses, inflicting payback, and lashing out, all of which are ultimately forms of self-protection. The ego is also a fan of avoidance—assuring us that we're fine, pretending that it doesn't matter, that we're impervious. We adopt a pose of indifference or stoicism, or we deflect with humor and cynicism. *Whatever. Who cares? None of this matters anyway.*

When the bouncers are successful—when anger, blame, and avoidance push away real hurt, disappointment, or pain—our ego is free to scam all it wants. Often the first hustle is shaming others for their lack of "emotional control." The ego can be a conniving and dangerous liar when it feels threatened.

Offloading Strategy #3: Numbing Hurt

We talked a lot about numbing in the section on the armory. The important thing to note here is that in addition to numbing being a popular form of armor, we can offload emotion through it as well.

Offloading Strategy #4: Stockpiling Hurt

There's a quiet, insidious alternative to chandeliering, bouncing, or numbing hurt—we can stockpile it. We're not erupting with misplaced emotions or using blame to deflect our true feelings or numbing the pain. Stockpiling starts like chandeliering, by firmly packing down the pain, but instead of unleashing it on another person, we just continue to amass hurt until our bodies decide that enough is enough. The body's message is always clear: Shut down the stockpiling or I'll shut you down. The body wins every time. Midlife and midcareer are when we often start to see the effects of having stockpiled emotion for too long. The body is holding down the emotional fort, and as a result, we can experience many symptoms including anxiety, depression, burnout, insomnia, and physical pain.

Offloading Strategy #5: The Umbridge

I named this strategy after J. K. Rowling's character Dolores Umbridge in *Harry Potter and the Order of the Phoenix,* and I find it to be one of the most difficult offloading strategies to experience. Played brilliantly by Imelda Staunton in the films, Umbridge wears cutesy pink suits and pillbox hats, adorns her pink office with bows and trinkets decorated with kittens, and is a fan of torturing children who misbehave. Rowling writes about her, "A love of all things saccharine often seems present where there is a lack of real warmth or charity."

Too many cheery claims, like "Everything is awesome" or "I

just never really feel angry or upset" or "If you're just positive, you can turn that frown upside down" often mask real pain and hurt. What's true but seems counterintuitive is that we don't trust people who don't struggle, who don't have bad days or hard times. We also don't develop connection with people we don't find relatable. When light and dark are not integrated, overly sweet and accommodating can feel foreboding, as though under all that niceness is a ticking bomb.

Offloading Strategy #6: Hurt and the Fear of High-Centering

Don't google the term "high-centered." More than likely you'll pull up an image of a cow stuck on top of a fence, legs dangling on both sides, unable to go forward or backward. It's disturbing. I learned the term because my grandmother's driveway in San Antonio was two parallel cement strips with a mound of dirt and grass in the middle. Every now and then, my grandmother would say, "The dirt and grass are getting too high. I'm gonna get high-centered in my car," and we'd dig out and flatten that center strip with a shovel. High-centered here meant that the center of the car would be higher than the four tires and she'd get stuck.

One reason we deny our feelings is the fear of getting emotionally high-centered—that is, getting stuck in a way that makes it difficult to go forward or backward. If I recognize my hurt or fear or anger, I'll get stuck. Once I engage even a little, I won't be able to move backward and pretend that it doesn't matter, but moving forward might open a floodgate of emotion that I can't control. Recognizing emotion leads to feeling emotion. What if I recognize the emotion and it dislodges something and I can't maintain control? I don't want to cry at work, or on the battlefield, or when I'm with my students. Getting high-centered can be the worst because we feel a total loss of control. We feel powerless.

STRATEGIES FOR RECKONING WITH EMOTION

This is going to sound weird, but the most effective strategy for staying with emotion instead of offloading it is something I learned from a yoga teacher. And from a few members of the military Special Forces. It's breathing. The yoga teacher called it **box breathing.** The soldiers called it **tactical breathing.** Turns out they're the same thing. Former Green Beret Mark Miller explains tactical breathing this way:

1. Inhale deeply through your nose, expanding your stomach, for a count of four.
2. Hold in that breath for a count of four.
3. Slowly exhale all the air through your mouth, contracting your stomach, for a count of four.
4. Hold the empty breath for a count of four.

We don't take enough deep breaths at work. We don't pause enough and check our body. I'm a breath holder, and sometimes, when things get really hectic and I'm in firefighting mode at the office, I just stop and trace a square on my desk: *In for four, hold for four, out for four, hold for four.* I swear just two or three of these breathing sessions rewires me. I even taught my kids and students how to do it. Breathing is also the key to another strategy for reckoning with emotion, and one of the most underrated leadership superpowers: practicing calm.

I define **calm** as **creating perspective and mindfulness while managing emotional reactivity.** Calm is a superpower because it is the balm that heals one of the most prevalent workplace stressors: anxiety. When it comes to anxiety, my greatest teacher is psychologist Harriet Lerner. In her book *The Dance of*

Connection, Dr. Lerner explains that we all have patterned ways of managing anxiety; some of us respond by *over*functioning and others by *under*functioning. Overfunctioners, like myself, tend to move quickly to advise, rescue, take over, micromanage, and get in other people's business rather than look inward. Underfunctioners tend to get less competent under stress. They sometimes invite others to take over and often become the focus of family gossip, worry, or concern. They can get labeled as the "irresponsible one" or the "problem child" or the "fragile one." Dr. Lerner explains that seeing these behaviors as patterned responses to anxiety, rather than truths about who we are, can help us understand that we can change. For those of us who overfunction, our work is to become more willing to embrace our vulnerabilities in the face of anxiety. For folks who underfunction, the goal is to work on amplifying strengths and competencies.

Whether we over- or underfunction, practicing calm creates the clearing we need to get emotionally grounded. The bad news is that anxiety is one of the most contagious emotions that we experience. This explains why anxiety can so easily become a function of groups, not individuals. It's too contagious to stay contained in one person. We've all had the experience of one person sending a group into a tailspin.

The good news? Calm is equally contagious. Over the past twenty years, the most proficient practitioners of calm that I've interviewed all talked about the important (and weird) combination of breathing and curiosity. They talked about taking deep breaths before responding to questions or asking them; slowing down the pace of a frantic conversation by modeling slow speech, breathing, and fact finding; and even intentionally taking a few breaths before asking themselves a version of these two questions:

1. Do I have enough information to freak out about this situation?
2. If I do have enough data, will freaking out help?

In addition to curiosity and breathing, don't forget permission slips. Sometimes we have to give ourselves permission to feel—especially if we come from a family where exploring and discussing emotion was either explicitly off-limits or just not modeled.

Imagine how different my conversation with Steve would have been if I had paid attention to my anger and hurt, taken a few deep breaths, and become curious.

The Rumble: Conspiracies, Confabulations, and Shitty First Drafts

If the reckoning is how we walk into a tough story, the rumble is where we go to the mat with it and own it.

The rumble starts with this universal truth: **In the absence of data, we will always make up stories.** It's how we are wired. Meaning making is in our biology, and when we're in struggle, our default is often to come up with a story that makes sense of what's happening and gives our brain information on how best to self-protect. And it happens a hundred times a day at work. Our organizations are littered with stories that people make up because they don't have access to information. If you've ever led a team through change, you know how much time, money, energy, and engagement bad stories cost.

Robert Burton, a neurologist and novelist, explains that our brains reward us with dopamine (that "aha" moment) when we recognize and complete patterns. Stories are patterns. The brain recognizes the familiar beginning-middle-end structure of a story and rewards us for clearing up the ambiguity. Unfortunately, the brain rewards us for a good story—one with clear good guys and bad guys—regardless of the accuracy of the story.

The promise of that *Aha! I've solved it!* sensation can seduce us into shutting down the uncertainty and vulnerability that are often necessary for getting to the truth. The brain is not a big fan of ambiguous stories that leave unanswered questions and a big tangle of possibilities. The brain has no interest in *Maybe I have a part* or *Am I blowing this out of proportion?* The part of the brain that goes into protection mode likes binaries: Good guy or bad guy? Dangerous or safe? Ally or enemy?

Burton writes, "Because we are compelled to make stories, we are often compelled to take incomplete stories and run with them." He goes on to say that even with a half story in our minds, "we earn a dopamine 'reward' every time it helps us understand something in our world—even if that explanation is incomplete or wrong."

The first story we make up is what we call the "shitty first draft," or the SFD. (If you're not comfortable with *shitty,* I call it the "stormy first draft" with kids. They totally get this concept and love talking about their SFDs because, after a hard experience, it gives them the opportunity to confirm that we love them and that they still belong.)

The idea of a "shitty first draft" comes from Anne Lamott's exceptional book on writing, *Bird by Bird.* She writes:

> The only way I can get anything written at all is to write really, really shitty first drafts. The first draft is the child's draft, where you let it all pour out and then let it romp all over the place, knowing that no one is going to see it and that you can shape it later.

When it comes to our emotions, the first stories we make up—our SFDs—are definitely our fears and insecurities romping all over the place, making up worst-case scenarios. For example, *Steve is a total jerk. He doesn't think I'm capable of running my business and being a great partner and mother. He's sick of me and the stress. The past thirty years have been a giant lie.*

Instead of plowing into the kitchen like a bull in an emotional china shop, I wish I had noticed my reaction to the ham comment and become curious about the emotions enveloping me. Had I taken the time to surface my SFD, I could have walked in and said, "I heard the ham comment, and the story I'm telling myself is that you're sick of me and all of the stress of my work right now."

I've known Steve for more than thirty years, and I'm 99 percent confident that he would have pulled me in for a hug and said, "I know you're overwhelmed. What can we do?"

Yes, the conflict worked out okay, but relationships can take only a certain amount of what I pulled in the kitchen before they're affected by it.

In our SFDs, fear fills in the data gaps. What makes that scary is that **stories based on limited real data and plentiful imagined data, blended into a coherent, emotionally satisfying version of reality, are called conspiracy theories.** Yes, we are all conspiracy theorists with our own stories, constantly filling in data gaps with our fears and insecurities.

In work cultures where there's a lot of change and confusion afoot, teams go crazy with SFDs. However, if you are operating in a culture of courage, you give people as many facts as you can, and when you can't tell them everything, you acknowledge that you're telling them as much as you can and that you will continue to keep them in the loop with information as you have access to it and have permission to share. Clear is kind. And clarity absolutely reduces story making and conspiracy theories.

Daring leaders ask for SFDs. They create the time, space, and safety for people to reality-check their stories. In the past, when we've had to let people go, we've met privately with the immediate team affected, made the announcement to the larger group, then invited people to come see us during a blocked-out time to "talk, ask questions, and check SFDs." Keep in mind: You can spend a reasonable amount of time attending to feelings and fears (and conspiracy theories), or you can squander an unreasonable time managing unproductive behaviors.

In addition to attending to conspiracy theories, we also have to watch for confabulations.

Confabulation has a really great and subtle definition: *A confabulation is a lie told honestly.* To *confabulate* is to replace missing information with something false that we believe to be true.

In his book *The Storytelling Animal,* Jonathan Gottschall explains that there's growing evidence that "ordinary, mentally healthy people are strikingly prone to confabulate in everyday situations." In one of my favorite studies described in his book, a team of psychologists asked shoppers to choose a pair of socks from a set of seven pairs and then to give their reasons for choosing that particular pair. Every shopper explained their choice based on subtle differences in color, texture, and stitching. No shopper said, "I don't know why this is my choice," or "I have no idea why I picked that one." All of them had a full story that explained their decision. But here's the kicker: All of the socks were identical. Gottschall explains that all of the shoppers told stories that made their decisions seem rational. But they really weren't. He writes, "**The stories were confabulations—lies, honestly told.**"

Confabulation shows up at work when we share what we believe is factual information, but it's really just our opinion. It's when I look at my colleague and say, "We are all getting laid off in September. This whole group is being shut down and let go." Everyone panics and asks me how I know. "I know, I heard, I know it's true."

The information might have no basis in truth, none at all; it's a confabulation. I believe it's true, but it's really my fear, combined with what might be a little bit of data. And it's dangerous.

With the SFD, we need to stop and capture that first story, that conspiracy, that confabulation, that scribbled mess in our heads. "Oh, my God, she looked at me like that in the meeting because she doesn't trust me. She thinks my ideas are stupid, and she is probably plotting to get me taken off this project."

It is incredibly important to grab hold of those before the myth making gets completely out of control. Today, I try to use my phone to capture my SFD before I act on it. I write it out when I have the opportunity simply because 70 percent of the risers we interviewed write down their SFDs. Nothing elaborate, just some variation of:

The story I'm making up:
My emotions:
My body:
My thinking:
My beliefs:
My actions:

James Pennebaker, a researcher at the University of Texas at Austin, has found that because our minds are designed to try to understand things that happen to us, translating messy, difficult experiences into language essentially makes them "graspable." Storytelling is another vehicle for sharing the story you're making up. If you have a friend or colleague you trust who has the skills and patience to listen, you can talk through your SFD.

Writing down your SFD doesn't give it power—it gives us power. It gives us the opportunity to say, "Does this even make sense? Does this look right?" Writing slows the winds and calms the seas. And if you're completely mortified by the thought of someone finding your SFD because it's blamey, pissy, immature, and a full-on rant, you've done it well. Unfiltered is powerful when it comes to the SFD.

The author Margaret Atwood writes,

> When you are in the middle of a story, it isn't a story at all, but only a confusion; a dark roaring, a blindness, a wreckage of shattered glass and splintered wood; like a house in a whirlwind, or else a boat crushed by the icebergs or swept over the rapids, and all aboard are powerless to stop it. It's only afterwards that it becomes anything like a story at all. When you are telling it, to yourself or to someone else.

To move from what Atwood calls "a wreckage of shattered glass and splintered wood" to a true story that you can address, these are the questions that risers need to rumble with:

1. What more do I need to learn and understand about the situation?

What do I know objectively?
What assumptions am I making?

2. What more do I need to learn and understand about the other people in the story?

What additional information do I need?
What questions or clarifications might help?

Now we get to the more difficult questions—the ones that take courage and practice to answer.

3. What more do I need to learn and understand about myself?

What's underneath my response?

What am I really feeling?

What part did I play?

Answering #1 and #2 means having the courage to address the conspiracies and confabulations. Answering #3 requires emotional literacy—being able to recognize and name emotions—the same skill set required in empathy and self-compassion.

Imagine how powerful it would be to catch ourselves making up an SFD, rumble with it for a few minutes, then check it out with a colleague: "Hey. Tough meeting today. You were quiet, and I'm making up that you were pissed about your team having to do all of the work for the next sprint. Can we talk about that?"

FYI: If you walked up to me and said that, my trust and respect for you would skyrocket.

Let's say my response is "No, I'm not mad at all. I'm exhausted. Charlie's sick and he was throwing up all night. But I appreciate you checking in." This gives you the opportunity to practice empathy: "I'm sorry. That's hard. Can I get you a cup of coffee?"

Now let's walk through the situation of this alternate reply: "Yes. I'm super frustrated! This is not our project and we don't have the resources to own the work. It's total bullshit." This gives you the opportunity to say, "Okay. Let's sit down and talk about it."

Win-win. Either way, this is connecting and trust-building. It sounds like a cure for lunatic behavior, but this making up stories and conspiracy theories is something we all do. Gottschall writes, "Conspiracy is not limited to the stupid, the ignorant, or the crazy. It is a reflex of the storytelling mind's compulsive need for meaningful experience." The problem is that rather than rumbling with vulnerability and staying in uncertainty, we start to fill in the blanks with our fears and worst-case-scenario planning. I love this line from Gottschall: "To the conspiratorial mind, shit *never* just happens."

The power of "the story I'm telling myself" is that it reflects a very real part of what it means to be a meaning-making human. It's disarming because it's honest. We all do it. This is why it works across diverse environments and with all people.

For example, we recently facilitated the Daring Leadership program at Shell, with an elite deep-sea engineering team called SURF (Subsea Umbilical Risers and Flowlines).

Gwo-Tarng Ju, or GT as he's more commonly known, bravely led his executive leadership team through the work. Like GT, who has a Ph.D. in aerospace engineering, most of the leaders were engineers or project managers. Part of the focus of our work together was examining how their leaders give performance feedback or lead setback debriefs as directives rather than facilitating conversations that lead to a deeper understanding of skill gaps, communication issues, and structural barriers.

After spending time drilling down on the differences between systemic vulnerability (which is not good) and relational vulnerability (which is a prerequisite for courageous leadership), the team started building skills that enabled them to engage in difficult conversations with one another and their direct reports. Speaking to this new skill set, GT writes:

> We have been able to achieve more constructive performance feedback sessions after learning the rising skills of reality-checking the stories we all make up during conflicts or setbacks. Circling back also allows us to gain clarity and minimize the negative emotion that often frames the feedback process. By surfacing dilemmas swiftly and constructively, leaders can help resolve conflicts in a timely manner.

> This is critically important given the complex and high-risk environments where we work.

Without real conversation around feedback, there is less learning and more defensiveness. Because it's human nature to turn on some level of self-protection when dealing with setbacks and receiving feedback, it's important to circle back with employees to ensure that the intention of the message matched what was actually heard, and to reality-check SFDs.

And for organizations that use a forced ranking system in employee evaluations, it's essential to create a culture in which circling back and checking out stories is safe and built into the evaluation process. You can do this by scheduling two meetings—one for the initial conversation and one for the story checking.

Another example comes from Melinda Gates, whom you met earlier. Melinda is someone who often sees curiosity and asking the right questions as a leadership superpower, and her story resonated deeply with me. She writes:

> For the longest time, the story I was making up was, *That expert is ignoring me or condescending to me because I'm not Bill.* But after years of feeling that sting, I started to realize that something else was underneath. I was worried that I didn't know enough science to lead world-renowned experts in global health. And it kept me from asking questions and from fully engaging. I was feeling like an imposter in a new field in which I didn't have a degree.
>
> Once I was able to face the fact of my insecurity, I was able to start chipping away at it. What I now believe is, *I know just the right amount: enough to ask good questions, and not so much as to be distracted by minute details.* Rewriting that story means that I feel confident asking seem-

ingly "stupid" questions, because I've learned that they are rarely stupid and often the most important ones to raise.

Both of these are great examples of finding the courage to own hard stories so we can write new endings.

In addition to affecting trust and connection in relationships and teams, the stories we tell ourselves can also crush our self-worth. **The three most dangerous stories we make up are the narratives that diminish our lovability, divinity, and creativity.**

The reality check around our lovability: Just because someone isn't willing or able to love us, it doesn't mean that we are unlovable.

The reality check around our divinity: No person is ordained to judge our divinity or to write the story of our spiritual worthiness.

The reality check around our creativity: Just because we didn't measure up to some standard of achievement doesn't mean that we don't possess gifts and talents that only we can bring to the world. And just because someone failed to see the value in what we can create or achieve doesn't change its worth or ours.

THE DELTA

The difference—the **delta**—between what we make up about our experiences and the truth we discover through the process of rumbling is where the meaning and wisdom of this experience live. The delta holds our key learnings—we just have to be willing to walk into our stories and rumble.

In the ham fold-over debacle, I had to rumble with shame, vulnerability, and trust. My key learnings: (1) When I'm struggling and things are falling apart, I'm much more likely to shame and blame myself. I can't think of even one instance where Steve has done that to me. (2) I have to get better at asking for help.

(3) I sometimes offload emotion—I'm especially good at bouncing hurt with anger.

Because I had the "I'm making this up" tool and was starting to put what I had learned researching *Rising Strong* into practice, Steve and I were able to take an angry almost-fight during an extremely stressful time and turn it into a moment of connection and trust.

As we start to integrate what we learn from the Learning to Rise process into our lives, we get better at rumbling. In our office, we probably check the stories we're making up with each other ten times a day. Now it's shortened to "I'm making up that they're still holding the redline because their lawyers haven't reviewed it yet," or "I'm making up that no one is going to want to sit through that presentation on Friday afternoon." It's so much more honest, vulnerable, and disarming than making proclamations that are really just conjecture.

Personally, I have found that sometimes the Learning to Rise process takes five minutes to get from "facedown in the arena" to the delta to key learnings—but sometimes it takes five days, and for the big life stuff it can take months. The more you practice rumbling with vulnerability, the better and faster you get.

When we own a story and the emotion that fuels it, we get to simultaneously acknowledge that something was hard while taking control of how that hard thing is going to end. We change the narrative. When we deny a story and when we pretend we don't make up stories, the story owns us. It drives our behavior, and it drives our cognition, and then it drives even more emotions until it completely owns us.

THE STORY RUMBLE

One of the most useful applications of the Learning to Rise process is how we can use it when an organization, or a group within an organization, experiences a conflict or a failure or a fall. We call this the **Story Rumble**.

Everyone who reads this book and puts the work into practice will have the basic tools for the Story Rumble. If necessary, you can even train people to facilitate the process or bring in one of our Certified Dare to Lead Facilitators to help. We've used this in the wake of failure to understand and address growing frustration and resentment on a team and across teams, and, most recently, to get to the bottom of a major project stall.

This is the Story Rumble process: Bring as many of the courage-building tools, skills, and practices we've discussed into the room as you can—especially shared language, curiosity, grounded confidence, your integrity, your values, and the trust you're building. You'll need them all, and you'll marvel at how they pay off.

1. Let's set the intention for the rumble and make sure we are clear about why we're rumbling.
2. What does everyone need to engage in this process with an open heart and mind? *Container-building is important, even if there's established trust in the group.*
3. What will get in the way of you showing up?
4. Here's how we commit to showing up: *from #2 and #3.*
5. Let's each share one permission slip. *More container- and trust-building.*
6. What emotions are people experiencing? *Let's put it out there, and let's name emotions.*
7. What do we need to get curious about? *Building more trust and grounded confidence by staying curious.*
8. What are your SFDs? *The Turn & Learn is very helpful here. These are vulnerable rumbles, and having someone with more influence go first, versus having everyone write their thoughts down and put them up on the*

wall at the same time, can change the outcome for the worse.

9. What do our SFDs tell us about our relationships? About our communication? About leadership? About the culture? About what's working and what's not working? *Stay curious, learn to resist needing to know.*
10. Where do we need to rumble? What lines of inquiry do we need to open to better understand what's really happening and to reality-check our conspiracy theories and confabulations?
11. What's the delta between those first SFDs and the new information we're gathering in the rumble?
12. What are the key learnings?
13. How do we act on the key learnings?
14. How do we integrate these key learnings into the culture and leverage them as we work on new strategies? What is one thing each of us will take responsibility for embedding?
15. When is the circle-back? Let's regroup so we can check back in and hold ourselves and one another accountable for learning and embedding.

Own the story and you get to write the ending. Deny the story and it owns you.

The Revolution

I'm not afraid of the word **revolution,** I'm afraid of a world that's becoming less courageous and authentic. I've always believed that in a world full of critics, cynics, and fearmongers, taking off the armor and rumbling with vulnerability, living into our values, braving trust with open hearts, and learning to rise so we can reclaim authorship of our own stories and lives is the revolution. Courage is rebellion.

In fact, in 2010, I wrote:

> *Revolution* might sound a little dramatic, but in this world, choosing authenticity and worthiness is an absolute act of resistance. Choosing to live and love with our whole hearts is an act of defiance. You're going to confuse, piss off, and terrify lots of people—including yourself. One minute you'll pray that the transformation stops, and the next minute you'll pray that it never ends. You'll also wonder how you can feel so brave and so afraid at the same time. At least that's how I feel most of the time . . . brave, afraid, and very, very alive.

If you asked me to boil down everything I've learned from this research, I would tell you these three things:

1. The level of collective courage in an organization is the absolute best predictor of that organization's ability to be successful in terms of its culture, to develop leaders, and to meet its mission.
2. The greatest challenge in developing brave leaders is helping them acknowledge and answer their personal call to courage. Courage can be learned if we're willing to put down our armor and pick up the shared language, tools, and skills we need for rumbling with vulnerability, living into our values, braving trust, and learning to rise.
3. We fail the minute we let someone else define success for us. Like many of you, I spent too many years taking on projects and even positions, just to prove I could do it. I was driven by a definition of success that didn't reflect who I am, what I want, or what brings me joy. It was simply accomplish-acquire-collapse-repeat. There was very

little joy, very little meaning, and tons of exhaustion and resentment.

In *The Gifts of Imperfection*, I wrote about the importance of a "joy and meaning" list and the power of actually thinking through these questions: When things are going really well in our family, what does it look like? What brings us the most joy? When are we in our zone?" For my family, the answers included things like sleep, working out, healthy food, cooking, time off, weekends away, going to church, being present with the kids, a sense of control over our money, date nights, meaningful work that doesn't consume us, time to piddle, time with family and close friends, giving back, and time to just hang out—real white space.

What was shocking for me and Steve was comparing this list to how we had defined success: There was no time for joy and meaning because we were too busy achieving. And we were achieving so we could buy more joy and meaning, but those require time, and time—that precious unrenewable resource—is not for sale.

Make your joy and meaning list and make sure that you use it as you define success for yourself. I stray from my list way too often, and I'm still adding to it—it's a lifelong practice. But it's been the best filter for making choices when bright and shiny opportunities come my way. Now, I can ask myself if taking something on moves me closer to what brings me joy and meaning. This alone is a revolutionary act.

As you think about your own path to daring leadership, remember Joseph Campbell's wisdom: "The cave you fear to enter holds the treasure you seek." Own the fear, find the cave, and write a new ending for yourself, for the people you're meant to serve and support, and for your culture. Choose courage over comfort. Choose whole hearts over armor. And choose the great adventure of being brave and afraid. At the exact same time.

ACKNOWLEDGMENTS

More than any other book I've written, this one was a serious crash and a huge team effort. Everyone on these pages has touched this book in a significant way. I am deeply grateful.

The BBEARG Team

To Ellen Alley, Suzanne Barrall, Cookie Boeker, Ronda Dearing, Linda Duraj, Lauren Emmerson, Margarita Flores, Cydney Ghani, Barrett Guillen, Sarah-Margaret Hamman, Zehra Javed, Jessica Kent, Charles Kiley, Hannah Kimbrough, Bryan Longoria, Murdoch Mackinnon, Madeline Obernesser, Julia Pollack, Tati Reznick, Deanne Rogers, Ashley Brown Ruiz, Teresa Sample, Kathryn Schultz, Anne Stoeber, Tyler Sweeten, Meredith Tompkins, and Genia Williams: Keep being brave, serving the work, and taking good care. You make me a braver person and I learn from all of you every single day. Thank you. #theworkwedo

To Murdoch: Let's do the damn thing!

The Random House Team

To my editor, Ben Greenberg: Thank you for making me laugh and helping me make sense of my thoughts and words. Charlie normally doesn't like it when I go into book-writing mode, but now he just wants you to come back to Houston so y'all can eat Torchy's and play Fortnite.

To the Random House team of Gina Centrello, Susan Kamil, Andy Ward, Molly Turpin, Theresa Zoro, Maria Braeckel, Melissa Sanford, Erin Richards, Leigh Marchant, Jessica Bonet, Benjamin Dreyer, Loren Noveck, Susan Turner, Joe Perez, Sandra Sjursen, Emily DeHuff, Lisa Feuer, and Karen Dziekonski: It's a great privilege to work with such a wholehearted team. Thank you.

To Elise Loehnen: Deeply grateful for your gifts. I know it's all brains, hard work, and practice, but you make it feel like magic.

The William Morris Endeavor Team

To my agent and friend, Jennifer Rudolph Walsh: Thank you for always believing. #pickles

To Tracy Fisher and the entire team at William Morris Endeavor: I'm grateful for the guidance and grind.

The DesignHaus Team

To Wendy Hauser, Mike Hauser, Jason Courtney, Daniel Stewart, Kristen Harrelson, Julie Severns, Annica Anderson, Kyle Kennedy: Thank you for the rumbles and the art. I'm proud of our partnership and the work we do together.

To Kristin Enyart: Thank you for rocking it! Our house is your house.

The Newman and Newman Crew

Thanks to Kelli Newman, Linda Tobar, Kurt Lang, Raul Casares, Boyderick Mays, Van Williams, Mitchell Earley, John Lance, Tom Francis, and Dorothy Strouhal.

The Home Team

Love and thanks to Deanne Rogers and David Robinson, Molly May and Chuck Brown, Jacobina Alley, Corky and Jack Crisci, Ashley and Amaya Ruiz; Barrett, Frankie, and Gabi Guillen; Jason and Layla Brown, Jen, David, Larkin, and Pierce Alley, Shif Berhanu, Negash Berhanu, Margarita Flores, and Sarah-Margaret Hamman. To Polly Koch: I miss you.

To Ashley and Barrett: I never take for granted that we get to work together every day. Thank you for laughing with me and keeping it uncomfortably real.

To Steve, Ellen, and Charlie: You are my heart. To Lucy: You are my weird dog. And my heart.

NOTES

a note from Brené

xiv **It was like reading *Old Hat, New Hat***: Stan and Jan Berenstain, *Old Hat, New Hat* (New York: Random House / Bright and Early Books, 1970).

xvii **In 2010, two years after that event**: Brené Brown, *The Gifts of Imperfection: Let Go of Who You Think You're Supposed to Be and Embrace Who You Are* (Center City, MN: Hazelden, 2010).

xvii **Two years after that**: Brené Brown, *Daring Greatly: How the Courage to Be Vulnerable Transforms the Way We Live, Love, Parent, and Lead* (New York: Gotham Books, 2012).

xvii **The epigraph of *Daring Greatly***: Theodore Roosevelt, "Citizenship in a Republic," speech at the Sorbonne, Paris, April 23, 1910.

xviii **My TEDxHouston talk**: Brené Brown, "The Power of Vulnerability," filmed June 2010 in Houston, TX, TEDxHouston video, 20:13, ted.com/talks/brene_brown_on_vulnerability.

xviii **I followed up *Daring Greatly***: Brené Brown, *Rising Strong: The Reckoning. The Rumble. The Revolution* (New York: Random House, 2015).

xix **The next year brought**: Brené Brown, *Braving the Wilderness: The Quest for True Belonging and the Courage to Stand Alone* (New York: Random House, 2017).

introduction: BRAVE LEADERS AND COURAGE CULTURES

7 **"What stands in the way becomes the way"**: The original source of this quotation is unknown, but it is generally attributed to Marcus Aurelius.

10 **to listen with the same passion:** Harriet Lerner, *Why Won't You Apologize?: Healing Big Betrayals and Everyday Hurts* (New York: Touchstone, 2017).

part one: RUMBLING WITH VULNERABILITY

section one: THE MOMENT AND THE MYTHS

22 **"To love at all is to be vulnerable"**: C. S. Lewis, *The Four Loves: The Much Beloved Exploration of the Nature of Love* (San Diego: Harcourt Books, 1960/1991).

24 **"When we were children"**: Madeleine L'Engle, *Walking on Water: Reflections on Faith and Art* (Colorado Springs: WaterBrook Press, 2001).

25 **"To grow to adulthood"**: John T. Cacioppo, "The Lethality of Loneliness (TEDxDesMoines Transcript)," published electronically September 9, 2013, singjupost.com/john-cacioppo-on-the-lethality-of-loneliness-full-transcript/.

33 **"What I've found through research"**: John Gottman, "John Gottman on Trust and Betrayal," published electronically October 29, 2011, greatergood.berkeley.edu/article/item/john_gottman_on_trust_and_betrayal.

36 **Google's five-year study**: Charles Duhigg, "What Google Learned from Its Quest to Build the Perfect Team: New Research Reveals Surprising Truths About Why Some Work Groups Thrive and Others Falter," published electronically February 25, 2016, nytimes.com/2016/02/28/magazine/what-google-learned-from-its-quest-to-build-the-perfect-team.html.

36 **"Simply put, psychological safety"**: Amy C. Edmondson, *Teaming: How Organizations Learn, Innovate, and Compete in the Knowledge Economy* (San Francisco: Jossey-Bass, 2012).

39 ***Boundaries* is a slippery word**: Kelly Rae Roberts, "What Is and Is Not Okay," published electronically March 22, 2009, kellyraeroberts.com/what-is-and-is-not-okay/.

40 **"Seek first to understand"**: Stephen Covey, *The Seven Habits of Highly Effective People* (New York: Simon and Schuster, 1989).

43 **"It's very hard to have ideas"**: Amy Poehler, "Ask Amy: Negativity," *Amy Poehler's Smart Girls,* 2:54, January 13, 2013, amysmartgirls.com/ask-amy-negativity-cec8eb81e742.

43 **"We are not necessarily thinking machines"**: Antonio Damasio, "Self Comes to Mind," YouTube video, 5:49, November 10, 2010, youtube.com/watch?v=Aw2yaozi0Gg.

section two: THE CALL TO COURAGE

49 **it made me think immediately of Luke Skywalker**: Gary Kurtz (producer) and Irvin Kershner (director), *Star Wars, Episode V: The Empire Strikes Back,* motion picture on DVD (San Francisco: Lucasfilm, Ltd. / Century City, CA: 20th Century–Fox Home Entertainment, 1980/2004).

52 **"The cave you fear to enter holds the treasure you seek"**: *A Joseph Campbell Companion: Reflections on the Art of Living,* edited by John Walter (San Anselmo, CA: Joseph Campbell Foundation, 1991), contains a passage alleged to be Campbell's words, as recorded by his associate Diane K. Osbon in her journal, that expresses in more poetical form the concepts that have since become condensed into this more commonly cited (though not authoritatively sourced) maxim.

56 **This insight took us straight to the pages**: Jim Collins, *Good to Great: Why Some Companies Make the Leap . . . and Others Don't* (New York: HarperBusiness, 2001).

section three: THE ARMORY

71 **"In the past, jobs were about muscles"**: Alain Elkann, "Interview with Minouche Shafik," published electronically April 1, 2018, alainelkanninterviews.com/minouche-shafik/.

71 **I have a thirteen-year-old son**: Kevin Feige (producer) and Ryan Coogler (director), *Black Panther* (Marvel Studios / Walt Disney Studios, 2018); James Gunn (director), *Guardians of the Galaxy* (Marvel Studios / Walt Disney Studios, 2014).

72 **"engaging in our lives from a place of worthiness"**: Brené Brown, *The Gifts of Imperfection: Let Go of Who You Think You're Supposed to Be and Embrace Who You Are* (Center City, MN: Hazelden, 2010), 1.

74 **"that thin wafer of consciousness"**: James Hollis, *Finding Meaning in the Second Half of Life: How to Finally, Really Grow Up* (New York: Gotham Books, 2005), 11.

74 **"We are not here to fit in"**: James Hollis, *What Matters Most: Living a More Considered Life* (New York: Gotham Books, 2008), xiii.

78 **"As children we found ways to protect ourselves"**: Brené Brown, *Daring Greatly: How the Courage to Be Vulnerable Transforms the Way We Live, Love, Parent, and Lead* (New York: Gotham Books, 2012), 112.

79 **Perfectionism is correlated with depression**: Paul L. Hewitt, Gordon L. Flett, and Samuel F. Mikail, *Perfectionism: A Relational Approach to Conceptualization, Assessment, and Treatment* (New York: Guilford Press, 2017).

84 **Globoforce worked with Cisco**: Globoforce, "Bringing Smiles to Hershey," published electronically, August 2016, globoforce.com/wp-content/uploads/2016/08/Hershey-Case-Study_final_8_16.pdf; "Connecting People: How Cisco Used Social Recognition to Transform Its Culture," published electronically, July 2017, globoforce.com/wp-content/uploads/2017/07/Case-Study_Cisco.pdf; "The Secret to Double Digit Increases in Employee Engagement," published electronically, 2012, go.globoforce.com/rs/globoforce/images/exec-brief-double-digit-engagement-increase_na.pdf; "Linking Social Recognition to Retention and Performance at LinkedIn," published electronically, 2018, resources.globoforce.com/case-studies/case-study-linkedin.

85 **According to the National Council on Alcoholism**: Sandy Smith, "Drug Abuse Costs Employers $81 Billion per Year," *EHS Today,* published electronically March 11, 2014, ehstoday.com/health/drug-abuse-costs-employers-81-billion-year; National Council on Alcoholism and Drug Dependence, "Drugs and Alcohol in the Workplace," published electronically April 26, 2015, ncadd.org/about-addiction/addiction-update/drugs-and-alcohol-in-the-workplace.

88 **"Shadow comforts can take any form"**: Jennifer Louden, *The Life Organizer: A Woman's Guide to a Mindful Year* (Novato, CA: New World Library, 2007), 43.

88 **"It's not what you do; it's why you do it"**: Ibid., 42.

90 **"All too often our so-called strength comes from fear, not love"**: Joan Halifax, *Being with Dying: Cultivating Compassion*

and Fearlessness in the Presence of Death (Boston: Shambhala Publications, Inc., 2008), p. 17.

93 **hope isn't a warm and fuzzy feeling**: C. R. Snyder, *Handbook of Hope: Theory, Measures, and Applications* (San Diego: Academic Press, 2000).

94 **"Despair is the belief that tomorrow will be"**: Rob Bell, "Despair Is a Spiritual Condition," presentation at Oprah Winfrey's "The Life You Want" Weekend Tour, various U.S. cities, 2014.

96 **In their publication *Making Change Happen***: Just Associates, *Making Change Happen: Power; Concepts for Revisioning Power for Justice, Equality and Peace.* Just Associates, 2006, justassociates.org/sites/justassociates.org/files/mch3_2011_final_0.pdf.

97 ***Power with* "has to do with finding common ground"**: Ibid., 6.

98 **As Ken Blanchard . . . explains**: Ken Blanchard,"Catch People Doing Something Right," published electronically December 24, 2014, howwelead.org/2014/12/24/catch-people-doing-something-right/.

106 **The work of Dr. Stuart Brown**: Stuart Brown and Christopher Vaughan, *Play: How It Shapes the Brain, Opens the Imagination, and Invigorates the Soul* (New York: Avery / Penguin Group USA, 2009).

107 **"The opposite of play is not work"**: Ibid., 126.

107 **"True belonging is the spiritual practice"**: Brené Brown, *Braving the Wilderness: The Quest for True Belonging and the Courage to Stand Alone* (New York: Random House, 2017), 40.

109 **Bill Gentry talks about**: William Gentry and Center for Creative Leadership *Be the Boss Everyone Wants to Work For: A Guide for New Leaders* (Oakland: Berrett-Koehler, 2016).

113 **"This is not really a moment to, like, celebrate"**: Karma Allen, "#Metoo Founder Tells Trevor Noah: Harvey Weinstein Indictment Isn't 'Moment to Celebrate,'" published electronically May 31, 2018, abcnews.go.com/US/metoo-founder-tells-trevor-noah-harvey-weinstein-indictment/story?id=55552211.

section four: SHAME AND EMPATHY

123 **Researchers Tamara Ferguson, Heidi Eyre, and Michael Ashbaker**: Tamara J. Ferguson, Heidi L. Eyre, and Michael Ashbaker, "Unwanted Identities: A Key Variable in Shame—Anger Links and

Gender Differences in Shame," *Sex Roles* 42, no. 3–4 (2000): 133–57.

127 **Current neuroscience research**: Naomi I. Eisenberger, Matthew D. Lieberman, and Kipling D. Williams, "Does Rejection Hurt? An fMRI Study of Social Exclusion," *Science* 302, no. 5643 (2003): 290–92.

128 **The majority of shame researchers and clinicians**: For the most comprehensive review of the shame and guilt literature, see June Price Tangney and Ronda L. Dearing, *Shame and Guilt: Emotions and Social Behavior* (New York: Guilford Press, 2002). Additionally, I recommend Dearing and Tangney, eds., *Shame in the Therapy Hour* (Washington, D.C.: American Psychological Association, 2011).

129 **While shame is highly correlated with addiction**: Ronda L. Dearing, Jeffrey Stuewig, and June P. Tangney, "On the Importance of Distinguishing Shame from Guilt: Relations to Problematic Alcohol and Drug Use," *Addictive Behaviors* 30, no. 7 (2005): 1392–404; Dearing and Tangney, eds., *Shame in the Therapy Hour;* Jeffrey Stuewig, June P. Tangney, Stephanie Kendall, Johanna B. Folk, Candace Reinsmith Meyer, and Ronda L. Dearing, "Children's Proneness to Shame and Guilt Predict Risky and Illegal Behaviors in Young Adulthood," *Child Psychiatry and Human Development* 46 (2014): 217–27; Tangney and Dearing, *Shame and Guilt.*

130 ***Humiliation* is another word that we often confuse with *shame***: D. C. Klein, "The Humiliation Dynamic: An Overview," *Journal of Primary Prevention* 12 (1991): 93–122.

142 **Theresa Wiseman, a nursing scholar in the UK**: Theresa Wiseman,"Toward a Holistic Conceptualization of Empathy for Nursing Practice," *Advances in Nursing Science* 30, no. 3 (2007): E61–72; Theresa Wiseman, "A Concept Analysis of Empathy," *Journal of Advanced Nursing* 23, no. 6 (1996): 1162–67.

142 **I added a fifth attribute**: Kristin D. Neff, "Self-Compassion: An Alternative Conceptualization of a Healthy Attitude toward Oneself," *Self & Identity* 2, no. 2 (2003): 85–101.

144 **"If people in powerful positions continue to hire"**: Beyoncé Knowles, "Beyoncé in Her Own Words: Her Life, Her Body, Her Heritage," *Vogue,* August 2018.

148 **"taking a balanced approach to negative emotions"**: Kristin Neff, "Self-Compassion," self-compassion.org/the-three-elements-of-self-compassion-2/.

153 **There's a fun animated short**: Brené Brown, "Brené Brown on Empathy," Royal Society for the Encouragement of Arts, Manufactures and Commerce shorts, 2:53, December 10, 2013, brenebrown.com/videos/.

157 **Dr. Kristin Neff of the University of Texas**: Kristin Neff, *Self-Compassion: Stop Beating Yourself Up and Leave Insecurity Behind* (New York: William Morrow, 2011).

158 **"being warm and understanding toward ourselves"**: Kristin Neff, "Self-Compassion," self-compassion.org/the-three-elements-of-self-compassion-2/.

160 **"that suffering and personal inadequacy is part"**: Kristin Neff, "Self-Compassion," self-compassion.org/the-three-elements-of-self-compassion-2/.

161 **When we have understanding**: Linda M. Hartling, Wendy Rosen, Maureen Walker, and Judith V. Jordan, "Shame and Humiliation: From Isolation to Relational Transformation (Work in Progress No. 88)," Wellesley, MA: Stone Center Working Paper Series, 2000.

163 **"We are the ones we have been waiting for"**: June Jordan, "Poem for South African Women," read by the author to the United Nations General Assembly, August 9, 1978.

section five: CURIOSITY AND GROUNDED CONFIDENCE

170 **"Unfortunately, the trend in many organizations"**: Mary Slaughter and David Rock, "No Pain, No Brain Gain: Why Learning Demands (a Little) Discomfort," *Fast Company,* published electronically April 30, 2018, fastcompany.com/40560075/no-pain-no-brain-gain-why-learning-demands-a-little-discomfort.

171 **A study published in . . . the journal *Neuron***: Matthias J. Gruber, Bernard D. Gelman, and Charan Ranganath, "States of Curiosity Modulate Hippocampus-Dependent Learning Via the Dopaminergic Circuit," *Neuron* 84, no. 2 (2014): 486–96.

171 **"Curiosity is unruly. It doesn't like rules"**: Ian Leslie, *Curious: The Desire to Know and Why Your Future Depends on It* (New York: Basic Books, 2014), xiv.

172 **"If I had an hour to solve a problem"**: The original source of this quotation is unknown, but it is generally attributed to Albert Einstein.

172 **"It's not that I'm so smart"**: The original source of this quotation is unknown, but it is generally attributed to Albert Einstein.

174 **In his 1994 article**: George Loewenstein, "The Psychology of Curiosity: A Review and Reinterpretation," *Psychological Bulletin* 116, no. 1 (1994): 75–98.

175 **"To induce curiosity about a particular topic"**: Loewenstein, "Psychology of Curiosity," 94.

part two: LIVING INTO OUR VALUES

187 **"If you have more than three priorities"**: Kimberly Weisul, "Jim Collins: Good to Great in 10 Steps," *Inc.*, published electronically May 7, 2012, inc.com/kimberly-weisul/jim-collins-good-to-great-in-ten-steps.html.

193 **"But I'll be looking for eight"**: Terry Stafford and Paul Fraser, "Amarillo by Morning" (1973), recorded by George Strait on the album *Strait from the Heart* (Los Angeles: MCA Records, 1983).

197 **"Spirituality is the deep human longing"**: Pittman McGehee, "Interview with Dr. J. Pittman McGehee," Consciousness NOW TV, 44:30, April 6, 2016, youtube.com/watch?v=4–2pnDpBOT8.

197 **"Love is not a victory march"**: Leonard Cohen, "Hallelujah" (1984), recorded by Leonard Cohen on the album *Various Positions* (New York: Columbia Records, 1984).

198 **I know I'm ready to give feedback when**: Brené Brown, *Daring Greatly: How the Courage to Be Vulnerable Transforms the Way We Live, Love, Parent, and Lead* (New York: Gotham Books, 2012), 204.

part three: BRAVING TRUST

222 **"choosing to risk making something you value vulnerable"**: Charles Feltman, *The Thin Book of Trust: An Essential Primer for Building Trust at Work* (Bend, OR: Thin Book Publishing, 2008), 7.

222 **"what is important to me is not safe"**: Ibid., 8.

222 **In a *Harvard Business Review* article**: Stephen M. R. Covey and Douglas R. Conant, "The Connection between Employee Trust and Financial Performance," *Harvard Business Review*, published electronically July 18, 2016, hbr.org/2016/07/the-connection-between-employee-trust-and-financial-performance.

223 **"While few leaders would argue against the idea"**: Ibid.

224 **"Knowledge is only rumor until"**: Original source of quote unknown.

238 **"I don't trust people who don't love themselves"**: Maya Angelou, Distinguished Annie Clark Lecture, 16th Annual Families Alive Conference, Weber State University, Ogden, Utah, May 8, 1997.

part four: LEARNING TO RISE

242 **Today, with millennials making up 35 percent**: Richard Fry, "Millennials Are the Largest Generation in the U.S. Labor Force," *FactTank: News in the Numbers,* published electronically April 11, 2018, pewresearch.org/fact-tank/2018/04/11/millennials-largest-generation-us-labor-force/.

249 **the song "Riser" by Dierks Bentley**: Travis Meadows and Steve Moakler, "Riser" (2014), recorded by Dierks Bentley on the album *Riser* (Nashville: Capital Records Nashville, 2014).

254 **I named this strategy after . . . Dolores Umbridge**: J. K. Rowling, *Harry Potter and the Order of the Phoenix* (New York: Scholastic Books, 2003).

254 **"A love of all things saccharine"**: J. K. Rowling, "Dolores Umbridge," pottermore.com/writing-by-jk-rowling/dolores-umbridge.

256 **1. Inhale deeply through your nose**: Mark Miller, "Tactical Breathing: Control Your Breathing, Control Your Mind," published electronically April 14, 2018, loadoutroom.com/2778/tactical-breathing/.

256 **In her book *The Dance of Connection***: Harriet Lerner, *The Dance of Connection: How to Talk to Someone When You're Mad, Hurt, Scared, Frustrated, Insulted, Betrayed, or Desperate* (New York: HarperCollins, 2001).

258 **Robert Burton, a neurologist and novelist**: Robert A. Burton, *On Being Certain: Believing You Are Right Even When You're Not* (New York: St. Martin's Press, 2008).

259 **"Because we are compelled to make stories"**: Robert Burton, "Where Science and Story Meet: We Make Sense of the World through Stories—a Deep Need Rooted in Our Brains," published electronically April 22, 2013, nautil.us/issue/0/the-story-of-nautilus/where-science-and-story-meet.

259 **"The only way I can get anything written"**: Anne Lamott, *Bird by Bird: Some Instructions on Writing and Life* (New York: Anchor Books, 1995), 22.

261 **"ordinary, mentally healthy people are strikingly prone"**: Jonathan Gottschall, *The Storytelling Animal: How Stories Make Us Human* (New York: Houghton Mifflin, 2012), 109.

261 **"The stories were confabulations"**: Ibid., 110.

262 **James Pennebaker, a researcher**: James W. Pennebaker, *Writing to Heal: A Guided Journal for Recovering from Trauma and Emotional Upheaval* (Wheat Ridge, CO: Center for Journal Therapy, 2004).

263 **"When you are in the middle of a story"**: Margaret Atwood, *Alias Grace* (London: Bloomsbury, 1996), 345–46.

264 **"Conspiracy is not limited to the stupid"**: Gottschall, *Storytelling Animal,* 116.

265 **"To the conspiratorial mind"**: Ibid.

271 **"*Revolution* might sound a little dramatic"**: Brené Brown, *The Gifts of Imperfection: Let Go of Who You Think You're Supposed to Be and Embrace Who You Are* (Center City, MN: Hazelden, 2010), 126.

INDEX

ABOUT THE AUTHOR

BRENÉ BROWN, PHD, LMSW, is a research professor at the University of Houston, where she holds the Huffington Foundation–Brené Brown Endowed Chair at the Graduate College of Social Work. She has spent the past two decades studying courage, vulnerability, shame, and empathy and is the author of five #1 *New York Times* bestsellers: *Dare to Lead, Braving the Wilderness, Rising Strong, Daring Greatly,* and *The Gifts of Imperfection.* Her TED talk—"The Power of Vulnerability"—is one of the top five most-viewed TED talks in the world with more than thirty-five million views. Brown lives in Houston, Texas, with her husband, Steve, and their children, Ellen and Charlie.

brenebrown.com
Facebook.com/brenebrown
Twitter: @brenebrown